Architectural Technology

Stephen Emmitt
Leeds Metropolitan University

Sheffield Hallam University
Learning and Information Service
WITHDRAWN FROM STOCK

KT-514-115

b

**Blackwell
Science**

Cornwall College

149315

© 2002 by
Blackwell Science Ltd
Editorial Offices:
Osney Mead, Oxford OX2 0EL
25 John Street, London WC1N 2BS
23 Ainslie Place, Edinburgh EH3 6AJ
350 Main Street, Malden
    MA 02148 5018, USA
54 University Street, Carlton
    Victoria 3053, Australia
10, rue Casimir Delavigne
    75006 Paris, France

Other Editorial Offices:

Blackwell Wissenschafts-Verlag GmbH
Kurfürstendamm 57
10707 Berlin, Germany

Blackwell Science KK
MG Kodenmacho Building
7-10 Kodenmacho Nihombashi
Chuo-ku, Tokyo 104, Japan

Iowa State University Press
A Blackwell Science Company
2121 S. State Avenue
Ames, Iowa 50014-8300, USA

The right of the Author to be identified as the Author
of this Work has been asserted in accordance with the
Copyright, Designs and Patents Act 1988.

All rights reserved. No part of
this publication may be reproduced,
stored in a retrieval system, or
transmitted, in any form or by any
means, electronic, mechanical,
photocopying, recording or otherwise,
except as permitted by the UK
Copyright, Designs and Patents Act
1988, without the prior permission
of the publisher.

First published 2002

Set in Aldine 401BT and News Gothic and
produced by Gray Publishing, Tunbridge Wells, Kent
Printed and bound in Great Britain by
MPG Books Ltd, Bodmin, Cornwall

The Blackwell Science logo is a
trade mark of Blackwell Science Ltd,
registered at the United Kingdom
Trade Marks Registry

DISTRIBUTORS

Marston Book Services Ltd
PO Box 269
Abingdon
Oxon OX14 4YN
(*Orders:*   Tel: 01235 465500
                 Fax: 01235 465555)

USA
Blackwell Science, Inc.
Commerce Place
350 Main Street
Malden, MA 02148 5018
(*Orders:*   Tel: 800 759 6102
                          781 388 8250
                 Fax: 781 388 8255)

Canada
Login Brothers Book Company
324 Saulteaux Crescent
Winnipeg, Manitoba R3J 3T2
(*Orders:*   Tel: 204 837 2987
                 Fax: 204 837 3116)

Australia
Blackwell Science Pty Ltd
54 University Street
Carlton, Victoria 3053
(*Orders:*   Tel: 03 9347 0300
                 Fax: 03 9347 5001)

A catalogue record for this title
is available from the British Library

ISBN 0-632-06403-X

Library of Congress Cataloging-in-Publication Data
Emmitt, Stephen.
    Architectural technology/Stephen Emmitt.
        p. cm.
    Includes bibliographical references and index.
    ISBN 0-632-06403-X
    1. Architecture–Technological innovations.
    2. Architecture and technology 3. Architectural
    design–Technique. I. Title

    NA2543.T43 E46 2001
    721′.09′049–dc21   200037962

For further information on
Blackwell Science, visit our website:
www.blackwell-science.com

CORNWALL COLLEGE
LIBRARY

Contents

Foreword

BIAT

**British Institute of
Architectural Technologists**

397 City Road
London
EC1V 1NH

Telephone: 020 7278 2206
Facsimile: 020 7837 3194
Email: info@biat.org.uk
Website: www.biat.org.uk

British Institute of Architectural Technologists (BIAT) is the largest non-chartered and independent professional body representing the construction industry in the UK. Fully qualified architectural technologists (MBIAT) play a key role in the construction process, and are frequently exploited to introduce and put into operation innovative and effective design solutions.

In the 6 years since I took up office as Vice President Education I have seen the number of degree courses in Architectural Technology expand from six to some thirty currently on offer in the United Kingdom. The development of complementary courses in the Republic of Ireland, Hong Kong, Singapore and Australia will ensure that the profession continues to expand and gain the recognition it deserves.

During my own studies the role of an architectural technician (as it was known then) was a functional role. At BIAT we are proud that modern architectural technologists are seen as having a pivotal role in the construction process and are at the leading edge in terms of innovative technical design solutions.

We are looking towards a very positive future and are certain that the next generation of architectural technologists will take the profession and its institute to even further heights.

This book will be an excellent tool for those progressing to a professional qualification in architectural technology, many of whom retain their passion for their profession throughout their career. We also hope that it will be an interesting and compelling read for those who wish to find out more about this exciting profession, an increasingly distinct specialism within an already specialised construction industry.

On behalf of BIAT, I would like to thank the author Stephen Emmitt for producing the manuscript and wish you all every success in your studies.

The Qualifying Body in
Architectural Technology

VAT No. 681 6419 17

Incorporated in London
as a Company
Limited by Guarantee
No. 1231038

Robert Mason MBIAT
Vice President Education

Preface

Human beings have a natural tendency to make things. Inventing, making, using, refining, redefining, abandoning and reinventing require constant effort and organisational skills. We make and remake buildings to house our enterprises, shelter us from the elements and to provide a secure environment. Buildings are designed, made, adjusted, altered and eventually dismantled (hopefully maximising recyclable elements), relying on the ideas, knowledge and practical skills of a vast number of people. In their own way, these diverse people and multi-skilled organisations are all concerned with matters of detail. Our buildings and associated engineering works are the result of careful consideration, compromise and co-ordination – the result of human beings using and applying technology, both to realise design intent and to maintain the artefact in a serviceable condition.

Over the last 50 years a succession of government reports and an enormous volume of research have urged all those involved in building to work together towards a joined-up industry. Paradoxically, the trend has been towards greater specialisation and increasingly more complex relationships, which has led to greater barriers to effective communication between the project participants. As information has become easier to access through information technology, it too has become more specialised and hence more compartmentalised, further supporting specialism and fragmentation. More recently the separation of technology from architecture, both in education and in practice, has resulted in the growth of a relatively new professional discipline, architectural technology. As a practitioner and more latterly as a researcher and educator it became apparent to me that a book which addressed architectural technology in a holistic manner, and that was also suitable for my students, did not exist. Hence this book – a modest attempt at trying to answer some of the usual questions that invariably arise and to try and bring together, often disparate, fields of literature under one cover.

This book is for students of building design: architecture, architectural technology, building, construction management, interior design and surveying. By 'students' I refer to those just embarking on a course of study related to building, and the professionals who deal with detail design issues on a daily basis. When we start to question how buildings are created, assembled and used, we begin a lifelong process of collecting, assimilating, adjusting and reinventing our practical knowledge base – perpetual students of our subject. Design knowledge is grounded in an understanding of how buildings are put together, used and eventually taken apart – knowledge that evolves with every new project. It is a process of gathering information, turning it into knowledge and using it to make the process of building more effective, with the ultimate aim of pleasing our clients and providing exciting, vibrant and healthy environments for all those who use them.

The absence of typical construction details in this book is deliberate and considered. This is not another construction technology book; rather, it aims to bring together philosophical, technical, legal and social issues, often taught as separate subjects, to provide a constructive link between manufacturer, designer and builder. An attempt has been made to integrate and encourage an environmentally responsible approach to design, construction, use and re-use throughout the text – i.e. essentially a holistic approach to the issues faced by building designers in their daily work. A number of case studies are used throughout the book to illustrate some of the issues; these are not meant to be representative, instead they help to show that there are different approaches to building, the benefit of one over another being an issue of circumstance and personal preference. The book is not designed to provide all the answers, but to highlight some of the challenges and opportunities that make architectural technology such an interesting subject. Examples of famous buildings by well-known designers are conspicuous by their absence. This also is deliberate, partly because there are plenty of excellent books that are building or designer specific, and partly because I feel it is important that the readers take the issues raised in this book and apply them to their own particular design approach (which invariably will be different to the next person's) without being tainted by my own likes and dislikes. For ease of readership this book is arranged in three parts. Part I deals with the background issues that colour the manner in which we build. Part II takes a journey through the life of a typical building project, from briefing and assembly, to building use and eventual disassembly. Part III aims to tackle some of the underlying issues facing those involved in aspects of architectural technology, concluding with a theory for practice.

Good architecture has always been difficult to achieve. Balancing the holistic with the physical and manipulating abstract ideas towards solid artefact through the use of robust technologies to design buildings that are beautiful, comfortable and enjoyable to experience, can become addictive. Designing and realising buildings that respond to, rather than compete with, ecological systems, that are humane, timely and of course simple to assemble and use, is a commendable objective. To do so requires a thorough understanding of building technologies, design and management. I hope this book will encourage, assist and stimulate those who strive for 'quality'.

Stephen Emmitt
Leeds Metropolitan University
s.emmitt@lmu.ac.uk

PART I: A PRIMER

Previous page shows Barcelona Museum of Modern Art

1 Setting the agenda

Individuals, groups and organisations responsible for building design and construction are essentially concerned with interpreting a client's requirements: exploring, exploiting and enhancing those requirements in the form of a design which satisfies planning legislation and building codes; is buildable within a defined budget and within a defined time period; satisfies user demands and also recognises ecological constraints. By way of an introduction this chapter provides an overview of the main considerations for building designers. To set the agenda the chapter starts with a look at detail design issues, followed by a discussion about the importance of enclosure and functional requirements. This is followed by some fundamental issues concerning ease of assembly, quality and drivers for more ecologically responsible buildings. The chapter concludes by addressing the human factor, because whatever technologies, tools and methods employed in the design, assembly, use, re-use, and eventual disposal of a building, the entire process involves people.

1.1   A matter of detail

It is impossible to detach ourselves from detail design decisions in everyday life. Every time we turn the hot water tap on, every time we go in and out of our front door, we are interacting with products that have been designed, detailed and manufactured to precise standards, products which have then been selected by designers, purchased by a contractor and assembled on a particular site by people (fitters and fixers) using a variety of machinery and tools. Normally we are relatively unaware of such detail until something goes wrong – the tap starts to drip or the door starts to stick – necessitating some form of repair or replacement. Sometimes our attention to detail is focused through the process of re-designing and refitting our kitchens or bathrooms; the choice of units, equipment, finishes, etc., seems endless, limited only by one's imagination and financial budget. Whatever the building type, be it an office, warehouse, factory, leisure centre, school, hospital or house, they are all used (and abused) by people. Decisions about detail design affect us all; poor detailing will be noticed and inappropriate product selections will lead, either directly or indirectly, to problems which may compromise the durability and functionality of our buildings, necessitating some form of remedial action sooner than anticipated. With the exception of the growing do-it-yourself (DIY) market, the majority of these detail design decisions are made by professional designers and implemented by skilled workers. Many individuals earn their living by design, manufacture, assembly, maintenance, alteration, demolition and recycling of buildings, or parts of buildings, working in an industry known as 'building' or 'construction'. Building is a major economic activity throughout the world, employing significant numbers of people, consuming significant quantities of (often finite) resources and adding to the pollution of our natural habitat, through both the process of building and the energy consumption of the building during its lifetime. The balance between improving our built environment, encouraging economic activity and limiting environmental impact is difficult to achieve in practice.

1.1.1   *The art of building*

Building design and construction encompasses a series of complex tasks that are undertaken by a wide range of specialists. Architects, engineers, interior designers, technologists and surveyors are all, to lesser or greater extents, concerned with issues concerning the integration of design, technology and management. Professionals need to understand the relationship between manufacture, detail design and assembly, in short the ability to apply available technologies and manage the process to ensure a quality product. One of the most challenging tasks for the design team, and the contractor, is the enormous range of materials, products, structural solutions and architectural styles from which to choose. These decisions lie at the heart of the design process during which designers, working individually or as part of a team, make decisions which affect architectural expression and which rely on technical knowledge for their realisation.

Before the Industrial Revolution the designer's choice of materials was largely limited to locally sourced materials: stone, bricks and timber were the principal structural materials and organic materials such as reeds were used for finishes. These materials had been used for centuries and the knowledge required for working and applying the materials had been handed down from master to apprentice. Legislation and the enforcement of rules was minimal compared with those in place today and shoddy building was commonplace. Buildings could, and did, collapse, and accidents on the building site were only too common in an age when human life was cheap. Although the choice of materials was limited there was a clear understanding of materials' properties, strengths and limitations. Vernacular architecture resulted in harmonious developments which relied for the most part on sustainable materials. Necessity and ease of use resulted in the re-use of materials such as timber and stone from redundant buildings; recycling was often a necessity rather than an option. With the Industrial Revolution came change. Transportation allowed materials to be moved greater distances relatively cheaply and also created a market for new building types, such as railway stations. Rapid advances in manufacturing and materials development, along with developments in tools and machinery used on building sites, resulted in new ways of doing things with new materials. At the start of the 21st century designers are faced not only with a bewildering choice of materials and procurement routes from which to choose, but also with an enormous volume of information relating to building. This information includes both the physical behaviour of buildings and the behaviour of their occupants over time. Designers also face new pressures. The increased threat of litigation may well inhibit or limit the range of materials used, while pressure to act in a more environmentally responsible manner may lead to the use of new details and materials to reduce the environmental impact of the building. The importance of the existing building stock is now recognised and social pressures are very much directed towards conservation, re-use and recycling of existing buildings. To bring brown-field sites (those previously built on) back into use in our towns and cities is a desirable policy in terms of sustainable development. Yet to do so raises a whole raft of technical and social challenges, such as dealing with contaminated ground and adjacent structures, and with economic and planning issues.

1.1.2   *Architectural technology*

Technology has its root in a Greek word *techne* referring to art and skill; the art of making. From this architectural technology is the art of building, a discipline that aims to bring together artistic, practical and procedural skills; the fusion of three separate worlds (Fig. 1.1). The artistic component is the domain of the designer – creative, difficult to quantify objectively and always subjective. The practical component is the domain of the builder – assembling physical materials, technical, physical and quantifiable. The procedural component is the domain of the manager – pulling together artistic and practical skills in an ordered manner. Design can be a complex matter in practice, yet the overall aims are very simple. They are to provide enclosure, for an agreed cost, in the agreed time, to an agreed standard of performance and quality, respecting environmental concerns and satisfying both client and building user.

Architectural tectonics is the art and process of producing practical and aesthetically pleasing buildings – the ability to take the conceptual design through the detail design and construction phases without losing design intent. Of paramount importance are the joints between the selected materials and the synergy between design and production – the domain of the architectural technologist, the individuals with an eye for detail and the ability to take conceptual design through to practical completion on site. For the professional there are underlying concerns over liability, ethics, sustainable design and responsibility to clients and society at large – concerns that sometimes conflict. For the professional designer the challenge is to achieve a balance through integration and synthesis, to design a building that is functional and is also a delight to use. Those involved in building design are faced with a number of interrelated issues, expressed in Fig. 1.2, namely enclosure and functional requirements, buildability, quality and

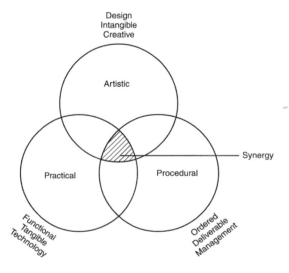

Figure 1.1   Architectural technology.

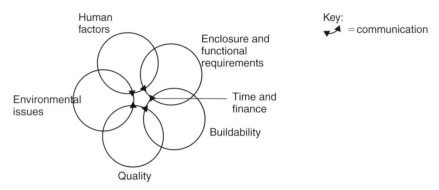

Figure 1.2 Detail design factors.

environmental issues – all within a set period of time and within a defined budget, and all dependent on the action of humans.

1.2 Enclosure and functional requirements

Building design is first and foremost concerned with the creation of enclosure, the building envelope. Separating inside from out, warm from cold, light from dark, results in a building comprised of elements common to all: floor(s), walls, windows, doors and a roof. The completed enclosure may not necessarily be ideal (most of us would like a bigger house or a more comfortable office environment) but functional, i.e. it must be fit for its intended purpose. Whether it is a new build project or work to an existing structure, building design is concerned with building up the separate elements into a connected whole. The skill is putting the various elements together in such a way as to be both functional and aesthetically pleasing.

Building designers are faced with a new set of problems every time they work on a project. The site will have its own special characteristics and the client's requirements, expressed in the form of a design brief, will also be specific to a particular project. That the design challenge is different from previous projects does not mean that the designer has to start from scratch every time. He or she will draw on existing precedents and previously used details, combining new ideas with old to create the design concept from which the detailed design work follows. There are a number of interrelated core elements of every design project which must be considered, and each element carries with it a certain amount of historical baggage which may constrain and inspire the designer. The core elements of the design challenge are expressed in Fig. 1.3. They comprise the following:

- *The brief.* Arguably this is the most important document because it sets the agenda for the events that follow. The brief should clearly identify the functional requirements and technical parameters for the design. Programme, cost, quality and professional relationships are established at this stage. Design life, service life and issues of ecological design should also be addressed here.
- *Conceptual design.* Achieving synergy between the brief and the conceptual design from which all other, more detailed, design decisions flow is not easy. The process relies on effective communication, co-operation and collaboration.

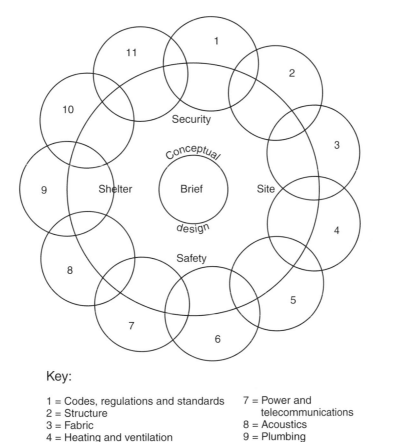

Figure 1.3   Enclosure and functional requirements.

Key:

1 = Codes, regulations and standards
2 = Structure
3 = Fabric
4 = Heating and ventilation
5 = Servicing
6 = Lighting
7 = Power and telecommunications
8 = Acoustics
9 = Plumbing
10 = Fire protection
11 = Furnishings and equipment

■ *Site, shelter, security and safety.* These four factors are essential design generators and are discussed in greater detail later in the book.

The elements are as follows:

■ *Codes and regulations.* Configuring the building design so that it complies with current codes, regulations and standards is a major concern for the design team. Codes, regulations and standards vary with location and are revised and updated over time as knowledge increases. Their roots lie in providing safe accommodation for building users, although the scope of the regulations has widened over recent years.
■ *Structure.* Structural systems need to be considered in abstract while the conceptual design is being developed. Many designers use 'rule of thumb' to gauge the approximate spans and the size of structural members before a structural engineer has been appointed, although the earlier the appointment the less the possibility of abortive work. Synergy between designer and structural engineer

is important if the scheme is to develop into a cost-effective product. Once the concept has been agreed the structural consultant can proceed with the detailed structural design, i.e. the sizing and spacing of structural members in accordance with regulations and codes.

■ *Fabric.* Deciding on the materials which will envelop the building structure and form the external and internal finishes with which we interact is closely related to the structural system employed. This is especially true of the interaction or fixing of the fabric to the structure. Embodied in the choice of surface finishes is that of fire resistance and surface spread of flame, requiring careful selection of materials and components.

■ *Heating, ventilation and air conditioning (HVAC).* The provision of a comfortable and healthy internal environment for building users is a primary concern. Consideration of natural ventilation, e.g. passive systems, in preference to mechanical systems should be encouraged. Natural ventilation is cheaper and gives building users more control over their immediate environments. Where mechanical systems are used, the positioning of mechanical plant and provision of adequate space to service it are a constant challenge. Heating should be specified with the user in mind and 'smart systems' considered to conserve energy in use.

■ *Servicing.* Access to the site will be determined by the physical constraints of the site, the wishes of the local highway authority and any legal constraints which may directly affect access. Horizontal servicing of the site is also required for refuse, deliveries and access for fire fighting equipment in the event of an emergency. Vertical servicing is required for buildings over one storey high. Stairs, ramps, escalators, elevators and dumb waiters provide routes for the transfer of people and equipment.

■ *Lighting.* Natural lighting must be considered early in the design process. Daylight is preferable to artificial lighting and is supplied free of charge. Unfortunately it is unreliable: too little and we have to resort to artificial lighting, too much and we suffer from glare and solar gain. Light levels are known to affect our health and are important in the workplace. Sizing and positioning of windows, as well as the positioning, type and size of artificial lighting, need careful consideration to maximise the potential of the building design.

■ *Power and telecommunications.* Electricity, gas and telecommunications need to be supplied to the building. Sustainable sources of power (e.g. photovoltaic cells) should be considered where possible.

■ *Acoustics.* As a general rule hard surfaces reflect sound energy, while soft materials absorb sound energy. Sound isolation (keeping sound in, or keeping sound out) is a major concern in situations where buildings are very close together or joined via a party wall or party floor. Input from acoustic engineers may be required in all but the simplest of designs if a quality acoustic environment is to be achieved.

■ *Plumbing.* Supply and removal lie at the heart of plumbing systems, i.e. cold and hot water supply, waste water removal and/or recycling. Waste water, both foul and surface, is removed through the drainage system, although with increased awareness of environmental issues there is a move towards recycling water.

■ *Fire protection.* Fire prevention, protection and management are important considerations for designers and for which extensive legislation and guidance is available.

■ *Furnishings and equipment.* No building would be complete without furnishings and equipment, the domain of interior designers. Furnishings can and sometimes do pose a fire hazard – not just in the materials used for their manufacture but also by blocking circulation and escape routes. Care in their selection is required at the design stage and at subsequent upgrade and replacement stages. Awareness of such issues is, therefore, important for owners, managers and future design teams.

1.2.1   *Technical integration*

Comparisons between functional requirements are very useful, but only form part of the process. Designers are also concerned with architectural style and expression, meeting the requirements of legislative codes and regulations, keeping the building watertight yet allowing enough ventilation, meeting financial budgets and keeping to tight time schedules for both the design work and the assembly of the building. The order in which these issues are tackled by the design team may well vary because of the size and/or complexity of the project being addressed. Indeed, different designers are known to have quite different approaches to solving design problems. The important point is that they are tackled and are integrated during the design process to avoid problems during

Figure 1.4   Integration – the end result.

construction and subsequent use. Various design guides have been published to aid the designer through the design process. The core elements all have a certain amount of design, management and technological input. Designers also need to consider 'how' the building will be assembled and 'how' it is to be maintained, dismantled and recycled. Achieving a consistent level of synthesis is a constant challenge for all concerned; quality and buildability are two important drivers in this regard. The quality of the building is determined by the skills of the individuals involved in the project, the comprehensiveness of the detailed drawings, specifications and schedules, and the ability of those charged with assembling disparate parts to form the whole. Throughout the design process thought has to be given to the manner in which the building will be assembled, maintained and eventually disassembled: its buildability.

1.3   Buildability

Buildability (or constructability) is an approach to design which seeks to eliminate non-productive work on site, make the production process more simple, and provide the opportunity for more efficient site management. Thus designing and detailing for buildability requires an understanding of how components are manufactured off site as well as how the building is to be assembled on site for the buildability philosophy to be adopted with any real effectiveness. During the early 1980s the Construction Industry Research and Information Association (CIRIA) published *Buildability: An Assessment* (CIRIA 1983) which defined buildability as 'the extent to which the design of the building facilitates ease of construction, subject to the overall requirements for the completed building'. This work highlighted the separation between design and production in the British building industry, identified in earlier reports (e.g. *Emmerson Report* 1962) and still highlighted as a problem in more recent publications (e.g. Egan 1998). To many designers the term buildability is synonymous with good design and good detailing, and something they have always taken seriously. However, with the development of different procurement routes and increased competition for work from new players in an already busy market the trend over the past 50 years or so has been for greater specialisation, greater complexity and increased detachment of designers from the building site. Architects and technologists often talk of 'making buildings' but very few build in a physical manner. The buildings they design and detail are built by others in a process where architectural intent represented by drawings, specifications, schedules and models is used to translate intent to physical artefact. In all but a few procurement routes the designer is disengaged from the physical act of building. A number of attempts at simplifying the process from a procurement angle have been made, although it is debatable as to whether these alternatives to the traditional method have improved the quality of the process or the quality of the product. The core message of buildability as advocated by CIRIA is more simplicity, greater standardisation, and better communication between designer and builder. These themes are summarised below and developed throughout the book.

(1) *Simplicity.* Experienced designers will willingly concede that it is easier to make something complicated than it is to make it simple. Arguably, many of

the best ideas, products and processes are simple in their inception, manufacture and use. Such simplicity has usually taken an enormous amount of effort. Simplification should not be confused with standardisation because many standardised systems are quite complex in the technologies employed and the skills required for successful implementation.

(2) *Standardisation.* Standardisation is a word that tends to conjure up images of conformity and monotonous repetition, a landscape of identical houses. It is a strategy central to manufacturing and becoming increasingly common in building through improved pre-fabrication methods. Because building projects are bespoke the amount of standardisation may be limited for some design problems, but for clients who depend on a certain amount of repetition, such as the mass house-builders, the potential of standardisation and pre-fabrication is considerable. However, no matter how good the quality of the manufacture off site there is still a reliance on people, the fixers and fitters, to assemble the components on site to form the whole, and careful control is required to maintain quality standards.

(3) *Better communication.* Communication between different building disciplines and between different stages in the project must be as smooth as possible, although this is never quite as straightforward as many would like to think. Because of the large number of specialists involved, combined with the tendency for the design stages to be segmented and hence divorced from manufacturing and assembly, the potential for ineffective communication is always present regardless of the effectiveness of the managerial systems in place. An ability to recognise potential hurdles to achieving effective communication is a desirable quality.

These three principles also relate to the eventual disassembly of the building. Thus the designer must consider the ease of buildability and the ease of disassembly at some unspecified future date, e.g. 50 years hence. In essence we are referring to the 'art' of detailing a building.

1.4   Quality

So far the word 'quality' has been used rather loosely. Trying to define quality is a real challenge when it comes to construction, partly because of the complex nature of building activity and partly because of the number of parties who have a stake in achieving quality. Individuals and organisations concerned with achieving quality range from government bodies (regulations, standards and codes), clients (individual and client bodies), manufacturers and suppliers (materials, products and systems), designers (architects, engineers, etc.), assemblers (craftsmen, tradespeople and construction managers), building users (often different to the client and changing over time), insurers and investors. Each group's perception of quality will vary depending on their particular position in the development 'team'. Not surprisingly there is a great deal of confusion when people talk about achieving quality in construction, despite a growing body of literature addressed specifically at such issues. Usually the word 'quality' is used in a subjective manner, rather than in an objective sense that can be tested and benchmarked. To confuse the issue further, provision of a quality service does not necessarily mean quality work, nor does a quality building necessarily have to be the product of a quality service. The two should, however, be inseparable (Maister 1993). In terms of the finished artefact Cuff (1991) argues that there are three principal judges of any building's quality: first, the consumers, the building users and the public at large; second, the participants in the design and assembly process; third, the architectural profession. These groups all have different criteria for determining quality, so an 'excellent building' is one perceived as excellent by all three groups. For the purposes of this book quality is considered under three, well-established headings, namely quality control (QC), quality management and quality of the finished building.

1.4.1   *Quality control*

QC is a managerial tool that ensures work conforms to predetermined performance specifications. Although QC has been developed by and is still very much associated with manufacturing, it has more recently been transferred to the service industry as part of a quality management system. For manufacturers the achievement of quality production, with long runs of products in a controlled and stable environment, is obtainable and, assuming the technology and personnel are correctly deployed, easy to maintain at a constant standard. When it comes to achieving QC on site the parameters are different. First, much of the work is carried out without the benefit of shelter from the weather and emphasis on programming work to achieve a weather-proof envelope as early as possible in the assembly process is a prime concern. Second, the physical arrangement of the building changes on a daily, or even hourly, basis as work proceeds, which inevitably creates problems for ensuring safe working conditions – what was void becomes solid, solid becomes void – necessitating constant vigilance. Third, the number of different operatives present on site at any one time (sub-contractors and sub-sub-contractors) makes the monitoring of quality particularly time consuming for both the construction manager and the clerk of works – work can be completed and covered up without anyone other than those responsible for doing it assessing the work for quality. Thus various initiatives to move as much production to the factory by way of pre-fabrication, leaving only the assembly to be done on site, have been tried over the years with varying degrees of success. For professional service firms such as architects and engineers, QC is more concerned with checking documentation against predetermined standards. Checking drawings, specifications and associated documentation before issue, and the checking of other consultants' documentation for consistency with the overall design concept, will help to control the quality of the information provided to the builder. QC is also achieved by adherence to current codes, standards and regulations.

1.4.2   *Quality assurance*

Quality assurance (QA) is a formally implemented management system that is certified and constantly monitored by an independent body, such as the British Standard Institution (BSI), to ensure compliance with the ISO 9000 series (formerly BS 5750). Quality management evolved from early work on QC in the American manufacturing industry but it was the Japanese who took quality management to new heights, inspired by the work of Deming and Juran. From the 1950s they contributed to the Japanese revolution in continuous quality improvement, a revolution which has spread world-wide. Widely adopted in manufacturing, quality management systems have taken longer to gain widespread acceptance in the building industry, although many contractors and professionals now have certified quality management systems in place or claim to be working towards QA. Provision of a quality service is fundamental to the competitiveness of a modern organisation, whether it is concerned with manufacturing, assembly, service provision or a combination of activities. Attempting constantly to please the client or customer is central to the total quality management (TQM) philosophy. As a step-by-step approach to continuous improvement, known as *Kaizen* in Japan, TQM has gained widespread acceptance. It is a people-focused management concept that aims at continual improvement and greater integration through a focus on client satisfaction – essentially a soft management tool involving pride in one's work and the constant desire to improve upon past success.

1.4.3   *Quality of the finished artefact*

QC, the use of quality management, and the adoption of a total approach to quality from everyone involved in the construction process will be instrumental in determining the finished quality of the building. Quality for each individual building project will be determined by the following constant variables:

- assembly of the design and construction teams (procurement route)
- effectiveness of the briefing process
- effectiveness of the design decision-making process
- effectiveness of the assembly process
- effectiveness of communications
- time constraints
- financial constraints.

When so much effort is often expended on the design and construction process it is crucial to understand quality from the perspective of the building users. While space and facilities are critical to ensuring user satisfaction, so too are the materials that form the finishes. Quality materials and craftsmanship carry a higher initial cost than cheaper and (possibly) less durable options, yet the overall feel of the building and its long-term durability may be considerably improved.

1.5   Time and costs

Closely associated with the achievement of quality is the amount of time available to complete the task within the project's financial constraints. Arguably, time and cost are the two most contentious issues with any project. Clients want a quality building for as little financial outlay as possible, and (of course) they want it delivered in a very short period of time. From the designer's perspective the financial budget is never quite generous enough to use good quality materials and the time frame to achieve a quality building is always too tight. Builders are often on the receiving end of cost cutting exercises and very tight programmes, which (contrary to much anecdotal evidence) they manage to achieve much to everyone's relief. With careful planning and tight managerial control the majority of projects are delivered on time and within budget, but when things do start to go wrong it invariably leads to additional time and/or additional expense. An argument often tabled when the project has exceeded its programme is that 1 or 2 weeks in the life of a building, say 100 years, are negligible. So it is, but the argument should be made at the briefing stage, not when the project is starting to run behind schedule because of poor managerial control.

1.5.1   Time

Of all the resources, time is the most precious and the one thing that no one ever appears to have enough of. No matter what the task, we would all have liked longer to complete it (or do it better); there is nothing unusual in this. However, time has an economic value and for commercial concerns the quicker they can get their building completed, or reopened if being refitted, the greater the financial return. Building designers and builders able to minimise the amount of time required to assemble a building, from inception to legal possession by the client, hold competitive advantage over those who cannot, a service clients are willing to pay a premium for. To do so requires extensive knowledge of design, manufacturing, assembly and managerial skills. For building design projects the time required can be divided into a number of main phases:

- time to develop the brief
- time to develop the design and acquire all necessary statutory consents
- time to select an appropriate contractor
- time to construct the building
- time to assess the consequences of the project, i.e. feedback.

1.5.2   Costs

In addition to a building's basic functions of providing shelter and security (regardless of technical sophistication), the site and the structure temporarily residing on it are economic assets. There are three principal costs to be considered at the outset of a construction project: the initial building cost, the cost of the building in use, and the recovery cost.

(1) *Initial cost.* Also referred to as the acquisition cost or the development cost, the initial cost covers the entire cost of creating, or remodelling, the building. For many clients this is their primary, and often only, concern. Initial costs cover land/building acquisition costs, professional consultants' fees, the cost of the materials that comprise the completed building, and the cost of putting it all together. Cost reductions may be possible by limiting the number of professionals involved in the development team (and hence reducing the professional fees), selecting less expensive building materials and reducing the amount of time required to assemble them on site.

(2) *Cost in use.* Otherwise known as the running cost or operating cost, this cost is set by the decisions made at the briefing stage and the subsequent decisions made during the design and assembly phases. For many years running costs were only given superficial attention at the design stage, although this has changed with the use of life cycle costing techniques which help to highlight the link between design decisions and costs in use. Materials and components with long service lives do cost more than those not expected to last so long and designing to reduce both maintenance and running costs may result in an increase in the initial cost. However, over the longer term, say 15 years, it will cost the building owner less than the solution with lower initial cost. It is a question of balancing alternatives at the design stage and educating the client about building costs in use because many clients will need some encouragement to part with their money 'up front'.

(3) *Recovery cost.* There is a third cost that is rarely considered – the cost of demolition and materials recovery. Partly, this is because the client may well have sold the building (or died) long before the building is recycled, and partly because such costs are traditionally associated with the initial cost of the future development. Again this may be of little concern to the current client who is looking for short-term gain with minimal outlay. However, if we are to take environmental issues seriously then the recycling potential and ease of disassembly must be considered during the design phases and costed into the development budget.

1.6 An environmental agenda

One of the most important concerns for all members of the building team is that of sustainability. At the start of the new millennium attention is once again focused on sustainable issues. The planet's resources are being consumed at a rate which is not sustainable and the amount of waste we produce is equally unsustainable. Building has a lot to answer for in terms of the amount of natural resources consumed, the amount of pollution created, the amount of energy wasted and the amount of waste generated. It is widely accepted that a more environmentally responsible approach to building design, construction, use and re-use is required. Such concerns are not new. Writing in 1954 Richard Neutra noted that mankind was becoming too detached from the natural world, and in doing so he raised similar concerns expressed some time earlier by Ruskin and his contemporaries. In 1962 Rachel Carson published *Silent Spring*, which is widely acknowledged as the catalyst to the world-wide environmental movement and increased public awareness of environmental issues. In 1965 James Lovelock put forward the Gaia hypothesis (Lovelock 1990), that organisms interact with their environment to produce a self-sustaining equilibrium, a different perspective to that of natural evolution. Thus if humans disturb the environment (e.g. pollute it) they will disturb the equilibrium (e.g. changing weather patterns), a pattern that is only too evident now. During the 1970s government concerns over oil supply resulted in attempts to conserve fuel resources through increased standards for thermal insulation. In the late 1970s and the early 1980s governmental policy shifted towards energy economy. By 1992 concern was focused on the reduction of CO_2 emissions. The term 'sustainable development' came into common usage following publication of the *Brundlandt Report* (World Commission on Environment and Development 1987) and further attention was generated by the Rio Earth Summit conference of 1992 and the widespread adoption of *Agenda 21*. In 1997 the Kyoto conference resulted in agreement to reduce greenhouse gas emissions by 20% (based on 1990 levels) because of concerns over global warming. These are issues that those involved in building cannot afford to ignore.

1.6.1   An environmentally responsible approach to building

It is important to recognise that decisions which affect the environment cannot be divorced from the everyday decision-making processes of the makers and users of buildings. For many designers, builders and users, it means doing something different to that which is familiar and routine, breaking existing habits and taking time to consider the consequences of their decisions. To adopt an environmentally responsible approach to building construction, use and re-use requires the commitment of all concerned. It also places an emphasis on designers and users having the relevant information to be able to make informed decisions. Issues surrounding 'green building' are complex and continue to change as developments are made and more information is made available to the designer. A wide variety of demonstration projects have been built over the years, although their uptake on a larger scale has, to date, been slow. There are an increasing number of buildings that are promoted as being environmentally friendly, such as the Queens Building at Simon de Montfort University in Leicester and the Business Promotion Centre in Duisberg, Germany, by Norman Foster and Associates. Less publicised are the buildings which incorporate small, but collectively significant, contributions to sustainable building: a quiet, yet collectively effective, approach to environmental concerns. Both existing and new technologies offer the opportunity for designers, builders and users of buildings to do their bit to help enhance the environment and take an environmentally responsible approach. Involving potential users in the briefing, design and management of buildings is an important consideration, especially in terms of users' evaluation of environmental issues. An ecological approach to building requires an integrated and balanced approach. It will, however, raise questions about how we, as designers, practise our vocation: we need to question and challenge existing building protocols and our existing habits. Actions taken to reduce the level of embodied energy, minimise pollution, conserve non-renewable resources, reduce energy consumption, etc., often place conflicting demands on the design team – it is a question of balance.

1.7   The human factor

Before proceeding further an important, albeit obvious, point needs to be made. Whatever technologies, tools and methods are employed in the design, assembly and use of a building, the entire process involves people. Buildings are designed, detailed, scheduled, assembled, maintained, refurbished, dismantled, used and misused by people. From a design perspective the human scale is important, although it has been overlooked in favour of new technologies in the past. People should be the strongest link in the quality chain, although they are often the weakest, prone to making errors under pressure and intent on doing things their way regardless of evidence to the contrary. Sometimes, even the most competent designers working in a well-managed office will make mistakes, as will experienced tradespeople working under ideal conditions. Some may be picked up by effective QC and/or quality management systems, and some may slip through the net, no matter how tight the mesh, leading to the possibility of disputes as people argue over who should pay to correct the error. Some errors are not always obvious at the time of design and construction and may manifest themselves in the form of a latent defect when the building is in use. Errors may occur through ignorance, misinterpretation of the information, and/or through inept building practices, although many can be traced back to trying to achieve too much in too little time.

1.7.1   *Murphy's Law*

Alternatively known as 'Sod's Law', the principle that 'if something can go wrong, it will' has been around for a long time. It was not until 1949, however, that Captain Edward A. Murphy's name became associated with this truism (Matthews 1997). He was the designer of a harness, fitted with electrodes, which was used to monitor the effects of rapid deceleration on aircraft pilots. During one of the tests on volunteers the harness failed to record any data. When Murphy investigated he found that every one of the electrodes had been wired incorrectly. This prompted his statement: 'If there are two or more ways of doing something, and one of them can lead to catastrophe, then someone will do it.' Now a familiar working assumption in safety engineering, this statement should be at the back of a designer's mind when detailing a building. The simpler the connections, joints and assembly sequence, the less the chance of someone doing it wrong – a philosophy advocated by this author in architectural practice and one advocated in this book.

1.7.2   *A question of liability*

Perhaps it is a sign of the times that liability is raised so early in this book, but whatever the background of a building designer he or she carries a considerable amount of responsibility for his or her actions. All decisions have consequences. Fortunately the majority of decisions taken by the design team have good consequences, but things do go wrong, some things could have been done better, and no matter how good we think we are at our jobs mistakes are made. As construction has become more complex so has the potential for error, and the threat of legal action is something that all those involved in building need to be aware of. Professional designers' legal obligations and responsibilities are governed by both statute and common law. Those which deserve the greatest attention are breach of contract and negligence:

■ *Breach of contract.* The design organisation will enter into a contractual relationship with the employer. In doing so the organisation agrees to carry out the work in a professional and workmanlike manner to the accepted standards of the profession. Failure to meet these standards may result in problems which lead to additional expense and delays – the organisation will be in breach of contract and may be liable for the damages.

■ *Negligence.* Professionals are also responsible for the consequences of their negligent behaviour, even in situations where no contractual arrangement exists. The duty under the law of torts depends on the duty of care which is owed to others.

In all cases it is the 'reasonable standard of care' as established under common law against which a defendant's performance will be judged. The law is a complex issue with rules and procedures affecting and controlling the actions of individuals and groups. Most professional design offices are now required to carry professional indemnity (PI) insurance as a condition of membership of their respective professional institution and/or governing body. Professional institutions also maintain and enforce codes of conduct to which their members must adhere. These codes vary with professional institution, but their aim is to try and ensure a certain standard of performance and behaviour by all members for the benefit of the profession and the public. For example, registered architects are bound by the Architects Registration Board (ARB) and (if they belong) by the Royal Institute of British Architect (RIBA); architectural technologists are bound by British Institute of Architectural Technologists (BIAT) Code of Conduct.

Further reading

Groák, S. (1992). *The Idea of Building: Thought and Action in the Design and Production of Buildings*, E & FN Spon, London.
Schmitz–Gunther, T. (ed.) (1998). *Living Spaces: Sustainable Building and Design*, Konemann, Cologne.

2 Evolving architectural technology

Technological change in building has long been a subject of interest to researchers and practitioners alike. Paradoxically, building has a reputation for being innovative but also slow to change established habits; as some observers have remarked, building is unlike other industries. This chapter starts by looking at the nature of building and technological change, explores the relationship between architecture and technology, and looks at the issue of detail design from both a theoretical and practical standpoint. It concludes with an overview of the evolution of the architectural technology discipline, tracing its development from the Oxford conference of 1958 through to the present day.

2.1 Building

Perhaps it is force of habit, or mere convenience, but we tend to use the term 'building industry' (or construction industry) and in doing so give the misleading impression that there is a homogeneous, well-defined industry with established relationships and supply chains, like, for example, the automobile industry. What we refer to as the 'industry' is in fact a massive network of manufacturers, suppliers, consultants, etc., brought together for specific projects. Some manufacturers produce materials and products that are specifically made for building, others supply their products to a wide variety of industries, supplying building as and when economic circumstances are favourable. We have an industry which is not, nor can it be, clearly defined, is extremely diverse in its output and in which relationships between parties are tenuous and which are often set up for one particular project. Regardless of these facts, the 'industry' has to be defined for purposes of economic analysis and employment statistics. When it is defined we find that building is the second most important industry in the majority of individual nations' economies (see Harvey and Ashworth 1993). Building activities both affect and are themselves affected by a country's economy and also by international economic trends. For example, the collapse of financial markets in the Far East towards the end of the 20th century had implications for the American and European markets, investment was delayed or suspended indefinitely and the building work associated with it stopped or delayed.

Buildings affect our health, both during the actual process of building and through the act of living and working in them. The industry has a poor record when it comes to health and safety on site, which recent legislation in the form of the Construction Design and Management (CDM) Regulations has tried to address. Links between poor health and inadequate housing were highlighted in a report by the Department of Health and Security working group *Inequalities in Health* (1980), better known as the 'Black Report', and again in the government's White Paper *Saving Lives: Our Healthier Nation* (1999). With 1.5 million homes considered to be below the current fitness standards and 2.5 million homes in the UK cold enough to cause ill health during the winter months, such concern is understandable. *Saving Lives* states that 'homes should be safe, warm, dry and well ventilated with amenities which meet minimum standards' (1999: 50), essentially matters of detail design which can be prevented and/or resolved through the correct application of technology as part of the complex jigsaw which makes up housing provision.

2.1.1　An industry of assembly

There has been a move more recently to see building as a manufacturing industry, rather than a craftsmanship based one. In some respects building has always relied very heavily on manufacturing processes and mass production. Clay bricks are perhaps the best example of a mass produced product, although they tended to be manufactured for local use until the development of effective transportation systems allowed their widespread distribution throughout the country and export abroad. Pre-fabricated buildings have been an essential part of building for a long time. As early as the 1780s portable cottages were being transported to the colonies, first exploiting timber frame technology, then corrugated iron and later cast iron (see Herbert 1978). Developments in patent glazing and glazed framed buildings can be traced back to the genius of Paxton. He was the chief gardener at Chatsworth House where he built the Great Conservatory between 1832 and 1848, which provided the experience to supervise and organise the erection of the Crystal Palace. Built as a temporary structure for the Great Exhibition of 1851,

Figure 2.1　Paxtonian glasshouse detail.

Paxton's design is regarded as the first major pre-fabricated building (Bowley 1960). Paxton was well versed in the potential of mass production, marketing his Paxtonian glass houses via mail order to the wealthier members of society.

Seaside pleasure piers also relied very heavily on mass produced components. The doyen of pier building, Eugenius Birch, an engineer, worked closely with manufacturers to realise his designs as elegant structures, building 16 pleasure piers between 1853 and 1884, the majority of which relied heavily on mass produced components in cast and wrought iron which were largely selected from standard components listed in the manufacturers' catalogues. Birch was an individual who understood the potential and limitations of the materials he selected (timber, cast and wrought iron) and exploited then to produce some elegant structures, most famously Brighton's West Pier and Blackpool's North Pier, a trait common among the world's best designers.

During the 20th century there were many attempts to harness industrial processes for the benefit of building and the building user. The Bauhaus movement is one of the best known, a movement which advocated mass production and repetition at the heart of its design philosophy. In the UK the use of mass production of pre-fabricated homes ('prefabs') to house families after the Second World War was a triumph of manufacturing and assembly. Factories dedicated to the war effort soon switched their attention to the domestic housing market and materials not previously associated with housebuilding, such as aluminium, were used because they were readily available. This was followed by the trend for system building in the 1960s when 'efficiency' was the main priority, a period when many large panel system tower blocks were assembled, very badly, on site. Poor detailing and inadequate supervision of construction on site, combined with the social problems associated with the majority of high-rise blocks in the UK accelerated the demise of the tower block. The partial collapse of Ronan Point in East London in 1968, killing five people, gave system building a bad name. Yet pre-fabrication techniques were and still are used. More recently pre-fabrication techniques have been used by the food retail industry, with fast-food units appearing around the country on pre-prepared sites literally overnight, an example of the Egan Report's core message of faster, cheaper and better through the integration of design and production. As the use of mass produced components and products has increased, the labour has shifted from the building site to the factory, to be replaced by robotic manufacturing systems. Now much of the labour on site is concerned with placing and fixing machine-made products to predetermined positions and/or is involved in the supervision of the assembly process; there is little in the way of craftsmanship to be seen.

2.1.2   *Building characteristics*

There are a number of constant factors which affect building, namely the technologies available, the rate of change, the amount of demand, the extent of legislation and architectural fashion. Combined these factors influence, and are influenced by, the people who build and use buildings (see Fig. 2.2).

(1) *Technologies.* Advances in materials and mass production have given the designer incredible potential in terms of choice. Conversely they also require

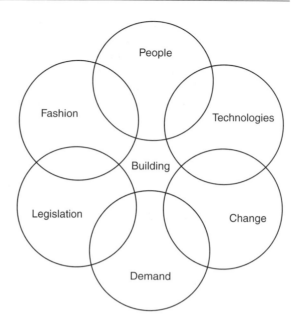

Figure 2.2 Characteristics of building.

the designer to have greater knowledge and understanding of materials and technologies. High-rise buildings were not just a result of developments in structural steelwork, the designs also required developments in fire protection and the development of the safety elevator. Other advances in services, such as air conditioning, have provided additional potential and choice for designers, as have advances in power distribution systems. Not so long ago many office buildings with shallow service zones were considered obsolete because of the need to accommodate many kilometres of cable for the computers, but now, with the growing use of laptops and infrared (IR) communication between machines, the requirement is no longer so great and buildings once considered obsolete are back in use. With the growth of information technologies (ITs) has come the potential for dealing with vast quantities of information provided through the monitoring of activities within a building: 'data mining' and other 'smart' technologies are essential tools for asset managers in their drive to save energy and manage resources through greater knowledge of the building in use.

(2) *Change.* Change in building has long been a subject of interest to researchers and practitioners alike. Paradoxically, some sections of building have a reputation for being innovative yet the industry as a whole has an equally deserved reputation for being slow to change established habits, which has led some observers to note that building is not backward, merely different to other industries (e.g. Ball 1988). In many respects the apparent paradox between a willingness to try innovative technologies and resistance to change can be explained by the fragmented, competitive nature of the industry. Yet change is ever present, changing procurement routes, changing building materials and technologies, and changing IT, such that what we term 'traditional' construction is, on closer examination, considerably less traditional than similar

construction undertaken 100 years ago, despite the fact that its external appearance may be very similar.

(3) *Demand.* Building activity is linked to demand, both social and economic demand. Changing living and working patterns have led to the development of new building forms, such as train stations and airports, whereas political pressure to rationalise services has led to the closure of the smaller hospitals and schools in favour of new, larger, buildings. The redundant buildings then become the focus of refurbishment projects, with redundant churches converted into flats and schools into restaurants and bars. Other sectors, such as housing, have long been a political football, with successive governments hoping to secure votes through promises of investment in new housing. Building is an economic activity and the assets need to be managed accordingly.

(4) *Legislation.* Legislation has developed largely in response to issues of public health and safety. It is constantly changing to respond to (and sometimes drive) technological advances and social change. Sometimes seen as hindering creative design solutions, sometimes as the generator of novel solutions, legislation cannot be ignored by the designer. Difficult to detach from political decision-making, especially in areas such as planning legislation and health and safety, legislation affects manufacturers, designers, builders and users to varying degrees.

(5) *Fashion.* Architecture has embraced technology as a badge of fashion. Buildings are described by the design teams' design philosophy, be it traditional, high tech, low tech, constructivist, de-constructivist, etc., approaches which influence the range and type of materials used to obtain the desired effect. At various points in time it may be fashionable to use brick, cladding or structural glass with the fashion set by the well-known designers and promoted by the architectural and building journals. There is a clear link between architectural fashion and developments in materials and technologies, although which leads the other is often open to debate. There is also a link between larger social concerns, such as sustainable development and architectural detailing.

(6) *People.* People are an important factor in the building equation, although largely ignored in many of the books which deal with building technology. People affect and are affected by technologies, change, demand, legislation and fashion. The behaviour of people influences the manner in which we build. For the technologist it is important not to be seduced by the technology; it must be remembered that people will have to build and assemble the details, building users will have to interact with the finished artefact and at some stage others will be faced with re-designing, re-using or demolishing and recyling the structure.

2.2   Architecture, technology and detail

Architecture and technology have a very special relationship, since without the technologies to realise the built form architectural design would exist only on paper. In education technology is usually taught as a separate subject to architectural design, coming together in the realisation of the design project. Yet technology is so completely tied up with architecture that in practice the designer is constantly juggling with the design concept, the technology to realise it and the management of that process, so much so that towards the end of the 20th century a new discipline, that of architectural technology, developed and continues to evolve (discussed below) – a discipline which aims to integrate three core areas, namely design, technology and management, in pursuit of quality buildings, i.e. architecture as the 'poetics of construction' to use Kenneth Frampton's (1995) terminology.

One question which is difficult, if not impossible, to answer is whether the design generates the detail or the technologies dictate the design. Perhaps it is best left unanswered. Generally speaking the great buildings of the world not only have a strong idea but also make use of the technology to realise the vision. This is equally so for the less famous, but equally important, buildings which fail to make it into the design journals, i.e. the vast majority of our building stock. As a society we have come to want more from our buildings than just shelter and comfort. Now even our homes are becoming complex in terms of the services which have to be provided and the quality of finish expected. Buildings are now more highly serviced than they ever have been as society responds to the market pull of ITs and the challenge of the information age. The 'pulling together' of different technologies into a completed building design is a complex task, involving the input and co-ordination of many different people, a process described as detail design where issues of buildability should be paramount in the designer's mind. Detailing for buildability, or more accurately, ease of assembly, is a constant challenge that all designers and builders must fully understand.

2.2.1 *Detail design methods*

The majority of published literature that has investigated the way in which architects make decisions has concentrated on the *design process* with emphasis on the resulting *design* (Rowe 1987). This body of literature goes back to the 1960s and 1970s and is commonly referred to as 'design methods' literature. It was concerned with creative problem-solving and sought to provide theoretical constructs based on information processing theory which in the event were poorly supported by observation of the actual processes. Not surprisingly design methods literature has been criticised by practising architects as irrelevant to their actual working methods (e.g. Mackinder 1980) and Peter Rowe (1987) has described it as an 'abject failure' since it was unable to describe the subtlety and profundity of problem-solving.

For many designers and researchers the conceptual design stage (RIBA stages A to D) is more interesting and not surprisingly more fully researched than the detail design stage. Heath (1984) was unable to describe how far the design process extended, but still separated schematic design from detail design. Separation of these two stages can also be seen in the larger architectural offices in which the design architect often delegates responsibility for the detail design to an architectural technologist whose primary skill is detailing. As Leatherbarrow puts it: 'many "designers" do not specify "details", as detailing is the work of architectural technicians' (Leatherbarrow 1993: 145). It would be easy to conclude from the design methods literature that the conceptual design stage is where the

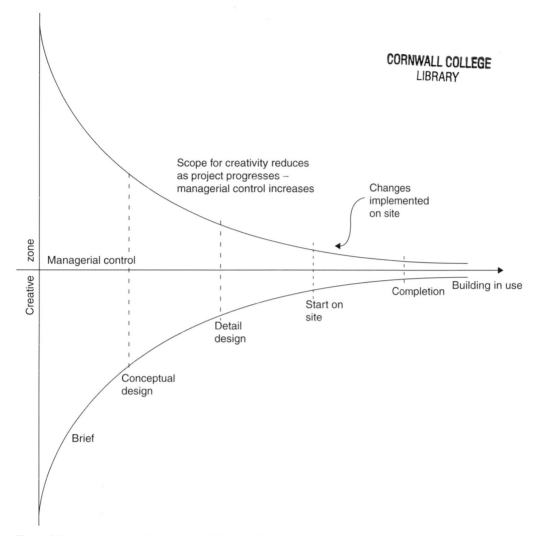

Figure 2.3   Design control (from Emmitt 1999: 112).

creativity takes place, ceasing at detail design. Such an assumption would be wrong; creativity still takes place – indeed the best detailers can come up with creative solutions to very difficult technical problems – it just has to be constrained (see Fig. 2.3). So while architects face information overload in terms of the literature dedicated to design theory, there is little which deals with detail design theory. Given the amount of time spent on this crucial stage of the design process, such an oversight may be surprising, although the observational work required to investigate detail design decisions is both time consuming and difficult to achieve without influencing the process (Emmitt 1997a). This leads to an interesting question. Is there a body of literature dedicated to detail design methods? The quick answer is no. The lengthier answer is that there is a lot of literature dealing with aspects of architectural technology, especially construction technology and materials technology, much of which is concerned with detail design but which does not form a coherent body of literature.

Given that the detail design stage is the most time consuming, the most demanding of resources and arguably the most critical in determining the long-term durability and serviceability of the building, such oversight is a little surprising. A small number of researchers have attempted to analyse the amount of time dedicated to conceptual and detail design and then assessed this against the overall cost of the project, finding that the major cost implications are related to the conceptual design stage, rather than the detail design stage, which has led them to conclude that the detail design stage is of minimal importance when it comes to cost. I disagree for a number of reasons. First, such research is dogged (if not flawed) by the difficulty of making divisions between conceptual and detail design decisions. It is only in design offices where conceptual design is formally separated from detail design and undertaken by different individuals that such a comparison can be made. In offices run under a more traditional system such divisions are dependent upon the discretion and perception of individual designers who have been asked by a researcher to record their actions. Thus boundaries are problematical in terms of research methodology.

Research into the detail design process by Holness (1996) found that there were two distinct but parallel decision-making processes: a dominant intuitive one and a supporting rational one. Designers were found to introduce their detail design concepts at a very early stage in the design process based on their intuitive understanding of what seemed to be appropriate for a given situation. Thus detail design was seen to form an integral part of the designer's strategy for formulating design options and the separation of detail from conceptual design appeared unjustified because they were developed in parallel rather than sequentially, apparently supporting earlier observations reported by Mackinder (1980).

For the sole practitioner and for offices working on very small projects such an approach may be possible, but for many practitioners working in professionally managed organisations which harness the individual skills of their employees there is a need to separate conceptual design from detail design if the business is to stay viable and able to deliver an excellent service to its clients. In such situations the transfer of information concerning conceptual issues to another individual who is concerned with issues of detail becomes a critical matter and needs careful consideration and management, usually through effective design reviews.

2.3   Detail design in practice

Conceptual design can be, and often is, technology driven. However, it is during the detail design stage that the majority of decisions are taken to realise the design vision – a period during which technology is applied to abstract ideas and concepts. In practice the detail design phase is a complex process involving the co-ordination of diffuse information, the management of disparate consultants and the making of thousands of decisions which will affect both the appearance and design life of the building, not to mention its cost in use and its durability. For the professional service firm the management of the detail design stage poses one of the biggest challenges because even minor adjustments to the design can cause problems for the design programme and the cost-effectiveness of the detail design exercise. The design manager is faced with a number of challenges, not least that of ensuring effective communication between different disciplines and different stages in the design process, one during which QC is a primary concern. This stage is often viewed as being concerned with implementing the design quickly, accurately and as cheaply as possible, although to do so in practice is a constant challenge.

2.3.1   Constant challenges

Before proceeding further it may be useful to address a number of challenges that confront designers constantly. They relate to the pursuit of a solution to a problem, the existing knowledge base of building construction, and the detailing challenge.

(1) *There is only one solution to a detail design problem.* While such an ideal is worth pursuing, in reality the detail design solution will be a compromise, a choice from a number of possible solutions, and whether one was better than another for a given situation is often only revealed with the passage of time. For the designer the choice is usually determined by his or her previous experience, the amount of time available to investigate fully an alternative solution and the input of other project participants in the form of pressure from, e.g. the client, cost consultant, engineer, design manager or builder. Thus the solution chosen may not necessarily be the best solution when analysed by a third party (usually someone with a legal bent after some element has failed prematurely), but which was eminently sensible at the time. Such a statement is not meant as an excuse for ineffective detailing because designers and builders should get it right (see point 2 below). As technologies have advanced and become more readily available the number of choices available to the designer has mushroomed; not only has the choice of detailing solutions increased but so has the number of manufactured building products that (according to the manufacturer's literature at least) will suit the detail. In many respects the number of choices is equally as numerous to the detailer as to the conceptual designer – it is simply that the parameters in which decisions are made are more clearly defined during the detail design stage.

(2) *We know how to detail buildings.* If this is true, why are there so many building failures? For the majority of building projects we have standard and/or well-rehearsed solutions that we know will work and weather in an acceptable manner, but we still make mistakes. It has been argued that we must get better at applying what we know (or what others know) before we attempt to apply innovative technologies, i.e. we should use the knowledge we already have before we try and improve on it (Gumpertz and Rutila 1999). For those concerned with the long-term performance of buildings such an argument is very persuasive and would appear to be based on common sense. Equally, such an approach is sensible if a practice wishes to keep its exposure to risk to an acceptable level. On the other hand new standards and changes to legislation may force technological change onto designers who then have to innovate to deliver economic and buildable solutions. For example, brick cavity

wall construction was an innovation that diffused to become a traditional construction detail and which is now being replaced by new techniques to meet higher insulation standards. Furthermore, the opportunity to try something new, or do something a little differently, is central to many designers' character and the desire to be creative and/or use new materials and techniques has to be balanced against other concerns. Innovation in building is also driven by cultural issues and political pressure. Society requires, expects and enjoys technological progress, best exemplified by the Millennium Dome in London, which mirrors the radical structures built for the Festival of Britain, despite the tendency of the press to favour a conservational approach.

(3) *Detail design is less interesting than conceptual design.* This impression is generated in the majority of books that address design decision-making and magnified in the architectural design studio where the emphasis is more on creativity and conceptual issues than matters of detail (usually addressed separately in construction technology). In many respects it is the process of putting the concept through the detailed phase which is the most challenging. Conflicts of interest between the creatives and the technologists is inevitable: hard decisions have to be made which can be fudged during the more abstract period of design development. Synergy between concept and detail is vital to a successful building as epitomised by the Mies quote 'God is in the details'. Who does the detailing will depend upon the size and complexity of the project.

2.4 The evolution of construction specialists

Specialisation and professional diversity are characteristics of building. Indeed, it would appear that the trend world-wide is for increasing diversity and specialisation. With diversity comes opportunities for doing things differently, hopefully better. On the downside, increased fragmentation of the building industry may lead to increased problems with communication between specialists, a problem that can be mitigated through effective utilisation of IT. A brief overview of the development and evolution of construction specialists in the UK may help to understand the current position, especially calls for greater integration.

The relationship between building technology and structure on architectural design can be traced back to the Enlightenment and the Industrial Revolution, periods when advances in technology and science were seen as the way forward, and times of solid faith in progress. Architects needed a thorough knowledge of scientific matters (applied mechanics and materials properties) as part of their education and daily practice. However, it was the engineers who took up the technical advances and new ideas in building the quickest. Cast iron, concrete, steel and glass gave engineers great opportunities to build great structures, sometimes working alongside architects, sometimes with contractors. The unquestioning faith in science and technology that dominated earlier times has given way to increased scepticism and caution, represented in constant questioning of professionals (architects, doctors, scientists, etc.) and increased focus on the amateur as some would argue (dumbing down). In many respects professionals have themselves to blame, retiring behind the façade of their professional institutions and exhibiting a level of arrogance that many outside these special cultures have been wanting to destroy for a long time. At the time of writing this book it is difficult to turn on the television or read the newspaper without seeing a professional in trouble (for negligence) and lots of advice from amateurs as to how to do it in journals and DIY-type programmes.

As technologies multiplied in number and complexity the building profession started to fragment. Architects started to distance themselves from surveying and construction, and build walls around themselves in the form of their professional institutions. Divisions in responsibilities, especially between design and technology, are linked to the historical development of the professional institutions and the protectionism that they sought to afford their members. Increases in building activity brought about social and structural changes within the building industry (e.g. Bowley 1960). Surveying, structural engineering and design activities were separated with the development of the professional institutions. The Institute of Civil Engineers was formed in 1818, the Institute of British Architects in 1834 and the Surveyors' Institute in 1868. Other professional groups, such as planners, came about in response to governmental legislation to control development. The American Institute of Architects (AIA) was formed in 1859 and a clear line of demarcation was drawn between architecture and construction (Carpenter 1997). More recently architects have withdrawn further from technical issues, both in education and in practice (e.g. Cole and Cooper 1988, Carpenter 1997, Emmitt 1999a), leaving a gap for someone to fill. The history of the architectural profession is well documented. What is less well covered is the role of the architectural technologist, one that has grown out of architect's assistant, through technician, to the relatively new profession of architectural technology.

2.5   Architectural technology – a 'new' discipline

For many years the unrecognised work-horses of architectural practices, technologists have been at the heart of many a successful practice, forming the link between conceptual design and production, translating design intent into physical reality. But they have had to endure a territory devoid of status, where career progression and standing within the industry have traditionally been well below that of their design orientated colleagues. For many technologists their education is wrought in the Schools of Building, where technology, management and design are robust components of their syllabus, as it is for surveyors and construction managers. Technologists are the production workers, converting design intent into meaningful information that can be conveyed to the builder; as such they occupy an important and often unrecognised role as detailers and information providers, spanning the boundaries of design and production (see also Chapter 15).

Writing in the later half of the 19th century the architect and critic John T. Emmett (1880), who was highly critical of the 'strange and paradoxical profession' of architecture, made a particular point of highlighting the plight of the architect's assistant. He claimed that assistants were by far the most important members of the architectural profession, essential to the smooth running of their superior's office, but largely unseen and certainly unrecognised. Emmett went on to urge architects' assistants to form an association or institute, in partnership with the tradesmen and workmen, which would lead to 'perfectly instructed, practical, artistic craftsmen', and who would become masters of their own destiny in a 'joyful and dignified career'. His words were not heeded, and it took almost 80 years before the institute advocated by Emmett was formed, not by the assistants, but by the RIBA at the Oxford conference.

2.5.1 The Oxford conference

The Oxford conference of 1958 proposed the abolition of pupillage and part-time courses for architects, and with it the formal creation of the architectural technician discipline. This essentially created a two-tier system, those responsible for controlling design (architects) and those with practical skills (the architectural technicians), and to reinforce the distinction the technicians were given lessons in 'design appreciation' rather than studio-based design projects (Crinson and Lubbock 1994). Of course, the two-tier system was already in place in the majority of practices, but now it had been officially recognised, thus setting the scene for the events that were to follow.

The RIBA 1962 report *The Architect and His Office* identified the need for an institution (other than the RIBA) that technicians could join to ensure maintenance of standards for education and training (RIBA 1962). Technical design skills were identified as a missing component of architectural practice and the report urged the diversification of architectural education so that this shortcoming could be addressed, suggesting that architects who chose to specialise in technology (rather than design), the 'architechnologists', should still be allowed to join the RIBA (RIBA 1962). The report acknowledged that technicians were needed in architects' offices to raise productivity and standards of service, for which they would require education and training in the preparation of production information and technical administration; 'design' was specifically excluded from the technologist's training. In 1965 the Society of Architectural and Associated Technicians (SAAT) was formed and inaugurated as an Associated Society of the RIBA under Byelaw 75 of the RIBA's charter in 1969 (SAAT 1984). SAAT did not encompass all technicians (estimated at 20,000–25,000 by SAAT); many belonged to other societies, as reflected in its membership of 5300 in December 1983.

In May 1984 the SAAT published an influential report, *Architectural Technology: The Constructive Link,* which drew on existing research to develop a view of construction for the 1980s and beyond, highlighting the future direction for SAAT and its members. The report was important in establishing a sense of identity for architectural technicians since it helped to identify the technicians' role as one that was complementary to that of the architect. In particular the 'constructive link' has since been seen as the most important concept, at the heart of the modern architectural technology discipline, implicit in the reports by Latham (1994) and Egan (1998).

2.5.2 The British Institute of Architectural Technologists

From inception in 1965 SAAT quickly became established. In 1986 the members changed its name to the British Institute of Architectural Technicians and then to

BIAT in 1994. With the change of name from technician to technologist and the promotion of degree-level qualifications for its members, BIAT has started to redress the issue of status and its members can now compete with architects and other building professionals on more equal terms. Architectural technology has evolved into a distinctly separate discipline from architecture, one that both complements and threatens architects.

Building has seen significant changes since the Oxford conference, with traditional roles and relationships both challenged and re-defined. Increased competition and the introduction of new disciplines such as project managers, facilities managers, etc., have resulted in a wide variety of building procurement methods, offered by competing and diverse professional disciplines. Within this competitive marketplace it is widely accepted that the architect's role has moved from traditional team leader to one of designer. Coupled with this has been the abrogation of technical issues to others (Cole and Cooper 1988), notably to the technologists. Over a quarter of BIAT's 6500-plus members practise privately or are running businesses as either partners or codirectors with architects and other building professionals, often providing services in direct competition with architectural and surveying practices. The trend is similar to that in the USA where there has been, and continues to be, a shift from the architect to the architectural technologist in terms of responsibility for building detailing and management. The role of the architectural technologist is continuing to grow in both stature and importance and is likely to develop further as BIAT matures as a professional body and starts to increase its leverage in the marketplace. In a step towards professional acceptability and accountability BIAT made PI insurance a mandatory requirement of membership from September 1995.

2.5.3 *Partnerships and common frameworks*

Careful to bridge the contrary worlds of design and production, BIAT has developed a common framework in conjunction with the RIBA that allows students the opportunity to transfer relatively easily (theoretically at least) from architecture to architectural technology or vice versa. One academic institution has developed a common first year for architects and technologists, with students making an informed choice after their first year of study, taking a design – or technology – rich pathway for their final 2 years. Universities that employ modular schemes have found it more difficult to meet the common framework, since their architectural technology degrees have more synergy with their building surveying and construction management degrees than architecture. Similarity in syllabus content between the Chartered Institute of Building (CIOB)'s construction management degrees and the new degrees promoted by BIAT was reflected in an announcement that the two institutions have formed a 'partnership' and would be working together on several issues, including education (*Architectural Technology* 1997).

At this juncture, it is useful to look back to Emmett's work again. As mentioned above, he was very critical of the architectural profession, since he saw the architect as nothing more than an intermediary, taking commission and not actually 'working': architects had become businessmen, taking a commission and pandering to their uneducated patrons, to the disadvantage of architecture. He favoured the traditions of the craftsman and manual workers, whom he urged to free themselves from the architectural profession. Essentially, Emmett was writing about the sub-division of responsibility within building and its associated disintegration of the creative act through the 'downward spiral of delegation, subordination, exploitation and alienation' (Crook 1972). He was attempting to resist the loss of craftsmanship in building through the argument for integration. Emmett was a radical and largely unknown in his lifetime, but there is an unnerving familiarity to his arguments even now.

2.5.4   BIAT definitions

On the 25 July 2001 the British Institute of Architectural Technologists (BIAT) published its definition of an architectural technologist and an architectural technician, thus helping to clarify the role and responsibilities of the technologist over and above the technician. This is an area that has caused a degree of confusion for some time, thus the definitions are welcome. BIAT's definitions are:

- *Architectural technologist.* The architectural technologist will be able to analyse, synthesise and evaluate design factors in order to produce design solutions which will satisfy performance, production and procurement criteria.

  This will be achieved through the design, selection and specification of material, components and assembly and the management, co-ordination, communication, presentation and monitoring of solutions which perform to the agreed brief and standards in terms of time, cost and quality.
- *Architectural technician.* The architectural technician will be able to establish the purpose, methods and techniques for preparing detailed design solutions.

  This will be achieved by the preparation, co-ordination and communication of technical information including drawings, graphical information, reports and schedules, contributing to meeting relevant statutory regulations and controlling projects by monitoring agreed quality standards and obtaining, recording and organising information.

Further reading

Harvey, R.C. and Ashworth, A. (1993). *The Construction Industry of Great Britain*, Newness, Oxford.

Potter, N. (1989). *What is a Designer? Things, Places, Messages* (Third Edition), Hyphen Press, London.

3 Constructive links

Building designers occupy a challenging, if not enviable, position as the link between design, manufacturing and production. The focus of this book is on the building (the product) rather than the project, yet one must have an understanding of project issues if the design intent is to be translated into an artefact of quality. This short chapter discusses the issues surrounding integration and supply chains. The tectonic links between the project's different stages and differing participants are also addressed, focusing on concept to detail, detail to assembly, and assembly to feedback into new concepts. Here the emphasis is on synthesis and detail design.

3.1 Interfaces

In 1984 SAAT published *Architectural Technology: The Constructive Link*, which comprised an overview of the changing nature of construction and the challenges facing the architectural technician. Based on an overview of the available literature, especially the RIBA report *The Architect and His Office* (RIBA 1962), SAAT's own report was important in emphasising the link between detail design and the operations on site, the constructive link. A position recognised and explored in the report became topical once again following the reports by Latham (1994) and Egan (1998). If we look at the three main phases of a building project (putting aside the building in use for one moment), i.e. conceptual design, detail design and site assembly, it is clear that there are two quite distinct links or 'boundary conditions' that are crucial to the transfer of design intent from conception to completion – the constructive links. The better the contributors to the process are able to communicate, the better the process and the completed building, expressed in Fig. 3.1.

- *Conceptual design.* Largely the domain of the designers, the conceptual design will be developed from the client's brief and will colour the decisions that follow.
- *Detail design.* This forms the link between conceptual design and the assembly of the building on site. Traditionally the break between conceptual design and detail design is between architects and technologists. Relationships with manufacturing companies should be closest during this stage.
- *Site assembly.* Putting the different elements together on the site in the correct position and within a set time frame and to a set budget is a constant challenge. The greater the empathy between designer and builder the more likely the project will be built as intended.
- *Manufacturers' input.* Manufacturers of building materials, components and products come from a wide variety of backgrounds, each with their own distinct trade association and particular areas of expertise. For designers, the challenge is to incorporate the manufacturers' expert knowledge into the design at the most appropriate time, not too early and not too late.
- *Users' input.* It is important not to get too absorbed in the process at the expense of the end product, the building. Buildings are containers that house some

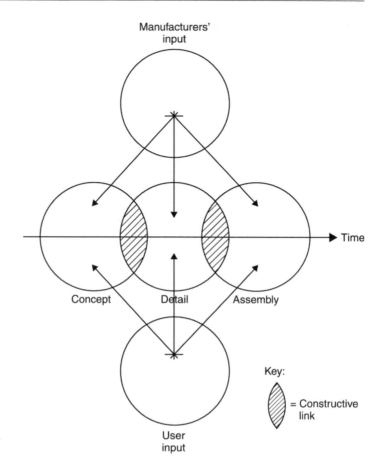

Time

Concept   Detail   Assembly

Key:

= Constructive
link

Figure 3.1 Interfaces.

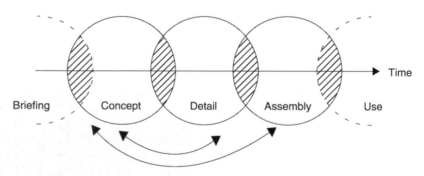

Time

Briefing   Concept   Detail   Assembly   Use

Figure 3.2 Feedback loops.

form of activity. They are designed, built and used by people. Thus user input at the various design stages is an important consideration, although not an easy objective to achieve for speculative projects.

These constructive links become more important with increased specialisation and fragmentation (see Fig. 3.2) and are discussed below.

3.1.1   *Concept to detail*

If design intent is to be converted to physical artefact then the link between the conceptual design and the detail design phase must be as seamless as possible. For sole practitioners working on small projects the transition from concept to detail should be relatively seamless simply because the concept is retained in their heads while they prepare the production information; changes are easy to accommodate. But for the majority of designers working on complex projects the distinction between conceptual design and detail design is more pronounced and often undertaken by individuals with quite different skills and objectives. It is at the detail design stage where collaboration between manufacturers and detailers is likely to be the most rewarding. Contractor involvement may also be necessary as the concept evolves in more detail.

3.1.2   *Detail to assembly*

At the detail design stage the technologist must work very closely to predetermined programme and cost constraints which were established during the conceptual design stage, while at the same time bearing in mind performance, durability, aesthetics and the client's initial brief. As with the conceptual design stage the designer will have a particular design approach which reflects personal

Figure 3.3   Steel framed building under construction.

aspirations, the design style of his or her design office and the overall vision of the client. The design is realised by combining knowledge of technology, design and management balanced against the previous experience of both individual and office. The end of the detail design process should result in information which describes how the building is to be assembled, and the type and the quantities of materials required to do so. It should also provide guidance on how the building is to be maintained and serviced through its design life, including the level of performance expected from each and every component and the health and safety implications of each.

3.1.3   Assembly, then back to new concepts

Assembling the building on site, the fixers and fitters working to a set of detail drawings, generates a lot of knowledge, knowledge that can and should be fed back into new concepts and detail designs to aid the buildability and quality of future projects. Because the majority of completed building projects are long lasting they provide an excellent source of reference material from which lessons can be learned with a view to improving the next project. The concept of continual improvement is well established in the literature on TQM and one designers would be foolish to ignore. Experience in the design of different building types and familiarity with the use of different building products are often embodied within an organisation's standard details and specifications. Generally speaking, designers do not have a particularly good record for returning to their buildings to get some feedback. If the client telephones it is usually to report a fault, so perhaps such reticence is understandable. But we do learn from our experiences and return we must, no matter how painful the experience. With increased attention focused on the building and the manner in which it is used by people over time, incorporating good quality information into the design process is a real possibility. Combined with owners realising that buildings are assets and the steady growth in asset management techniques have come more sophisticated monitoring techniques.

3.2   Tectonic models

Our source word tectonic is concerned with the joint between two or more materials, but it also refers to the equally important joint between two or more stages in the project. To take the design intention from inception through to successful completion is a skilled task, involving three major stages separated by two important links in the information chain. As noted by Richard Neutra (1954: 72), 'If aesthetic satisfaction is a matter of brains and nerves, the finished product and its mode of production – perceived or remembered – are closely linked.' So we need to concentrate our efforts on both the creative link and the constructive link when matters of detail design and the success of the project are being considered. Both demand creative yet firm managerial control (see Emmitt 1999a).

Successful design occurs when the conceptual design can be translated into detail design and then into production; it is the linkage between these different but interrelated areas that is important. An enormous amount of effort is involved in designing a building. Technological, design and management options need considering; teams have to be assembled and then managed to exploit their potential; information and knowledge have to be collated, analysed and applied. However, the manner in which a building is designed and then built is rarely a neat, ordered process. There are many changes to both the design and the programme as the individual project moves from conception to completed building. The most widely used framework to describe the design process is the RIBA *Plan of Work* which implicitly divides the process into a sequence of different events through which the design process should progress. Other models have been proposed, such as the triangular model, the supply chain model and environmental models, discussed in more detail below.

3.2.1   *The linear model*

If we take the RIBA plan of work as our starting point we are presented with a very clear model, interpreted in Fig. 3.4. Here the division between conceptual design, detail design and site operations is explicit. The implication of this model is that the designer (architect) deals with the creative stage, the technologist deals with the more technical aspects and contract documentation stage, and finally the builder assembles the disparate components to produce a finished building. This traditional view, reinforced during education, is used widely, and helps to position the technologist within the plan of work as the constructive link between design office and building site. The difficulty with this model is that it does not include the equally important contribution of the building product manufacturers. Although it has been criticised because it fails to recognise the iterative nature of design, the *Plan of Work* continues to be used by practitioners because it is a familiar guide for the organisation of projects in the design office and it provides a convenient guide for fee invoicing. A further criticism is the failure of the guide to acknowledge fully the life cycle construct associated with an environmentally responsible approach to design, construction, use and disassembly.

3.2.2   *The triangular model*

Building is essentially a process of assembly. The majority of building materials used in modern building come to site as manufactured products, supplied by building product manufacturers. Frequently ignored in literature dealing with building

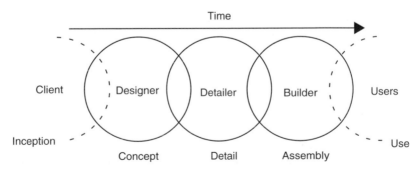

Figure 3.4   The linear model.

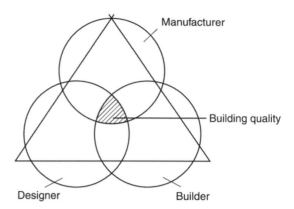

Figure 3.5 The triangular model.

and building design, they have an important part to play in the appearance and durability of the finished product. As such they have a close relationship with designers and builders. Figure 3.5 shows the relationship between the technologist, the building product manufacturer and the builder, all three contributing to the quality of the finished building, forming a constructive 'node', rather than a link.

3.2.3   Supply chain model

Now that we have the building product manufacturers in the frame we can look at the concept of the supply chain and supply chain management. And here our model becomes a little more realistic and at the same time a little more complex. The use of the term 'supply chain' has become popular since the publication of the Latham Report (1994) and the Egan Report (1998), although the concept and practice have existed for some time. Richard Neutra referred to design chains, producer chains and the chain of 'performers and artisans' in his 1954 publication *Survival Through Design*, although it is only more recently that the term has come into regular usage in the UK. At an elementary level there are three interrelated yet very different supply chains: the designer's, the manufacturer's and the assembler's. Depending upon career decisions the technologist may be charged with creating and maintaining efficient links between the supply chains or may be working for the designer, manufacturer or assembler in a detail design capacity. Supply chain management seeks to reduce the number of suppliers in the chain, developing a mutually beneficial relationship between a limited number of suppliers with the aim of reducing costs and improving quality of product and service. Such an approach may have drawbacks because it effectively removes competition and may hold dangers in 'putting all of one's eggs in the same basket'. Despite current hyperbole surrounding this method of procurement it is unlikely to achieve much without integrating the concept with an IT delivery system. IT provides individuals with the ability to network and deliver a building from anywhere in the world – thus service provision takes on a new dimension. The three primary chains are as follows (see Fig. 3.6):

(1) *The design chain.* The designer's supply chain is one of supplying information to other designers to develop the detail design and to those charged with

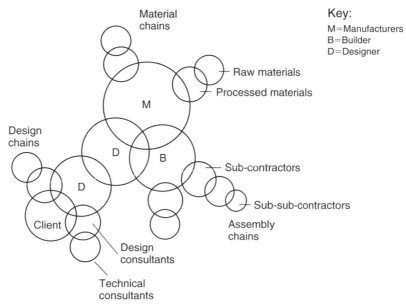

Figure 3.6 The supply chain model.

assembly. This chain should be closely linked to the manufacturers, many of whom contribute to the information chain through the input of technical details and product specifications.

(2) *The manufacturers' supply chain.* All building products and components supplied to the building site start life as raw materials, thus the manufacturers' supply chain is one of supplying manufactured products which are themselves the result of a highly organised design and production process. Some manufacturers also provide detail design services specific to their products, and some have a list of approved installers to carry out the work.

(3) *The chain of assembly.* Building is essentially an industry of assembly which is still dependent upon human labour. The assembler's supply chain is, therefore, one of supplying labour and equipment – the management of resources. This is usually undertaken by the main contractor who may employ staff directly, or more likely will manage the project via sub-contracted (and sub-sub-contracted) works packages.

3.2.4 *Environmental models and a project framework*

Criticism of many models lies in the fact that they have failed to take into account ecological issues. Over recent years this has been debated on the conference circuit and many different environmentally orientated models have been proposed. To discuss them here would be confusing and beyond the scope of this book. From a personal viewpoint one model that is applicable to the issues discussed between these covers and thus to those involved in architectural technology is that proposed by Schmid, and this is discussed in Chapter 4. An attempt to integrate environmental issues is represented in Fig. 3.7, a project model that

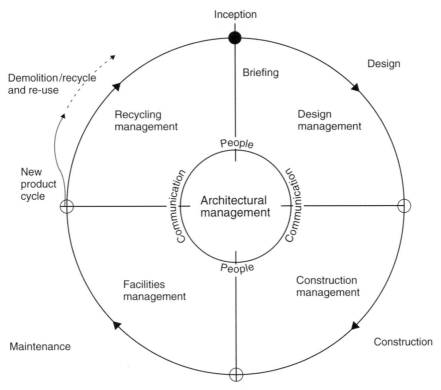

Figure 3.7 The project framework (from Emmitt 1999: 96).

incorporates and fully acknowledges the life cycle construct. For consistency this is taken from *Architectural Management in Practice* (Emmitt 1999a). It covers the project from inception, to design, construction, maintenance and eventual recovery. This model also helps to identify some of the management fields associated with individual projects.

3.3 Co-operation, integration and information

Synthesis, the process or result of building up separate elements into a connected whole, is central to the design process. Not only should the whole be greater than the sum of the parts, but the finished building should be more important than the process. Debate about which method of procurement is better than another will always be with us; however, the increased power and accessibility of IT represents a real opportunity for networking and co-operation. IT provides the means to control every aspect of the project and the finished building, i.e. an integrated delivery system that can include the client's financial models and cater for comprehensive asset management strategies.

3.3.1 Information requirements and sources

Design has been described as an information processing activity – searching, assimilating, assembling and transmitting. Building designers have a constant thirst for information, the extent of which will vary depending upon the tasks they are engaged in. For example, client briefing is an information gathering stage that needs constant reference during the development of the design. Information is central to making decisions and an essential tool to transfer design intent into physical artefact. The more relevant and complete the information, the better an individual is able to make an informed decision. Good quality information which is easy to access is a valuable resource for building designers. Information can be defined as data in a usable form: it allows people to make decisions and take action (Daniels 1994). Data have a cost and information value. The cost of researching, analysing, using, storing and transmitting is relatively easy to quantify compared with the value of the information to the user.

Design is an open-ended process of continual discovery during which a great deal of information is generated, some of which is used, and much of which is discarded as no longer useful. Information is exchanged during building through the process of communication. It can be effective in communicating between people who do not know one another and who have little personal basis for mutual understanding, a common situation in building. It is also key to the effective use, maintenance, remodelling and eventual recycling of the building. Paradoxically, with the growth of IT the speed of access to information has taken great steps forward, yet the amount of information has also expanded to such an extent that accessing relevant information is still a problem for busy designers. Furthermore, much of the literature produced today has become more specialised and hence more difficult to access. The biggest problem facing designers is that of information retrieval. Information has to be current, yet access to old (superseded) information will be required for work to existing buildings.

3.3.2   *Design in detail*

For some design offices and individual designers the constant threat of liability is a big enough incentive to adopt a very conservative approach to practice, using details and design solutions that are known not to fail. Those adopting a more innovative approach, specifying new products and creative solutions to their detailing, need to be aware of the enhanced risk they are taking. Whatever the approach adopted there is a constant need to access current information so that the decisions taken are informed ones. Information is a key resource for manufacturers, designers and builders. It has to be acquired quickly and thus the ability to carry out research and data collection is an essential skill. Steven Groák's (1992) philosophy of a building as flows of energy is an endearing one. Comparisons may be made with flows of information throughout the life of a building: that required for the project, and that required for the product.

Whatever the procurement route employed to secure a building, someone will be responsible for the design input. Architect, contractor, engineer, surveyor and technologist may be responsible for design, either individually or as part of a team. Design problems are generally large and complex spanning time scales of days, months and even years. Being large and complex, design problems have many parts, although because of the unstructured nature of design problem-solving the lines of decomposition are rarely clear. Instead, these lines of decomposition are dictated by the design organisation's managerial structure and/or the individual designer's experience of solving similar problems in the past. Thus familiar templates such as the *Plan of Work* are used as a guide and *aide-mémoire*.

Design involves making choices and, therefore, design decisions are based on a mixture of determination and compromise. Design problems do not have right or wrong answers, only better or worse ones. Whether or not a good or bad decision is made can only be determined with the benefit of hindsight. Bad decisions are easy to see, e.g. the detail as drawn cannot be constructed on site, while good decisions tend to be noticed less simply because they do not cause difficulties for building assemblers or users. There are costs associated with every action – the penalty for getting it wrong can be high. Components of the design problem are not logically interconnected; however, there are many physical interconnections between the parts. Input to the design process consists of information about physical things (physical generators) and the people who may use the building (social generators), the goals to be satisfied being a mixture of the client's wants and the design team's intent. Output consists of the building specification, represented by drawings, written specifications and models. A distinction needs to be made between the specification of the building and the specification of the construction method, because the building has to function independently of the design team. There has been a lot of debate about the incorporation of feedback into the design process, feedback that must be simulated or generated by the designer during the problem-solving exercise. Feedback from the world comes after the design and building are completed and occupied, too late for the decisions made but of use for future design problems. There is an old saying: 'if you do not know where you are going to, any road will get you there'. This is particularly so with detailing a building. The overall aim must be clear if the detailing is to achieve the objective. Detail design has been described by Wade (1977: 280) as 'the selection of mutually compatible components to solve some specific defined standard problem or some specific unique problem within a larger consistent design context', a theme developed in this book.

Further reading

Emmitt, S. (1999). *Architectural Management in Practice*, Longman, Harlow.

4 A question of detail

Successful designers consistently demonstrate a thorough understanding of the building site and the manner in which materials and elements are brought together as a whole entity. Before we investigate the typical life cycle of a building and the process behind its production, it is necessary to understand the physical and the social generators that underpin design decisions. An overview of the relationship between the structure and the fabric, materials and services, joints and connections, and then internal and external finishes follows. The chapter concludes by looking at the 'whole of the sum of the parts' and an environmental model to aid decision-making.

4.1 Physical and social design generators

There is a need to understand and recognise the environmental generators that lie behind all building design, design generators that are sometimes implicit and sometimes explicit. We build to provide enclosure and shelter, to provide a comfortable environment in which to live, work and play. Our buildings should be durable, economical to construct and maintain, weather-proof, secure, structurally sound, and easy to adapt and recycle as and when they reach the end of their service life. To design good quality buildings requires a clear understanding of the environment in which we live, and a useful starting point is to look at the primary generators of both design and detail design, i.e. the connection between our planet and our buildings.

4.1.1 Earth

In building design a lot of emphasis is, not surprisingly, placed on the site – the building's *genius loci*. Building designs are made for a specific place, in a specific environment, for a specific time. These contextual constraints will colour the design process and the finished artefact. The manner in which the design team deal with context will help to shape the conceptual design, and different designers will have their own way of dealing with given constraints. Buildings are shaped and influenced by their immediate surroundings because every site is different, to a lesser or greater extent, to that adjacent to it. Each has its own particular ground conditions, its own micro-climate, and its own physical design constraints such as access points, existing services and existing levels. Structures are expected to sit on, above or in the ground, and attention must be given to the existing ground conditions. Soil type and its load bearing capacity can vary significantly between locations, e.g. clay soils pose different problems to the foundation designer than do sandy ones. Using Newton's Law that to each and every force there is an equal and opposite reaction, foundations must be capable of transferring forces to the ground, and the ground must be capable of accommodating those forces if failure is to be avoided. Although many different types of foundations exist, there are essentially two types: those that distribute loads directly to the ground (strip footings and rafts), and those that rely on friction between structural element and soil (piles or caissons). Choice is determined by the ground conditions particular to the site. Bringing previously used sites (brown-field sites) back into use has placed even greater emphasis on existing ground conditions. Brown-field development brings its own special challenges because many of the sites are contaminated from previous use(s) and old foundations, cellars and services pose additional hazards for developers. Thorough investigation and testing is required before a decision to proceed with design can be made. The cost of dealing with contaminated ground, through removal to a licensed disposal site, and/or capping, is high, as is dealing with unwanted services, redundant foundations and forgotten cellars. The cost of dealing with existing ground conditions needs to be built into the feasibility study, with any restrictions on foundation and hence structural loading considered in the early stages of the design.

Sites do not exist in isolation – neighbouring buildings, structures and landscapes need to be considered as contextual issues. A site's history and context has implications for the type of development that can be undertaken. There may be planning constraints because of previous use and/or zoning policy, or simply because it is adjacent to a conservation area. Whether designers respond by trying to fit in with the existing grain, or attempt to contrast with it, is quite another matter. Responses to the site may vary depending upon prevailing fashions and social conditions. Earth sheltered housing is one response which is coming back into fashion. In areas of the world subject to seismic activity the building design must be capable of resisting sudden and extreme pressure if life and property are to be protected. Landscape formation and development is important in rural, semi-rural and urban environments, i.e. the relationship of the building to its landscape. Is the building to blend harmoniously with its neighbours or is it more a piece of sculpture, deliberately different and hence contrasting with its environment? Site boundaries are particularly important, providing visual privacy as well as views out, security as well as access, and where natural boundaries are used, habitats for birds and animals. Natural boundaries can provide a link to nature, a changing backdrop throughout the year in temperate climates.

Another factor that links the building to its site is the actual process of assembly – regardless of the amount of pre-fabrication carried out in the factory, the site will become the workplace of many different specialists during the period of assembly. Building materials, components, products and labour all need to be transported to the site, leaving behind a pollution trail in the process. Then, at some undetermined time in the future, alterations, repairs or even wholesale redevelopment will take place, leading to recycling and disposal of the separate elements which made up the building. In one way or another the raw materials that are manufactured into building products come from the earth. Extraction of raw materials has become a cause for concern because many of them are finite in supply. Organic, sustainable building materials have experienced a revival in their application as attention has shifted to sustainable design. For example, there is revised interest in timber, an organic and sustainable material (when managed), which can be used in conjunction with other materials, both organic and synthetic, as part of an environmentally responsible approach to building assembly.

4.1.2   *Weathering*

Physical site constraints will influence the orientation of buildings and access to them. Orientation will also influence the way in which the building responds to the site's climate. All built structures weather, or, more precisely, deteriorate, as a direct result of the environment acting upon the structure. Erosion, staining, discoloration and warping are a few of the visible signs that deterioration has occurred and will continue to occur; without adequate and regular maintenance and repair the building will eventually collapse. Combined the elements act on a building throughout its life weathering the external face. The earth that the building rests on may sink or heave placing pressure on the foundations, the wind will push and pull at the surface, the sun will degrade through ultraviolet (UV) radiation and induce stress and strain in materials through rises and falls in temperature, and water will try to enter the building through a variety of means, by rain or snow, in combination with the wind as driving rain, or failing that through rising damp. Add in damage from general use (and misuse) and malicious damage and the rate of deterioration is often faster than building owners would like to acknowledge at the design stage. The term 'building pathology' is one borrowed from the field of medicine. It signals the end of a component part of a building or the end of an entire building, and is a process that attempts to determine the reason(s) behind the failure of the whole building or a component. Designers must be aware of the four elements and the effect that weathering is likely to have on the completed building. It is only through consideration of these constant variables that effective detailing can be achieved.

(1) *Sun.* Apart from being an excellent source of renewable energy, solar radiation is a major contributor to the deterioration of the building fabric. UV radiation can cause materials to become brittle and thus liable to cracking, e.g. uPVC rainwater goods. Stains, dyes, paintings, etc., will fade through exposure to visible light. IR radiation is a source of radiant heat and can cause shrinkage of organic materials such as timber through the loss of moisture from the material. Careful consideration of building orientation and the materials to be used, together with shading through considered detailing, can help to prolong the life of materials.

(2) *Wind.* Over the centuries the wind has been harnessed as a sustainable source of energy, but it is a constant threat to buildings. Every winter extensive damage is caused by strong winds. In the UK the prevailing winds (and rain) come from the northwest and southwest, although there are variations depending upon the location of the site. Our traditional reaction to the wind has been to strap components to each another in an attempt to avoid one being ripped off another in a storm. In the tropics, where the temperature rarely gets too cold, the solution is to let the wind blow through the building, thus reducing the resistance to the wind and providing welcome ventilation. For climates where heat loss is undesirable air penetration is another factor to consider, a problem that becomes more acute the further buildings rise into the air. The solution is to wrap the inner wall in a material that is impervious to the wind (building wrap).

(3) *Water.* We cannot live without it, yet we struggle to live with it. The major part of the earth's surface area is covered by water and human bodies are made

up of approximately 70% water. Just as we depend upon water for our survival so do our buildings. Too little water and the fabric starts to show signs of stress, timbers will shrink and split; too much water and the fabric starts to dissolve. Water comes in three states, liquid, solid (ice) and gas (water vapour), and is one of the most serious threats to the building fabric. Rain, sleet, snow, ice and condensation are all issues to be considered at the detailing stage. We introduce water to our buildings during the construction process, e.g. in plastering, thus necessitating a period for the structure to achieve some form of stability in its environment. We also introduce water to our buildings in our daily activities. Technologies employed in the construction of buildings need to prevent the ingress of water yet allow the building to breathe without causing interstitial condensation.

(4) *Fire*. Fire is a constant threat to the occupants of buildings and legislative controls have been developed over the years in an attempt to safeguard a building's occupants and contain the spread of fire to neighbouring properties (see Chapter 7). Fires may start by accident, e.g. a faulty electrical appliance, by carelessness, e.g. a discarded cigarette, or they may be started deliberately, an act of arson. Designers can reduce the likelihood of fire through careful choice of materials, the relationship of these materials to one another, and the manner in which they are joined.

Some of these agents of destruction can be powerful on their own, e.g. fire, and some are more destructive in combination, e.g. wind and water or water and solar radiation. The way in which materials weather will be determined by the location of the site, the orientation of the building and the manner in which it is detailed. Effective detailing must consider the geographical location of the site, be it sheltered or exposed, and the orientation of the building to the prevailing wind and rain. There is a large body of literature that deals with building pathology, building failures, and this should be studied before detailing commences in order to avoid making the same mistakes that others have done previously. Thus detailing to mitigate the effects of the local climate with a view to durability should be a paramount consideration for designers.

4.1.3   *Social generators of design*

In addition to the physical design generators there are a number of what could be described as social generators, which may be as equally important as the physical constraints. These are not dependent upon physical properties pertaining to the site but upon softer, more volatile and less predictable issues concerned with and driven by the time in which we live. Just as every site is unique, so is the 'team' responsible for the design and assembly of the building, issues explored in Chapter 3. The point is that the social generators will influence the physical ones.

Changing fashions and technologies, combined with changes in legislation, make a career in building a challenging and fascinating one. The uptake of new technologies is dependent upon decision-makers, the clients and their design teams, i.e. people. These people have their own distinct, personal characteristics: some are clearly more adventurous than others and have a lower risk threshold; some will borrow technologies from other industries, such as yacht building, while at the other end of the scale there may be resistance to even the most established technologies (see Chapter 13). The modern movement's desire to design buildings that reflected an international style, rather than a more parochial one, led to the loss of local traditions and character. More recently the fashion for large international companies to reflect their brand image through their buildings, as well as through their product and marketing strategies, has given rise to the proliferation of 'identical' units, indifferent to their surroundings and local building traditions. Some planning authorities in England and Wales have tried to enforce a more endearing external appearance, but the brand image endures and pervades in the majority of cases. Designs, much like clothes, do come into fashion, fade away and then re-emerge some time later in a slightly different guise; indeed architectural styles and architects are prone to periods of neglect and stardom. Three principal social influences on design are design philosophy, social aspirations and legal liability:

(1) Design philosophy operates on two levels, that of the design office and that of the individual working within the organisation. Peer pressure is ever present.
(2) Social aspirations will influence the time and cost available, and hence impose constraints on the choice of materials and the design life of the building. There is a difference in approach between, e.g. a warehouse and a public building.
(3) Legal liability arises because building failures do occur. Sometimes they can be quite dramatic and life-threatening, but often the failure is minor and poses more of a problem for the professional. In an attempt to limit exposure to potential claims some designers use a limited range of materials.

4.2   Structure and fabric

Structure and building fabric have a very special relationship. In load bearing construction the materials forming the structural support often provide the fabric and hence the internal and external finishes. In framed structures the fabric is independent of the structure, applied to the load bearing structural frame. Many developments in structural form have come about through a series of trial and error, with engineers and designers learning from disasters and making codes more rigorous in an attempt to prevent the same fault arising again. Designers have continually been faced with problems that have required some form of creative solution, either through the application of new ideas and tools to old problems or through the resolution of new problems with limited means (Mainstone 1998). More recent developments in structural engineering, based on a growing understanding of structural behaviour and computing power, have increased the designer's freedom of choice with regard to structure and fabric (Mainstone 1998).

Structural design is the domain of the structural engineer, a professional who should work closely with the designers to ensure synergy between structure and fabric. That structural calculations and expert knowledge about the behaviour of building structures are the domain of structural engineers is no excuse for designers not having a sound understanding of structural principles and the main structural systems. There are a number of reasons for this. First, an appreciation of materials and their structural properties, e.g. clear span and depth of the structural members, is essential at the conceptual design stage when the use of 'rule of thumb' is a useful design aid, and one that will determine the structural grid. Second, much of a building's appearance will be affected by the choice of structural system chosen, e.g. framed structure or load bearing construction. Third, there is a very clear link between the structural system and the amount of fire resistance achieved. So having the capacity to design buildings with a notional structural system and approximate sizes of structural members can aid the development of the early design solutions in the knowledge that they will work.

4.2.1 Loading

For building designers one of the most important considerations is how forces are transferred within the structure, the relationship between design (architecture) and structure (engineering). Buildings need to resist loads and forces if they are to resist collapse. There are three types of loading:

(1) *Dead loads*. Dead loads remain relatively constant throughout the life of a building, unless it is remodelled at a future date. These loads comprise the combined weight of the building's construction materials and are transferred to the ground via the foundations. Because the weight of individual components is known the dead load can be easily calculated.

(2) *Live loads*. Live loads will vary. These comprise the weight of the people using the building, the weight of furniture and equipment, etc. Structural design calculations assume an average maximum live load based on the use of the building. If the use of a building changes then the live loads will need to be assessed against those determined at the design stage. Seasonal changes may result in (temporary) live loading from snow and rain.

(3) *Wind loads*. Maximum wind loads (gusts) are determined by considering the maximum recorded wind speed in a particular location and adding a safety factor. Wind loading is an important consideration for permanent structures and also for temporary structures to protect building workers from the elements.

4.2.2 Structural frames

Timber, steel and reinforced concrete are the main materials used for structural frames. The benefits of one over another need to be considered against a wide variety of design parameters, such as the following:

■ embodied energy and associated environmental concerns
■ extent of clear span required
■ fire resistance and protection
■ extent of pre-fabrication
■ availability of materials and labour skills
■ site access
■ erection programme and sequence
■ ease of fixing the cladding and associated fabric

- maintenance, future adaptability
- ease of demolition (disassembly) and recycling potential
- cost.

4.2.3   *Dimensional stability*

Stability of the building as a whole will be determined by the independent movement of different materials and components within the structure over time. Dimensional stability will be determined by individual components' dimensional variation when subjected to changes in moisture content and temperature changes.

(1) *Moisture movement.* Dimensional variation will occur in porous materials as they take up or, conversely, lose moisture through evaporation. Seasonal variations in temperature will occur in temperate climates and affect many building materials. Indoor temperature variations should also be considered. Some materials such as glass, plastics and steel are highly impermeable and are not prone to moisture movement.
(2) *Thermal movement.* All building materials exhibit some amount of thermal movement because of seasonal changes in temperature and rapid diurnal fluctuations. Dimensional variation is usually linear and will depend upon the temperature range the material experiences, its colour, its coefficient of expansion and its size. These factors are influenced by the material's degree of exposure and care is required to allow for adequate expansion and contraction through the use of control joints.

4.3   Materials and services

Design is a complex task. Drawings, models, specifications and schedules are interconnected pieces, useful for testing ideas and concepts, and essential for conveying design intent into construction. They all, to a lesser or greater extent, deal with the physical positioning, assembly and description of materials and services.

4.3.1   *Materials*

Materials form the basic ingredients from which designers select and successful designers have a thorough appreciation of the materials they use. Some use a very limited palate of materials, others are equally successful in combining many different materials to achieve their design ideal; their recipes for successful design. Rapid advances in technology, combined with cheap transportation, have led to a wide variety of building materials and manufactured products from which to choose. Designers must understand the nature of materials, their scientific properties, their structural properties, their characteristics in a fire, their interaction with other materials, their anticipated durability for a given situation, their cost, their maintenance requirements, their potential for recycling and other environmental issues such as embodied energy, their impact in terms of health and safety, and last but not least their aesthetic properties. With such a long list of considerations, it is, therefore, essential that designers welcome opportunities to handle and physically work materials.

Knowledge of materials is central to the philosophy of buildability and is critical in the creation of a high quality building. Materials differ in their physical properties and their environmental impact. The principal materials are only listed below because they are explored in detail in books dedicated to materials and their properties (e.g. Dean 1994, Lyons 1997).

- bitumen
- brickwork and blockwork
- cement and concrete
- ceramics
- glass
- metals
- paints, stains and varnishes
- plastics
- straw, reeds, canvas, hemp
- stone and artificial stone
- timber.

Many materials do not appear in their natural state, but are manufactured and invariably become components or building products that combine two materials or more (see Chapter 9).

4.3.2   Services

Buildings need to be serviced, and the integration of those services into a coherent whole is a constant challenge for designers. With increased awareness of both environmental and health issues there has been a tendency to move away from mechanical ventilation and artificial lighting to more natural forms of control, i.e. passive ventilation and natural lighting. Generation of electricity through sustainable technologies is becoming more cost effective and more widely available, e.g. the harnessing of solar energy (solar collectors, photovoltaic cells, etc.), wind power (wind turbines), and hydroelectric and geothermal energy sources are available and are being used. Furthermore, the conservation of important resources and their re-use has become a major design generator, e.g. the re-use of rainwater to flush toilets. Whatever the design approach adopted the comfort of the building users and the impact on the environment as a whole should be primary concerns. As with materials, services have been covered extensively in other books and, therefore, a list of main considerations only is provided here:

- water supply
- drainage and waste disposal
- heating, cooling and ventilation
- lighting
- cooking
- security and fire
- communications
- mechanical conveyance (of goods and personnel)
- refuse disposal and recycling.

4.3.3   *Ecological considerations*

How these materials are sourced and the implications of their specification, together with the design and specification of services, need to be understood in a wider environmental context. Particular attention should be given to the materials' embodied energy and ecological footprints. Ecological footprints is a concept devised to measure the amount of the earth's surface area taken up in sustaining the material (or service) being consumed (Wackernagel and Rees 1996). Design considerations fall broadly under three headings, namely embodied energy, energy in use and pollution prevention:

(1) *Embodied energy.* For building designers the concept of embodied energy is arguably the most important, yet paradoxically one of the most difficult to get accurate information on. The concept of embodied energy has been around for about 30 years and is a measure of the energy consumed in the production of a particular material, for which comparative charts are available to aid the designer. There is a strong link between embodied energy and embodied carbon dioxide (CO_2). Designers should consider the following:
  (a) Recovery and re-use of materials existing on site.
  (b) Re-using existing buildings wherever feasible through sensitive design.
  (c) Detailing for future disassembly and re-use.
  (d) The use of materials from managed, sustainable, sources.
  (e) Specifying locally produced materials to reduce pollution caused by transportation.
  (f) The use of materials and products that have low embodied energy levels.
  (g) The use of recycled materials wherever possible.
(2) *Energy in use.* Reduction of energy in use is influenced by the thermal efficiency of the building and the way in which the occupants use it. Thermal insulation plays an important role in energy conservation, both in the design of new buildings and in the upgrading of existing building fabrics. Designers can play their part by increasing insulation levels, and hence reducing heating costs, by specifying thermal insulation values in excess of those currently required by the Building Regulations. Control over how the occupants use a building, however, is more a matter for those charged with its day-to-day management. For example, providing energy for an office block that houses 1000 people generates 6000 tonnes of CO_2 emissions per annum (the equivalent of driving 1300 petrol cars around the world). Designing offices that are more energy efficient and that minimise energy consumption through careful consideration of the servicing requirements can help to minimise global warming. Designers should consider the following:
  (a) Specification of high levels of insulation (with low embodied energy rating) and adequate ventilation.
  (b) Design in passive and natural ventilation systems instead of mechanical systems.
  (c) Specification of low energy, low pollution heating.
  (d) Use of low energy lighting and appliances.
  (e) Employing smart technology to reduce energy consumption.
  (f) Specification of renewable energy sources wherever possible.

(3) *Pollution prevention.* Manufacture, assembly, use, re-use and eventual disposal all create pollution – pollution of our external environment and that of the environment within our homes, workplace and leisure buildings. Designers should consider the following:
   (a) The use of non-toxic materials.
   (b) Natural ventilation to all rooms.
   (c) Reducing dust and allergens.

4.4   Joints and connections

We tend to view buildings as static structures that suddenly exhibit signs of distress which need urgent repair. In reality a building is anything but static: it moves to accommodate, e.g. changes in temperature and/or humidity, it flexes to accommodate increased or decreased loads on the structure; and it has to breathe to expel moisture laden air if condensation is to be avoided. Failure and the development of defects is (with a few exceptions) a gradual process. As designers we need to recognise such characteristics in our detailing and choice of products. If we do not allow for thermal expansion and subsequent contraction then materials will exhibit stress and will eventually fail; if we do not allow for increased loads the structure may fail; and if we do not allow the building to breathe we will have serious problems with condensation and the health of residents will be affected. If we view a building as a living, dynamic structure we may be in a better position to understand its maintenance requirements and, therefore, enhance the durability of the structure.

There is a temptation to see detail design as a process of bringing together standard solutions to familiar problems, a tendency promoted by construction technology books and through education where the typical detail is frequently over-used. For many designers the prospect of detailing a building is anything but standard – the challenge comes with joints and connections, especially when different materials, products and/or systems are connected to one another to create the whole. Joining different pieces of the same material is usually relatively straightforward and has well-established fixing techniques, but it is a little unusual to assemble buildings exclusively from one material. When materials are combined numerous technical challenges are created, simply through the use of different materials in juxtaposition to each other, e.g. attaching cladding to the structural framework and in doing so creating weather-proof joints capable of accommodating movement, yet impervious to the passage of water. The construction process is essentially one of assembling parts together to form the completed building. The interface of the parts will be via a 'joint' or a 'connection'. A joint is the term used to describe the space between components; where these components are joined structurally then it is referred to as a connection.

4.4.1   *Joints*

Putting two or more components together will create a joint and the manner in which this is detailed will influence the appearance and durability of the fabric. Different trades have a variety of names for joints, e.g. 'dovetail joints' (carpentry), 'bed joints' (masonry), 'weather-struck joints' (brickwork), 'ball-joint' (plumbing). One of the most extensive books on the subject of jointing, *Joints in Buildings* (Martin 1977), provides a comprehensive overview of joint typologies.

4.4.2 Control joints

With the development of lightweight construction, increased standards of thermal insulation, new materials and construction methods, together with a move away from elastic materials there has come a greater emphasis on material movement. Movement in materials can be substantial and involve large forces. If these materials are restrained in such a way that they cannot move then these forces may exceed the strength of the material and result in failure. Control joints, sometimes described as 'movement joints' or 'expansion joints', are an effective way of accommodating movement and the associated stresses. One of the major causes of building failure is inadequate attention to material movement at the design stage. It is during the detail design phase that materials and components should be analysed for their potential to move in conjunction with others and with respect to the overall physical geometry of the building. Failure to position control joints correctly and/or failure to size and detail control joints correctly may lead to failure at a future date because the stresses cannot be accommodated within the materials. Aesthetically, control joints can look unsightly unless they are carefully detailed and positioned to minimise their visual impact. Carefully positioned rainwater downpipes can be used to cover otherwise unsightly joints. In other instances the control joint can form part of the architectural expression of the building, depending upon the materials used and the desire of the design team.

One of the most informative texts on the problems of movement is Philip Rainger's *Movement Control in the Fabric of Buildings* (1983). At the time of publication there had been a significant rise in the number of movement associated failures in buildings. Rainger's book helped to shed some light on the problem by identifying the main causes. First, the fashion for thinner building sections, with reduced thermal capacity, resulted in structures that responded faster to changes in temperature and thus were more prone to failure, a problem that becomes more acute with the use of materials with high thermal coefficients. Second, the use of larger components and thus fewer joints resulted in greater physical movement in the component and less opportunity to accommodate such forces. The third cause was the adoption of dry jointed assemblies and many materials with differing dimensional stability. The fourth cause was the trend towards higher stressed and slender structures which reduced the building's capacity to accommodate thermal and moisture related stresses. Rainger's book was important in raising awareness of the problems caused by rapid adoption of new building technologies without an adequate knowledge base.

4.4.3 Connections

The word 'connection' implies some form of physical joint between two or more elements. How and why separate elements are connected will depend upon the materials to be connected, the resources available (human labour and mechanical plant) and the manner in which the connection is detailed by the designer.

Designers should bear in mind the ease of disassembly at a future date, so connections that can be easily accessed and easily undone without causing damage to the connected components are preferred if the recovery of materials at the end of the building's life is to be efficient. The connection of different components or different planes is made considerably easier when one material is used. Timber is perhaps one of the most versatile of materials and one where an extensive vocabulary of fixing details has been established. Carpenters and joiners have a well-rehearsed vocabulary of joints and connections which are known to work. Many of these joints are easy to disassemble as and when alterations are made to a building. Connections may involve one or a combination of the following:

- adhesives
- bolts
- glues and resins
- mastic
- nails
- screws.

4.4.4   *Tolerances*

Building involves the use of labour, either in the factory, or on site, or in combination. Designers must consider those who are expected to assemble the various parts physically into a whole as well as those responsible for servicing and replacing elements in the future. In order to be able to place various parts in juxtaposition with other parts of the assembly a certain amount of dimensional tolerance is required. With the trend towards using a greater proportion of manufactured components on site the issue of tolerances needs careful consideration. With traditional construction the craftsmen would deal with tolerances as part of their craft, applying their knowledge and skill to trim, cut, fit and adjust materials on site to create the desired effect. Where materials are manufactured under carefully controlled conditions in a factory, or workshop, and brought to the site for assembly, the manufacturer, designer and contractor must be confident that the component parts will fit together. Because many materials cannot be produced to precise dimensions allowance must be made for variations in material, production and for positioning the components on site:

- Materials have to be worked by machine or hand and variation between component sizes is to be expected. For example, bricks vary in size because of the firing process.
- Materials may change their physical size after production. Components may shrink and expand because of changes in temperature and moisture content; some may twist and bow due to loading.
- Positioning materials on site is only possible when there is a gap to help manoeuvre components. The heavier and larger the component, the more difficult the operation, and hence the larger the gap required to enable the task to be completed safely and without damage to the component being manoeuvred or those adjacent to it.

Providing for variation is achieved by specifying allowable tolerances. Too small a tolerance and it may be impossible to move components into position on site; too large a tolerance will necessitate a degree of 'bodging' on site to fill the gap – for practical and economic reasons both situations must be avoided. A useful reference is *BS 5606: 1990 (1998) Guide to Accuracy in Building* which may assist the designer in the avoidance (and resolution) of problems of inaccuracy or fit and the likely achievement of specified tolerances. This standard also provides advice on the monitoring and controlling of work during construction to ensure compliance with the specified accuracy. There are three interrelated tolerances that the designer must specify.

(1) *Manufacturing tolerances.* Manufacturing tolerances limit the dimensional deviation in the manufacture of components. They may be set by a standard, by a manufacturer, and/or the design team. Some manufacturers are able to manufacture to tighter tolerances than those defined in the current standards. Some designers may require a greater degree of tolerance than that normally supplied, for which there may well be a cost to cover additional QC in the factory.

(2) *Positional tolerances.* Positional tolerances will depend on the accuracy of setting out and the technology employed to erect and assemble the component parts. Minimum tolerances are essential for convenience of assembly; however, whether the tolerances are met on site will depend upon the skills of those doing the setting out and the quality of their supervision.

(3) *Joint tolerances.* Joint tolerances are set by functional and aesthetic considerations. Functional requirements should allow for expansion and contraction as a result of changes in temperature and/or moisture content and structural movements caused by, e.g. wind loading. Buildings are not static and the component parts respond to changes by expanding and contracting and many materials will creep (experience plastic flow) over the longer period due to loading. Control joints at regular intervals or changes of plane and/or materials can help to accommodate such movement without signs of distress to the fabric. Aesthetic requirements may be determined by building traditions, architectural fashion and the designer's (or engineer's) own idiosyncrasies. However, smaller joints tend to be more aesthetically pleasing and are usually better than larger ones when it comes to keeping the weather out (functional requirements).

As a general rule the smaller (or closer) the tolerance the greater the manufacturing costs and the greater the time for assembly and assembly costs. When considering tolerances designers should refer to the relevant standards for the materials or components and also seek advice from the manufacturers, most of whom offer advice on tolerances. Manufacturers of proprietary systems, such as cladding or rainscreen systems, will provide a comprehensive performance specification that includes detailed information on tolerances, and many will produce design drawings as part of the package.

4.4.5 *Dimensional co-ordination*

Once the tolerances are understood and known it is possible to compose the drawings and details that show the building assembly in and the position of individual components. Those involved in the production of the contract information will be concerned with the dimensional co-ordination of many different materials to create the whole. The use of grid lines at regular intervals (in 2D or 3D) will assist with the placing of individual components for the designer when producing the drawing and those on site who physically have to put them in position. To avoid confusion it is standard practice to show all linear measurements in millimetres, with dimensions expressed in metres reserved for the site layout drawings.

Dimensional co-ordination is obviously important to ensure that the multitude of components fit together correctly. It is also important in helping to reduce waste on site through unnecessary cutting. Designers can readily access tables showing the sizes of standard components, such as timber, bricks and columns. An ability to work with standard production runs will save time during assembly and will help to reduce waste on site as components are cut to suit the dimension specified on the drawings – essentially a modular approach to building design.

4.4.6   Modular co-ordination

Modular co-ordination is essentially a form of dimensional co-ordination, based on a module, to which manufacturers and designers adhere. There have been many proponents of modular building over the years (perhaps best known is Le Corbusier's Modulor), closely related to the drive for increased standardisation and interconnectivity – sometimes referred to as 'rational' design. One of the aims is to reduce cutting and hence waste on site and many attempts have been made to persuade manufacturers to work to such a system and persuade designers to work to it. At the heart of the modular system is the modular unit, based on increments of 100 mm. Dimensional co-ordination is based on the 100 mm grid and the selection of building components that fit within these design constraints. In the UK the modular system has not been widely adopted. There are a number of reasons for this. First, manufacturers are reluctant to alter their existing manufacturing machinery from an imperial system (feet and inches) to one based on multiples of the 100 mm module. Second, until all suppliers of building materials change there cannot be full adoption. For example, timber and steel sizes do not fit well in a modular system. The third reason is one of tradition (and aesthetics): designers appear to prefer the size of a traditional brick to the modular one – indeed modular bricks were manufactured but were not liked by designers. Office standard details and specifications would need to be changed. Fourth, work to existing buildings requires the availability of traditionally sized materials to ensure compatibility. For designers with a more organic approach to building design the modular system is viewed as something akin to an unhealthy obsession with standardisation and modularisation which may be detrimental to the aesthetic appeal of the building.

4.5   Internal and external finishes

Finishes form the interface between building user and building. Surfaces are seen, touched and smelt by building users. Colour, or the lack of it, affects our psychology and the atmosphere of our buildings. There are two different types of finish to the building fabric: that which is inherent in the material and that which is applied to a background.

(1) *Inherent finishes.* Many materials such as timber, stone, brick and glass provide a natural finish without any need for further work – an inherent finish. Carefully chosen, materials with an inherent finish may help to reduce construction time and construction costs, furthermore their use is an important consideration when looking ahead to the eventual disassembly of the building and the recycling of materials.

(2) *Applied finishes.* Application of materials to existing backgrounds, such as paint to timber, is an applied finish. The durability of the finish will depend upon the material properties of the finish and the material it is applied to, as well as the bond between the two surfaces. Ecological design goals aim to minimise the pollution from applied finishes. Petrochemical paints, stains and varnishes should be avoided and preference given to products with natural pigments that are not harmful to animals, plants or people.

4.5.1   External finishes

External finishes are important in determining the aesthetic appeal of the building. The external finishes will also, in conjunction with the detailing, determine

Figure 4.1   Detail of stone cobbles to building facade.

how the building will weather over time. Thus the quality of the materials used for external finishes and the manner in which they are applied will determine the durability of the building fabric.

4.5.2   Internal finishes

Internal finishes are important in creating a sense of place. They are also important in helping to ensure a healthy indoor environment. Since we spend a great deal of our time within buildings, the internal environment is particularly important in ensuring a sense of well-being and enjoyment. Materials will be touched, experienced visually and will give off a scent, which combined with furnishings and appliances will influence our perception of the space in which we live or work.

4.6   An environmental model

Before proceeding further we need to consider the impact of our decisions on our host planet. Many models have been developed with the aim of helping the designer to make more responsible decisions regarding environmental sustainability; however, there is one model that deserves particular attention for its elegance and usability. This comprehensive guide for designing in an environmentally responsible manner is Schmid's 'basic model of the architectural detail' (Schmid 1986, Schmid and Pa'l-Schmid 1999). His model clearly illustrates an unavoidable dependency on the detail and serves as a simple, yet comprehensive, design aid. Figure 4.2 illustrates his matrix which has the architectural detail at its centre. The model incorporates the following:

- Central horizontal (material) axis:
  left – matter and energy, the building materials
  right – components and structure, the parts of the assembly
- Central vertical (non-material) axis:
  top – shape and form, the morphological factors
  bottom – production and the process, the time factor
- Top corners:
  left – goal and function, the use of the building
  right – indoor climate, the convenience of the building
- Bottom corners:
  left – nature and environment, the ecological factors
  right – human health, the human factors
- Centre:
  connections, details, joints – the knot or nucleus.

Schmid's matrix suggests an unavoidable dependency on the detail and, vice versa, the unavoidable influence of the detail on the finished building. As a design aid this graphic guide can help designers to consider the physical and human aspects of architecture in harmony, the material and non-material characteristics of building design. Architectural detailing is central to our desire for a more sustainable way of building, maintaining, re-using and recycling our buildings.

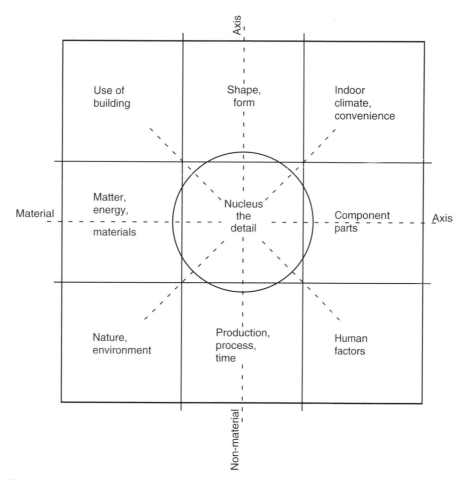

Figure 4.2   The 'basic' model of the architectural detail (adapted from Schmid 1999).

How do we put these building systems together in a more sustainable fashion? What about constructability? To what extent do we pursue dematerialisation? These are just a few questions that can be addressed through Schmid's holistic model. Indeed, answers to such questions are influenced as much by societal pressures as technological ones. In Part II of the book we turn our attention to the building and the process where the issues raised above are dealt with as an inherent part of the design process.

Further reading

Lyons, A.R. (1997). *Materials for Architects and Builders: An Introduction*, Arnold, London.

Mainstone, R. (1998). *Developments in Structural Form* (Second Edition), Architectural Press, Oxford.

Woolley, T., Kimmins, S., Harrison, P. and Harrison, R. (1997). *Green Building Handbook: A Guide to Building Products and Their Impact on the Environment*, E & FN Spon, London.

PART II: THE BUILDING AND THE PROCESS

Previous page shows traditional detailing, St Ives, Cornwall

5 Planning for life

M any detail design decisions are influenced by those made at the briefing and conceptual design stage during which the design agenda is set – a stage at which issues relating to the life and re-use of the building should be considered. The interface between conceptual design and detail design comes into focus with the preparation of the planning application, a stage during which important decisions that affect later material selection are made and where environmental impact must also be considered. Concern for detail at the planning stage is also discussed in relation to both the design and service lives of the building.

5.1 Briefing – setting the agenda

Irrespective of size or initial cost, all construction projects represent a significant capital investment for the sponsor of the project. Because of the large amount of capital investment required building projects are perceived as carrying a large amount of risk, a perception heightened by the apparent uncertain nature of building. Construction projects also represent a significant emotional investment on behalf of both the client and those engaged to fulfil the vision. Will the project turn out as intended, or will it end in litigation? Will the client be happy with the service provided and with the finished artefact? Will building users find the environment comfortable? Designers are faced with a given site and a fixed programme. The programme is sometimes fixed before the design team is assembled, sometimes after and sometimes early in the design process. Individual projects will take place within a given time span and to a pre-established budget, both of which are sometimes bettered and often exceeded. Because of the financial and emotional outlay it is important that clients seek and obtain professional advice and that the brief is developed to its full potential. It is through the selection of appropriate professionals and a thorough development of the brief that customer satisfaction can be delivered – a vital goal for all organisations regardless of size or market orientation. Important decisions need making early in the process. The type of procurement route selected may influence the quality of the finished building because of the resulting relationships and responsibilities. Constraints relating to time and finances will undoubtedly affect quality. Such decisions should be considered at the client briefing stage.

5.1.1 Inception

The first stage in any project is the identification of a need for some form of design and building activity, a phase known as 'inception' which is closely linked to briefing and the feasibility/viability of the proposal. It is here, early in the process, that a whole life approach to building design needs to be considered. The building sponsor, the client, must be able to communicate his or her wants and needs to the design team – stage A of the RIBA plan of work – the briefing stage.

Traditionally the list of client requirements is known as a 'brief', a document that specifies certain requirements to which the design team should adhere. Some clients will approach designers with a detailed brief already prepared, others who may be less experienced will look to their professional advisers to help them identify and clarify their requirements through the process of developing the brief. It is worth remembering that designers work with and for their clients, and are concerned with their clients' problems and goals, not their own (Potter 1989). Since the efficacy of the briefing process will set the tone for the ensuing design work it follows that its management requires particular interpersonal skills and should not be undertaken lightly. The resulting document, the brief, will form a detailed framework from which to develop the design.

A number of guides exist to help the design team in the development and progress of individual projects. One of the most extensive guides is the RIBA's *Architect's Job Book* (Cox and Hamilton 1995) which provides an excellent *aide-mémoire* based on the plan of work stages A to M. Other design guides are available and the one used will depend to a large extent on the professional background of the reader. Sufficient time needs to be made available for the briefing process to be completed in as much detail as is possible before proceeding any further with the project. It follows that there is never an 'open brief'. As Potter (1989) observes, there will always be limitations of contract or context, in addition to those of cost, materials and conditions of manufacture – it is the identification of such limits and conversion into a working brief that complements an analysis of building use and performance.

5.1.2   Client briefing

Without doubt, the most important phase in a building's life is the client briefing stage. It is here that fundamental decisions relating to building performance should be made. Arguments as to who should be involved in the briefing process have been around for a long time, the benefit of one approach over another as much a reflection of the characteristics of the designer as any theoretical argument. Regardless of professional background, those involved in the briefing stage must have good communication skills and be able to give informed advice with regard to three key areas, namely management, design and technology. Designers involved in briefing must be able to emphasise with both the client and also the design team if communication is to be effective. For small projects such skills may be present in one individual, but in larger or more complex projects it is likely that the briefing process will be a team effort, combining the skills of a number of individuals to produce a coherent document. In these situations the brief taker, often a senior member of a design organisation (or an independent project manager), must be capable of communicating with the client (to develop the brief) and communicating the result of that process to the design team as effectively as possible (Fig. 5.1). It is not uncommon in such situations that the client never communicates directly with the design team, thus emphasising the importance of communication channels. A comprehensive brief will guide the design and construction phases and minimise the potential for ambiguity and disputes.

Client briefing is a complex area and there are differing views as to how the brief should be developed. However, it is generally accepted that the better the briefing process, the better the resulting design: excellent briefing usually translates

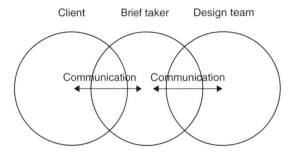

Figure 5.1 Communicating the brief.

into excellent design, and excellent building. Also, and arguably more crucially, the greater the involvement of the client during the briefing stage the greater the success of the outcome (Salisbury 1990). Briefing is expensive in terms of the amount of time consumed, but time spent on data gathering at this stage is seldom wasted because the majority of the information is needed before the design process can begin (see below).

Having suggested that the brief should be complete before the design process commences it may be useful to discuss the two schools of thought about briefing. The first believes that the brief should be established and agreed by the client before the design process begins. Thus briefing is a separate activity to the other stages in the design process, stages which can only begin once the brief has been fixed. Such an approach is seen as crucial in reducing the gap between client expectations and those of the design team and is central to a well designed and implemented quality management system. However, in practice, and despite everyone's best intentions, it is rarely possible to fix every element of the brief before design begins given the time pressures that are often brought to bear by the client and the enormity of the task. The second school of thought maintains that briefing occurs throughout the design process, an ongoing and evolving activity which extends throughout the design process (e.g. Salisbury 1990). In many respects this view represents the classic stereotypical image of design as a creative and chaotic process that is difficult to manage. Advocates of such a philosophy claim that it is only through keeping the briefing process fluid that creativity and hence architecturally stimulating buildings can develop. Both approaches are valid and whether one approach is adopted in preference to another will depend as much upon the approach of the design organisation as the wishes of the client (Fig. 5.2).

Briefing is a creative activity during which client and designer need fully to understand each other. If empathy is missing the briefing process can go wrong and lead to a design solution which does not meet initial expectations. The RIBA's own guide (*Architect's Job Book*, 1995) claims that briefing is a continuous process, from inception and feasibility (RIBA stages A to B) through to the detail design (stage E). Four distinct phases are identified which follow on from the identification of the client's objectives, or functional requirements, as summarised below.

5.1.3 *Client's requirements*

Establishment of functional requirements: environmental standards, levels of quality, life span and maintenance.

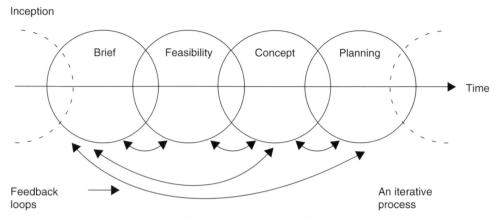

Figure 5.2 Briefing as a comprehensive document from which the design proceeds.

(1) *Initial brief.* This should be developed in sufficient detail to enable the feasibility studies to be carried out and should be presented as a document to be agreed by the client before proceeding further.

(2) *Project brief.* The project brief should cover the technical, managerial and design intentions, indicating how the requirements of the initial brief are to be met. It should cover:
   (a) feasibility studies
   (b) site and/or building surveys and associated reports
   (c) functional needs
   (d) environmental impact assessment (EIA)
   (e) statutory constraints, easements and legal restrictions
   (f) cost appraisal studies.

(3) *Design brief.* This is developed from the project brief and includes input from all relevant consultants and specialists, and the health and safety planning supervisor. It will require:
   (a) co-ordination of all relevant information
   (b) design studies and investigations
   (c) preparation of outline design proposal
   (d) preparation of a cost plan (and programme).

(4) *Consolidated brief.* This represents the definitive brief. This document should be agreed and then 'signed off' by the client. Presented in report format it should include:
   (a) introduction, purpose and scope
   (b) summary of the research
   (c) discussion of design options
   (d) description of proposed scheme design
   (e) cost plan and programme.

Time scale and cost constraints will influence the type of construction techniques employed and the materials used, especially if the project is to be fast tracked. Availability of components and special finishes will need checking here, or at least identifying as a design consideration, before proceeding further.

The RIBA's guide may be a little cumbersome for small projects, although the philosophy of developing the brief in a systematic manner for all projects is a professional approach and in keeping with quality management systems. Another advantage of segmenting the process is that the different phases can be linked into a schedule of design reviews. Planned design reviews held between the different briefing stages can help to identify any problems with communication and interpretation of the client's requirements. Criticism of the model illustrated above would be the lack of attention to recycling and disposal strategies, although these can be incorporated very easily.

5.1.4   *Briefing checklist*

A methodology for the design and management of processes used for delivering a service to customers and maintaining that important link through the adoption of a 'total' approach to the design and development of products is well established in engineering (e.g. Pugh 1991). Product design does not just entail technology and detail design, it also involves the satisfaction of customers, without which the product would be unsuccessful in the marketplace. Total design embraces and maintains the customer focus. Ramaswamy (1996) has applied these principles to the delivery of service processes and Emmitt (1999a) has used the philosophy for the delivery of building design services. For the design team the focus has to be on satisfying the client in the short term and also on satisfying building users over a much longer period. So service delivery is not just about delivering a building project on time, within budget and to predetermined quality parameters, it is also about delivering a building which will be enjoyable to use, cost-effective to service, easy to maintain, safe and secure, and has a clearly identified recycling/disposal policy. Extensive checklists are available that essentially deal with performance criteria and technical restrictions, for which a degree of balance has to be reached and individual design organisations tend to develop models that suit their approach to the design process. Once the briefing stage is complete the resulting briefing document should be agreed by the client and the design team and 'signed off', i.e. agreed and signed by all those party to the briefing stage.

5.1.5   *Briefing – a place for detail?*

The importance of getting the brief right was discussed above. How this is achieved is quite another matter (see Emmitt 1999a for a discussion about the management of the briefing process). How much detail should be included in the brief? The answer depends on the client. Many commercial clients have standard performance specifications which must be complied with, and many include lists of prohibited products and materials (usually because of fears over health and safety, sometimes from bad experiences on previous projects). The important point to recognise is that decisions made at a very early stage in a project will undoubtedly affect the choice of materials and technologies to realise the design. Consideration should be given to durability and performance issues:

(1) *Durability*. This needs consideration at the briefing stage. BS 7543: 1992 (1998), 'Guide to durability of buildings and building elements, products and

components', is a useful reference. This standard provides guidance on durability, required and predicted service life and design life, as well as guidance on presenting information when a detailed brief is being developed. At this juncture it is useful to make the distinction between design life and service life. Both must be considered at the briefing stage where the following question needs to be addressed. What are the client's requirements for the building's serviceability? The answer to this question will influence the design life of the materials, components and products subsequently selected. For example, a specified service life of 15 years will lead to the selection of different materials to those required to last 50 years. Designers also need to consider the extent to which the specified service life and specified design life will have on the routine cleaning, maintenance strategy and schedule of replacement.

(2) *A performance approach.* The concept of a performance is not new; however, there appears to be a global shift towards setting performance parameters in preference to prescriptive standards and regulations. Such trends can be seen in the way in which regulations are written (see Chapter 6) and the manner in which buildings are being procured and maintained. Performance standards are presented as a set of functional requirements which need to be met. For example, stating that the external wall of a dwelling should provide a U value of at least 0.35 leaves the choice of construction to the contractor, assuming of course that the U value can be met. So performance standards allow the manufacturer and/or contractor to decide how to meet the requirements laid down in the standard, i.e. they transfer the decision-making process from the designers and engineers to the manufacturers and contractors. The performance approach to procurement should improve communication between the different parties because they are brought together early in the development process so that performance standards can be agreed (Huovila 1999). Required performance standards for thermal insulation, noise insulation, fire resistance, etc., must be specified early – technical requirements that will influence both conceptual and detail design.

5.1.6   *Gross versus net building area*

Clients often express their requirements in terms of floor area (sometimes volume) and many are vague as to whether they are referring to gross or net floor area. Furthermore, many buildings are sold or leased according to the usable floor area and, therefore, the relationship between the gross building area and the net usable (lettable) area is an important consideration for both client and designer. Good detail design can help to maximise the net to gross ratio; indeed some designers obtain repeat commissions for commercial work because they are particularly good at maximising the ratio of net to gross floor space.

■ *Gross floor area* is usually measured to the external face of the external walls of the building, sometimes referred to as the building 'footprint'. The gross area includes the circulation areas, the mechanical/electrical equipment areas, and the area taken up by the construction materials. Planning authorities are concerned with the footprint of the building in relation to the overall site area and require gross floor areas to be clearly identified when applying for planning consent. Sometimes the 'gross area' should also include the extent of roof overhang, a requirement which usually leads to the loss of any significant overhang (to maximise floor area) and thus not only influences the architectural character of the building but may adversely affect the long-term weathering of the building.

■ *Net floor area* is usually measured to the face of internal walls. The net area excludes the circulation areas, the mechanical/electrical equipment areas, and the area taken up by the construction materials, including structural columns within rooms. Depending on whether one is buying or selling the net area may also exclude the depth of the skirting boards! Clients usually express their needs in terms of net areas; few are concerned with the depth of the walls, or their method of construction, unless it affects their potential income.

Problems arise when areas are specified without any indication as to whether they are gross or net. Disputes can and do arise from misunderstandings over what was measured when calculating the respective areas. In the design of commercial buildings part of the designer's brief will be to minimise the ratio of non-lettable space to lettable space, thus helping to maximise the owner's income from the building asset. In areas where land prices are high the requirement becomes a very important factor and can influence the manner in which the

Figure 5.3 Urban design solution.

building is detailed. Structural columns take up lettable space, thin wall construction is preferred to thick, and service zones, plant rooms and circulating space should be kept to a minimum.

5.2 Feasibility

Once the brief is complete, or has developed to such a stage as to allow the project to proceed, the design team will be able to assess the feasibility and viability of the project (RIBA stage B). At this stage an assessment is made of the feasibility of the scheme against the client's technical, time and cost constraints, i.e. can the brief be met? To answer this question usually requires a significant amount of work. A measured survey of the site will be required to ascertain physical constraints and any existing buildings will need to be surveyed and assessed for their condition and structural integrity. Provision, position and suitability of mains services (electricity, telecommunications, gas, water and foul drainage) need to be established and any adjustments in position or supply capacity costed. Legal documents will need to be checked to confirm the boundaries of the site and any conditions attached to the site, such as easements and right of ways, identified. The local planning authority will also need to be consulted to check for any use or development restrictions (see below). In the majority of cases a thorough ground investigation will also be required to determine soil conditions (for foundation design and costings) and the extent of any contamination (and an estimate of the time and cost of making the site fit for development). These independent and inter-dependent data collection exercises often involve many different consultants and are a necessary, but expensive, phase of the project. This phase of the project is an extensive information collecting exercise from which the conceptual design work will flow.

5.2.1 Design reviews

Before the project moves to the conceptual design stage there is a need to arrange a programme of design reviews. The design review is a formal assessment of the design against the client's brief to check that the design meets the client's requirements, is in line with the firm's own standards and conforms to relevant regulatory requirements. Design reviews are planned events, forming an important part of the programme and the project quality plan. These meetings should include the presence of the client and consultants working on the project so that the design is reviewed by the project team and any alterations are agreed by the team and recorded in the office plan. They work well because they bring people together to communicate, share views and agree a course of action in a supportive environment.

Design reviews are carried out at predetermined stages in the project and to work at their best should include the project team, consultants, the quality manager, the planning supervisor, and the client or the client's representative. The review system is essentially a series of gates in the design process through which the project cannot pass without a thorough check from the quality manager and the approval of the client. They are a tool for ensuring full understanding of the information available to the development team at a particular point in the project.

It is a very good system of detecting errors and omissions. It provides a checkpoint for ensuring that the design meets the client's requirements and the architectural practice's standards. It also gives the planning supervisor an opportunity to check the scheme for compliance under the recently introduced CDM Regulations. Perhaps, even more importantly, it also provides a window for debate, while feedback from (and for) other projects can be introduced at these reviews.

5.3   Conceptual design

Only after relevant information has been collected, assimilated and analysed should the design team consider any design possibilities, cost estimates and a programme of design and construction works. This assumes that all the relevant information is to hand, although this is rarely the case. It is not uncommon for the design team to proceed with design work without all the queries raised at the feasibility stage being answered, so assumptions have to be made and notified in writing to the client. For example, legal queries related to boundaries may take a long time to be resolved; thus reasonable assumptions made on the physical evidence from the site may have to suffice (and the client informed accordingly). Client and designer concerns are expressed in Fig. 5.4, namely the budget, aesthetics, buildability and functionality, all determined by time.

The design concept expresses the idea underlying the designer's vision and helps to direct the multitude of decisions that follow. Concepts embody architectural and cultural symbolism; they draw on a wide variety of sources such as previous experience, typologies and standard solutions; they are stimulated by the site and the client's brief. Concepts usually embody a certain amount of objective criteria and a fair subjective element. Concepts may be represented by a few single lines on a piece of paper that form a sketch, or represented in diagrammatic form, through to quite elaborate drawings, all of which may be supported by some textual annotation. The approach depends upon the personality and working method of the designer and the design office in which they work. Although some conceptual designs may look extremely simplistic, one should not lose sight of the fact that designers need to understand the issues that follow on from these

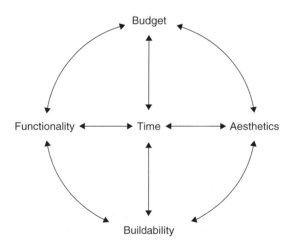

Figure 5.4 Client and designer concerns (leading to concept) – quality loop.

early visions (such as structural design, legislation, detailing, assembly, disassembly) if a workable concept is to be developed, an understanding of the issues developed in this book. It is not enough just to be a good designer – other issues cannot be ignored.

Conceptual designs lead into the design process proper, which although determined by time (programme) is not entirely linear. Design is an iterative process during which concepts are developed further and in greater depth alongside other members of the design team, solving problems (some anticipated, some not) as they go along. Throughout this process the original concept must be borne in mind and decisions made considered against the concept and the brief and modified accordingly (sometimes the brief/concept is modified). Thus the conceptual design is developed into a more formalised design for planning approval, bearing in mind buildability, cost, programme, functionality and quality. The manner in which various elements are put together will dictate the final appearance and functionality of the building. Designers' preferences, combined with office culture, will be influential in how the concept is developed. Design is a creative activity that draws on known solutions and the unknown, so a good framework is required so that the process can be managed effectively. The ability constantly to reassess, adjust and reflect, together with determination and persistence, are requisite qualities for designers.

5.3.1   Manufacturers' input

As concepts are developed and refined it may be necessary to invite manufacturers into the office to discuss the feasibility and cost of using their proprietary products. Early involvement of manufacturers, drawing on their expert knowledge of particular materials and products, can help to eliminate waste and keep costs to an acceptable level at an early stage. Establishment of such relationships can save time later in the design programme as specialist suppliers are familiar with the design philosophy of the design team and have developed a working relationship before detailing starts; thus the potential for effective communication and effective detailed solutions is much improved. Some design organisations have adopted such an approach (in line with supply chain ethos); others prefer to distance themselves from manufacturers until the design has been more fully developed.

It is common practice to seek advice from three competing manufacturers, from which an assessment can be made as to whom to work with during the development of the design. This decision is likely to be made on an assessment of the total service to be provided by a particular manufacturer. Product characteristics may be less significant than the quality of the technical support, guarantees and general supporting advice given (or promised) by the manufacturer. On the basis that there is no such thing as a 'free lunch', the service (sold as being 'free') is paid for in more expensive products. Whether the design team are able to confirm their choice of materials and major product specifications at an early stage will be dictated by the client, the project type and any planning restrictions. Specialist input from trade contractors and sub-contractors may be sought early in the design development stage, depending upon contractual arrangements and/or the complexity of the project.

5.3.2 *Value engineering*

Many of the principles enshrined in buildability are consistent with ensuring value for the client. In recent years there has been a trend to look at design solutions to assess their 'value' before the design gets to the contract stage, a process in which value is that perceived by the client, and one that may be interpreted differently if, e.g. one was considering the scheme in terms of its ecological value. Value engineering and value management techniques have become popular, but are often criticised for being nothing more than cost cutting devices. However, if carried out at the right time and by people able to make a comprehensive assessment of the project's buildability, such exercises can be effective in reducing waste. Arguably, the most critical factor in carrying out a value engineering exercise is timing. Cost permitting, the value engineering exercise should be carried out in conjunction with the briefing phase to identify the potential for saving resources before any design work has commenced. Further exercises to assess the design against predetermined functional and technical requirements can then be incorporated into a schedule of design reviews. Whether or not such exercises improve or compromise 'quality' is a debatable point, and one that will depend upon one's position in the larger scheme of things, whether client, designer, builder or user.

5.4 Town planning and development control

The extent to which the conceptual design is developed before discussions are held with the local authority planning department will depend upon the wishes of the client and the commercial sensitivity of the scheme; however, there will come a stage when planning consent has to be applied for. As development control has become more stringent so has the importance of acquiring planning consent. Planning is a major design generator because the materials to be used externally must be stated on the planning application and samples submitted for approval of the planning authority. Thus many major material specifications are made at the planning stage and carried through to the completed artefact.

Town planning has a long history, though our more recent legislation can be traced back to concerns for public health and more latterly concerns over land usage and development control. There are close links with the Building Regulations (see Chapter 6) and legislation is influenced by governments' political agendas and on an individual basis by local politics. For local authorities the challenge is to achieve a balance between economic growth and minimising damage to the environment, within the national planning framework and policy guidelines. Planning legislation continues to evolve in response to changing patterns of human activity, although as it stands at present in the UK, town and country planning seeks to restrict development to guidelines set by government. There was a presumption in favour of granting planning permission until 1991, but this changed with the Planning and Compensation Act 1991 which requires planning decisions to accord with a local authority's development plan unless material conditions indicate otherwise. Growing concern about our natural environment and increasing pressure to re-use and recycle previously used sites instead of pushing further into greenfield sites has placed additional pressures on the planning system. EIAs, planning policy guidance documents (PPGs) and increased participation from local pressure groups enrich the planning process even further. Before looking at the process of planning submissions and the implications for the detail design of a building it is useful to consider a brief overview of the development of planning legislation in England and Wales.

5.4.1   Early legislation

The UK underwent rapid economic and social change in the 19th century. The development of new technology and increased industrialisation led to a rapid growth in urban centres and public health became a major concern. Between 1800 and 1850 there was an enormous increase in the number of people living in urban areas all over the Western world. Rapid growth of the major industrial towns was accompanied by overcrowding, poor housing conditions and a lack of sanitation, leading to epidemics of waterborne diseases with pandemics of cholera in the 1830s and 1840s on both sides of the Atlantic. Medical statisticians soon found a link between mortality and overcrowded, dirty, poorly serviced and shoddily built housing areas. Although diseases tended to break out in the poorer areas of town the viruses spread rapidly and the better-off members of society were just as susceptible as the working classes. Necessity, being the mother of invention, led to a number of important reforms, legislation and large scale engineering projects to provide drainage to the burgeoning urban areas. The Sanitary Act, 1847, was an important piece of legislation in that it required the provision of sewers and drains to all new residential areas. One year later the Public Health Act, 1848, set out requirements for the design and construction of houses, e.g. a minimum ceiling height was stipulated in an attempt to improve the amount of daylight and air circulation within the dwelling. These Acts added to the cost of development and many builders and developers chose to ignore them.

Victorian towns and cities were not particularly healthy places to live. Not only was the internal environment of a poor standard, but also the external environment was deteriorating. There was little regard for the natural environment, with streams, rivers and the sea used as a convenient dumping ground for human and industrial waste, a legacy which has taken a long time to deal with. Use of the River Thames by Londoners as an open sewer eventually became unacceptable, with the 'Great Stink' coming from the River Thames forcing the adjournment of Parliament in 1852. In 1868 the Royal Commission on Sanitary Administration was set up with its final report leading to the Public Health Act, 1875. By the 20th century the great killer infections which had plagued urban centres of population, such as cholera, diphtheria, typhus, typhoid and tuberculosis, were in retreat in many parts of the Western world (Porter 1993). The Housing and Planning Act, 1919, led to a large scale council house building programme, specifically for soldiers returning from the First World War (1914–1918), and required local authorities to produce town plans with land use zonings for settlements of over 20,000 people. The interwar period witnessed a boom in private house building on the edges of existing urban centres, the growth of suburbia. In an attempt to control the expansion into the countryside the Town and Country Planning

Act, 1932, required local authorities to produce zoning maps and developers to apply for permission. It was largely ignored because the financial penalties were minimal and the local authority was required to pay compensation if permission was refused (Greed 1996). It was not until the end of the Second World War and the period of post-war reconstruction that British town planning started to evolve into a system that had to be taken seriously.

5.4.2   *Increased constraint*

From the late 1940s there has been a steady increase in the power of local authority planning departments. In 1947 an Act was passed which required all development to have planning permission and, just as important, the Act provided powers of enforcement. It was the Town and Country Planning Act, 1947, which set the scene for increasing governmental control over development. Since the early 1950s national and local governmental control has increased through a mixture of increased legislative powers and the imposition of planning policy guidelines. As pressure on space increases legislation will continue to change and become more onerous, a point many designers and developers are not particularly happy about. Environmental concerns, reflected in the adoption of *Agenda 21* and the increased use of EIAs has helped to focus the development team on ecological issues.

5.5   Planning permission

Apart from a few exceptions the development of land in the UK cannot be undertaken without first applying for and receiving planning consent from the local planning authority. Building, engineering, mining and other operations on, over or under land come under the term 'development', as does the change of use of buildings and/or land. There are exceptions, referred to as 'permitted developments', but these continue to change and are affected by neighbouring properties, so designers should check with the appropriate local planning department. The point was made above about planning becoming more restrictive and the need to involve consultants expert in planning law has become paramount on all but the simplest of developments. For clients and their development teams planning can be a major obstacle, especially when the site is located in or adjacent to a conservation area or the development does not accord with a local authority's development plan.

Development plans, represented by district plans, local plans and unitary development plans (UDPs), set out strategic development for a particular area. These plans differentiate different use classes for different areas of land, identifying existing use and that required by the planning authority. Such plans are useful for the development team in identifying whether or not their particular proposal accords with that wanted by the planning department. If the proposal is in line with that identified in the development plan, approval should be forthcoming. If the proposal does not accord with the development plan then permission is likely to be refused on policy.

As an aid to development the Use Classes Order, 1987, classifies buildings by their intended use. Any changes to the approved use, e.g. a dwelling house (C3)

CORNWALL COLLEGE
LIBRARY

although it is worth knowing the likely reasons for non-determination. They are as follows:

■ *Complexity of schemes.* Many schemes do not fall easily within a local authority's development plan. Authorities must consult with neighbours, must advertise the application, and consult with relevant departments, such as highways, landscape, etc. The more complex the scheme the more time is required to digest the information and make an informed recommendation to the planning committee.
■ *Complexity of legislation.* As planning legislation and PPGs have become more numerous the number of issues to be considered has mushroomed.
■ *Over-stretched planning department.* In periods where there is a lot of building activity taking place planning departments may become over-stretched and the period taken to determine applications will increase as a result. Other factors, such as staff shortages or poor management, may also contribute to delays. Some authorities have better records for dealing with applications on time than others.
■ *Poor quality of the information submitted.* Authorities may refuse to register the application if insufficient detail is provided with the application. Alternatively, there may be a request for additional information before they can complete the consultation process.

Assuming that all goes well, the application will be put to the next available planning committee with a recommendation for approval or refusal. This committee meets on a regular basis, every 3 weeks or so, to determine planning applications. The manner in which they operate varies between local authorities. Some welcome a presentation by the designers and client, others do not – a point worth bearing in mind when preparing the submission. Planning committees are made up of people with political interests, and there is no guarantee that an application recommended for approval by the planners will be approved, or, vice versa, that one recommended for refusal may be approved. For designers dealing with planning applications it is worth remembering that no guarantees can be made to the client because the committee's decision is beyond the control of the applicant and his or her agent.

5.6 Concern for detail

With the growth in importance of planning legislation and the move towards greater powers of protection for existing buildings comes the issue of design control. It can be an emotive area for designers (seeking to get the best design for their clients) and the planners (seeking to uphold their policies). There are two, connected, issues: those concerning legislative issues, such as planning policy documents and design guides, and the effect on product selection.

5.6.1 Design control

Conservation areas and listed building legislation have implications for designers, especially the architectural style adopted and the choice of materials to be used externally, discussed in more detail in Chapter 12. These are in place for good reason (in the majority of cases) and the design team know what to expect in terms of input from the planning authority and local user groups. What is a little more difficult to deal with is control over design when buildings are not in conservation areas or are not listed. Here PPGs provide planners and designers with a set of guidelines for specific issues.

Design guides, of which the Essex Design Guide is the most well known, are still about, and are important for designers because they set out detailed design requirements that should be followed to ensure consent is forthcoming. Manchester's Hulme Development Guide is one of the more recent. The Hulme Development Guide provided an urban vision and a mechanism for its implementation rather than creating a masterplan (Symes and Pauwels 1999). Proposals for traditional street design and physical massing, rather than specific detailed design, were the approach adopted, combined with policies for reducing the risk and fear of crime through natural surveillance, and promoting initiatives for sustainable design.

5.6.2   *Product selection*

There may be occasions when planning officers suggest, recommend or even insist on the use of specific external materials or products for certain projects. Both the external appearance of the building and the landscaping of the site (both hard and soft) are subject to close scrutiny by the planning authority. Anecdotal evidence of town planners' interference in this important area is easy to find and designers are quick to complain about such action. Research into the frequency and effect of such action is, however, harder to find. That which has been published has identified and commented on such action. Mackinder (1980) found that town planning officers did recommend that specific products be used on some projects. The Barbour Report (1993) highlighted the influence of town planning officers over product selection for materials to be used externally, observations that were confirmed in more recent research (Emmitt 1997a) where planning officers frequently recommended products by brand name. In a recent development familiar to the author the planning committee eventually granted approval to a housing scheme, but with conditions. One of these conditions stated that permission would only be granted if timber window frames (aluminium were specified) and natural stone (render specified) were used. This highlighted the personal preference of the planning department and the planning committee, rather than any architectural issues, because render and aluminium window frames had been used on buildings adjoining the site. Apart from the cost implications of the planners' requests, it was a clear illustration of the planners' influence on detail design decisions that affect the external appearance of buildings.

Clearly there will be a certain amount of give and take on many planning applications and the need for an objective and balanced approach on both sides is necessary if conflict is to be avoided. Where town planning officers are insistent that a specific product be used the designer has two options: to agree to the request or refuse (and possibly go to appeal). It must be remembered that the responsibility for product selection lies with the design office and therefore the specifier should exercise caution when considering such requests. Planners will be first and foremost concerned with the appearance of the external materials, durability will not be foremost in their concerns, while technical and financial considerations will be of no importance to them. It is the specifier who remains responsible for the selection of materials and products, not the other participants involved in the planning process.

5.6.3   Enforcement

Substitution of materials for cheaper or more easily available ones is relatively common. In circumstances where the external materials to be used have been approved, and hence are a condition of planning consent, the approval of the local authority planning department must be sought and obtained prior to changes being made. Failure to do so may lead to enforcement action being taken by the local authority. Approved drawings must be complied with; in many respects they set the agenda for the majority of the detail design decisions that follow planning approval.

5.7   Environmental impact

A large number of tools to aid decision-making have been, and continue to be, proposed. Perhaps the most important and well-established tool lies with the EIA. The European Union's first Directive on Environmental Assessment, Directive 85/337 EEC, was introduced in 1985 and approved for implementation in 1988. Use in the UK remains patchy, restricted to large or 'difficult' developments, and seen to be the domain of the town planners, so its potential as a decision-making tool to aid a more environmentally responsible approach to construction remains largely untapped. Nationally some local authorities use EIAs enthusiastically while others have not used them for fear of blighting economic development, and where they are used many developers view them as a 'means to an end' and forget about them once approval has been granted.

The introduction and development of EIAs around the world is well documented and guidance on how to deal with EIAs is extensive (e.g. Munn 1979, Walthern 1992, DoE 1994). The objective of an EIA is to provide decision-makers with an indication of the consequences of their actions and following this argument it could form an essential design aid for the development team. Although this does occur in the best examples, unfortunately it is more commonly seen as little more than an exercise that must be done to achieve planning approval, carried out once the main decisions have been taken; not surprisingly the documentation is often put together once the initial design proposals and planning application drawings have been completed. The result is that the planners are seen as the gatekeepers, the scope for participation is limited (since the design has already been agreed by developer and designer) and the process can become adversarial. It is essentially a reactive process, not a proactive one. At present EIAs are only required on major projects, the remainder being at the discretion of local authorities and voluntary use by the development team. EIA has potential to be extremely useful for all those engaged in the development process, from clients and designers to planners and local residents alike. Published in 1990, the *Rosehaugh Guide* provided excellent advice to designers, in which Tomlinson argued for the consideration of materials and products within the EIA, advice that seems to have been ignored. Others in the field have proposed comprehensive checklists for selecting 'environmentally sound' building products to assist the development team in the maximisation of recycled materials and the reduction in extraction of raw materials and waste (Friedman and Cammalleri 1995).

5.7.1   *Opportunities*

EIAs are carried out as a series of steps, or stages. These steps start with screening, i.e. asking whether an EIA is necessary, through scoping which determines the extent of the EIS, to consultation and then decision-making by the relevant (local) authority, to be followed by monitoring and auditing. Although some authors remain enthusiastic about EIAs, other researchers paint a picture of missed opportunities. For example, Thompson *et al.* (1997) found that the information dealing with ecological issues was so poor that it was impossible to assess the actual impact of the schemes reviewed.

EIAs do provide a tool to take a fuller, more integrated, approach to the ecological impact of buildings. Cole (1998) has suggested that the contribution of EIAs has been to acknowledge the importance of assessing buildings, and he places much greater emphasis on the importance of life cycle assessment (LCA), within the EIA process, to evaluate the performance of building designs and/or the completed building. The development team have a responsibility to consider the building and the smaller components that make up its assembly. For example, what proportion of the building's assembly comprises reclaimed materials, or recycled materials? What is the cumulative effect on local and global consumption? What is the embodied energy rating of the materials used? These are important questions often overshadowed by other concerns for the development team. Glasson *et al.* (1997) have argued that the 'process should be an iterative and dynamic one which provides the opportunity of improving projects and safeguarding the environment at every stage'. If we take this statement forward then the natural progression would be to consider the product and its detailed assemblage, within the EIA process, i.e. from briefing onwards.

Design in its widest sense can make an important contribution to environmental impact, but, showcase buildings aside, the majority of developments have failed to incorporate environmentally responsible ideals and practices (Emmitt 1997b, Mackenzie 1997). As creators of the building concept the design team set the scene for the detail design where individual decisions regarding product selection are made. It is usually too late by the time it gets to the planning consent stage since important design decisions have already been taken which influence the detail product selection. Attention to detail is important and central to LCA which aims to consider the environmental impact of materials and products from the cradle to the grave. But there is a large gulf between the theory and practice, primarily because it is so difficult to access relevant information. It is also very difficult to quantify the actual impact of all the individual materials and products that together form a finished product, as some are trying to address, e.g. the Building Performance Group (Bartlett and Moss 1999) and the Building Research Establishment (BRE) (Edwards and Anderson 1999).

There is clearly an opportunity to make the EIA and its associated EIS meaningful and useful for the whole life of the building, itself an ongoing process, a living document. Addressed as part of the briefing process and refined through to handover and eventual disposal, planning approval becomes one step in the process. Following this approach EIA and EIS become a natural and integral part of the design and development process, co-ordinated by the project manager and, most importantly, owned by the product. EIA as an underlying philosophy to development is one with enormous potential, but it requires a change in attitude and action by all members of the development team.

Further reading

Greed, C.H. (1996). *Introducing Town Planning* (Second Edition), Longman, Harlow.

6 Regulations, codes and standards

We live in a society bounded by laws, regulations and codes, and building has not escaped lightly. Building regulations, codes of practice, national and international standards, lie at the heart of the technologist's domain, essential design tools that are constantly changing. It is essential that practitioners maintain a working knowledge of relevant legislation. Often seen as something that hinders creativity, regulations, codes and standards are examined in this chapter as generators of creative detail design. Here we explore the development of legislation from a historical perspective and identify challenges for the future, such as designing for disassembly, and staying abreast of developments.

6.1 Control and creativity

In the previous chapter we looked at the first approval stage for a building project, planning consent, and the contribution that detail design can make at an early stage in the building design process. After the planning stage comes the detail design stage, RIBA stages E and F, during which the design team's work must be co-ordinated and consultants' input checked for potential conflict during the preparation of the production information. For the vast majority of building operations designers must also ensure proposals comply with current Building Regulations, and also, depending upon the type of project, with the National House-Building Council (NHBC) guidelines, insurance requirements and prevailing standards of best practice. Once planning permission has been granted the design team can proceed with the Building Regulation submission (discussed below). There may have been alterations made to the design in order to achieve planning consent and there may also be planning conditions that affect the detailing stage and hence the information to be produced for Building Regulation approval (see Fig. 6.1). Particular care needs to be taken to ensure that any materials approved by the town planners, and possibly specified by brand name, are included in the detail design phase.

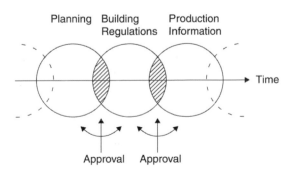

Figure 6.1 Statutory approvals.

Regulations are first and foremost concerned with ensuring safe buildings although more recently emphasis has shifted towards providing a healthy environment for all building users. Regulations, in whatever form, offer designers a familiar set of controls to work with. They also offer a series of constraints based on experience, research and common sense, essentially a guide to best practice. Whether or not such guidelines, whether obligatory or optional, are a barrier to innovative practice is explored in Chapter 14. Regulations, standards and codes are foremost in the designer's mind during the detail design stage and their impact on a design will have been considered at the conceptual design stage. Constraint is greatest at the detail design stage when the designer aims to convert the conceptual design into a set of detailed information which satisfies the brief and complies with the relevant prevailing legislation.

National and international regulations *must* be complied with, standards and codes *should* be complied with. Busy designers may well view regulations, codes and standards as a burden because they can be time consuming to read and act upon, yet one of the many skills of the building designer is his or her ability to keep up to date with current legislation and apply it in a creative and cost-effective manner to realise the design intent. Research by Mackinder and Marvin (1982) found that building designers tended to refer to written documentation only when they had to, preferring to rely on rules of thumb and their experience, until such time that they were forced to search for information. Clearly there comes a point when someone with technical knowledge will have to make the design work, including compliance with legislation and best practice. In some design offices this is carried out by the same person who crafted the conceptual design, in others the task of detailing and ensuring the design complies with prevailing legislation will be carried out by more technically orientated individuals.

Regulatory frameworks do vary between countries and regional variations are not uncommon in many countries. Globally the trend has been to move towards a performance approach in preference to a prescriptive one. Prescriptive regulations show or describe the construction required to achieve conformity. Performance based regulations stipulate a level which must be met (or bettered) but do not specifically indicate how this is to be done. Another difference between prescriptive and performance regulations is that the performance based focus on methods of conformity which consider buildings as whole systems, not elements in isolation. Thus trade-offs between component parts, e.g. in achieving the necessary minimum thermal insulation values, are allowed to achieve the given objectives. In theory the performance approach allows designers greater freedom of expression in the way in which conformity is achieved. Another approach is an objective based one, as adopted in the National Building Code of Canada (NBCC), which should allow greater opportunity to address matters of durability (Chown 1999). An objective based approach seeks to combine prescriptive, performance and functional requirements. Canada's code is based on a hierarchical structure of objectives comprising four elements: objectives, functional requirements, quantitative performance criteria and acceptable solutions.

Whether or not regulations, codes and standards stimulate or hinder technological advancement is open to debate. Do regulations encourage innovation? This was a question posed by the authors of a paper which focused on energy efficiency in housing (Gann *et al.* 1998). They noted that there had been very little debate about such relationships and raised a number of interesting questions for further research. On one hand changes to regulatory frameworks may provide the opportunity for manufacturers and designers to work in new ways, to innovate. For the manufacturers of building components and products the changes to the regulations set new standards of performance, often providing the stimulus for new product development and/or product development and improvement. On the other hand regulations could be seen as reinforcing current practice – which may not necessarily be best practice – and in so doing stifling innovation. An interesting feature of the current Building Regulations is the use of typical details to demonstrate methods of compliance. These details can be, and frequently are, copied (see Chapter 8).

6.1.1   *Jerry-building*

Regulations, standards and codes form an essential framework for ensuring a quality structure. Combined they provide clients, government regulators and fellow professionals with instruments to measure the quality of the finished product. On their own regulations and codes cannot bring about good quality and safe construction. Regulations have to be enforced and construction work closely monitored to ensure compliance with prevailing legislation. Throughout history there has been, and continues to be, evidence of shoddy workmanship and the flouting of legislation. For those professionals engaged in work to existing buildings it is not uncommon to find that the building was not built entirely in accordance with the approved drawings. Deviation by workers on site from the approved details can be annoying for both the designer trying to ensure quality and the client who may well end up paying for something that is inferior to that expected. Sometimes the failure to build in accordance with current building legislation can have serious consequences. For example, in Turkey the Izmit earthquake of 1999 resulted in widespread destruction of buildings and infrastructure and high loss of life despite the existence of stringent building codes. Allegations of shoddy construction, the failure to adhere to regulations and the failure to enforce the regulations soon followed – clear evidence that 'jerry-building' is still with us despite the proliferation of codes and regulations. Fitchen (1986: 44) makes the point that it is impossible to tell how many jerry-built structures have collapsed over the years, but that 'their numbers must be legion'.

In many respects building has always provided the less scrupulous with an environment in which to make a quick profit, regardless of the consequences to public safety and the durability of the finished product. Developers, builders and building professionals have all been tarred at some point or another with corrupt acts. Professional bodies and organisations have tried hard to stamp out jerry-building but it still exists. In modern parlance the term 'cowboy-builder' is used to describe jerry-builders. In addition to the major disasters which expose jerry-building there are more subtle forms which, again, are particularly difficult to quantify. For example, the penchant of contractors and sub-contractors for substituting inferior building products for those previously specified is not only dishonest, but may well compromise the durability of the structure. There is a clear need for someone to take responsibility for site supervision over and above the contractor's own, regardless of procurement route (see Chapter 11).

6.1.2   Sources of technical information

Building designers need access to a wide variety of information at the detail design stage. Some of the main sources for designers working in the UK are the following:

- Building Regulations and Codes
- British (BS), European (EN) and international (ISO) standards
- British Board of Agrément certificates
- BRE publications
- Manufacturers' technical literature
- Compendia of technical literature, e.g. *Specification*, *RIBA Product Selector*, *Barbour Index*, etc.
- Trade association publications
- Technical articles and guides in professional journals
- Previous projects worked on by the organisation
- Office standard details and master specifications.

This information has traditionally been held in the design office library as paper copies. More recently with the improvements in IT and a reduction in cost which has improved accessibility, many design offices have moved towards electronic information, held on CD ROM or accessed on-line, usually by subscription to the provider. This makes access to relevant information quicker and helps to ensure all members of the office are using up to date and reliable information, thus reducing the likelihood of mistakes attributable to old information.

6.2   Regulatory frameworks

Before looking at the current regulations it is useful to get some idea as to how and why building legislation came into force. We are conditioned to accept legislation without questioning its wisdom: do we, e.g. *always* need a damp-proof course in brickwork walls? A brief historical overview of the Building Regulations, codes of practice, British and international standards provides a useful point of reference.

6.2.1   The Building Regulations

The Romans first introduced some controls over building to the UK and control through local Acts aimed at reducing the consequences of fire was present in the Middle Ages. Our current legislation has its roots in the Great Fire of London of 1666 and the Act for the Rebuilding of the City of London of 1667 (the London Building Act). Building Acts only applied to London, the largest centre of population, although their effect on architectural detailing was copied by builders in other parts of the country who looked to the capital for the latest architectural styles. The Building Acts of 1707 and 1709 outlawed timber cornices and window frames that were flush with the external brickwork, and thus brought about the fashion for parapets and recessed window frames (Quiney 1989). With the growth of urban centres and the pressures created by overcrowding some builders were tempted to maximise their profits by cutting corners, thus endangering life both during construction work and after. Such practices were, and still are, known as 'jerry-building', a term used to describe shoddy practices which lead to substandard, unsafe structures, often flouting regulations by using inferior materials and inept workmanship (Fitchen 1986).

Concerns over the structural stability and poor quality of building work, combined with those over public health, resulted in further Acts for London. Effective laws to outlaw the jerry-builders and to reduce the risk of fire spread from one house to another came with the 1774 Building Act for London, although other towns had to wait some time for their own by-laws. The 1774 Act introduced four 'rates' of houses, the largest (and most expensive) being the First Rate houses, through Second and Third, to the smallest (and least expensive), the Fourth Rate. Detailed requirements for wall thickness, timber joist sizes and fire proofing measures were mandatory and related to the rate of the house to be constructed. Failure to comply could result in demolition of the building. Although the Building Act was relatively straightforward the description of the rates was full of contradictions and many of the pattern books of that period were devoted to explaining the effect of the rates (Quiney 1989). One of the effects of the Act was the further demise of wooden decoration to reduce combustibility and fire spread.

Problems of overcrowding and poor sanitation still remained along with frequent outbreaks of diseases such as cholera and typhus. In 1845 the first Public Health Act was passed which sought to address the problems endemic in housing of the time. Dampness, poor sanitation, fire risk, structural stability, and rights of light and ventilation were dealt with in the Act, elements at the heart of our present regulations. New foul sewage systems and better planning slowly followed (e.g. Sanitary Act, 1847; Public Health Act, 1848: Public Health Act, 1875), although reformers had to battle hard for the adoption and enforcement of local by-laws. In 1877 the first model by-laws were produced as a guide for local authorities, setting the first minimum standards for housing guidelines. Individual local authorities were responsible for setting and enforcing the minimum standards and not surprisingly variations developed in different areas. The major cities, such as Birmingham, Leeds and Manchester, were governed by local Acts of Parliament, although the best known and most important was the London Building Act of 1894. This Act was revised on a number of occasions, e.g. in 1930 with amendments in 1935 and 1939.

A change in approach from the prescriptive to the performance was signalled in 1952 when the 'deemed to satisfy' clauses were introduced via the Model By-laws, Series IV, primarily to allow greater freedom in the use of new construction methods (Yeomans 1997). These were adopted by local authorities throughout England and Wales, with the exception of Inner London, bringing with it a greater degree of consistency. The first national Building Regulations were introduced in 1966, which brought England and Wales under the same legislation for the first time and replaced the various local by-laws. Minor amendments followed along with comprehensive re-issues in 1972 and 1976. Fire continued to be a major cause for concern and the Fire Precautions Act, 1971, became an important piece of legislation relating to fire safety in buildings and was closely linked to the Building Act of 1984.

In 1985 the regulations were re-designed and re-published as a set of Approved Documents which sought to control the health and safety of the building's occupants and conserve energy under the Building Act of 1984. These regulations followed the government's White Paper *The Future of Building Control in England and Wales* published in 1981 (Cmnd 1981), and represented a major shift from a prescriptive approach to a performance one. The regulations are intended to provide guidance for some of the common forms of construction while encouraging alternative ways of demonstrating compliance. Designers and builders now have a choice: they can accept the suggested method in full, in part, or not at all if they can demonstrate an alternative method of compliance. In reality many designers and builders find it quicker, easier and more convenient to work to the solutions suggested and illustrated in the documents; alternatives are more time consuming and may well be rejected leading to delays. Many of the construction details illustrated in the current regulations are to be found in design organisations' standard details.

Since their re-design in 1985 there have been a number of revisions and additions to the Approved Documents, with a major revision in 1991, and ongoing updates. In their current form the Approved Documents form a useful *aide-mémoire* and detailed design guide. A summary of the requirements of Schedule 1 to the Building Regulations is provided below. (Those working in Scotland will need to refer to the Building Scotland Act, 1959 (as amended) and the Building Standards (Scotland) Regulations, 1990.)

Part A – Structure
   A1 Loading
   A2 Ground movement
   A3 Disproportionate collapse

Part B – Fire Safety
   B1 Means of escape
   B2 Internal fire spread (linings)
   B3 Internal fire spread (structure)
   B4 External fire spread
   B5 Access and facilities for the fire service

Part C – Site Preparation and Resistance to Moisture
   C1 Preparation of site
   C2 Dangerous and offensive substances
   C3 Subsoil drainage
   C4 Resistance to weather and ground moisture

Part D – Toxic Substances
   D1 Cavity insulation

Part E – Resistance to the Passage of Sound
   E1 Airborne sound (walls)
   E2 Airborne sound (floors and stairs)
   E3 Impact sound (floors and stairs)

Part F – Ventilation
   F1 Means of ventilation
   F2 Condensation in roofs

Part G – Hygiene
  G1 Sanitary conveniences and washing facilities
  G2 Bathrooms
  G3 Hot water storage

Part H – Drainage and Waste Disposal
  H1 Sanitary pipework and drainage
  H2 Cesspools and tanks
  H3 Rainwater drainage
  H4 Solid waste storage

Part J – Heat Producing Appliances
  J1 Air supply
  J2 Discharge of products of combustion
  J3 Protection of building

Part K – Protection from Falling, Collision and Impact
  K1 Stairs, ladders and ramps
  K2 Protection from falling
  K3 Vehicle barriers and loading bays
  K4 Protection from collision with open windows, etc.
  K5 Protection against impact from and trapping by doors

Figure 6.2 Steel and glass detail.

Part L – Conservation of Fuel and Power
L1 Conservation of fuel and power

Part M – Access and Facilities for Disabled People
M1 Interpretation
M2 Access and use
M3 Sanitary conveniences
M4 Audience or spectator seating

Part N – Glazing – Safety in Relation to Impact, Opening and Cleaning
N1 Protection against impact
N2 Manifestation of glazing
N3 Safe opening and closing of windows, etc.
N4 Safe access for cleaning windows, etc.

6.3 Standards and codes

National Building Regulations must be conformed to. Standards and codes provide guidance to designers based on best practice and research, and they should be complied with. They are an effective way of bringing research and development to practitioners thus aiding technology transfer and raising standards of quality. National research organisations such as the BRE in the UK and international research bodies such as the International Council for Research and Innovation in Building and Construction (CIB) are actively involved in the development of national and international standards through representation on various development committees. For example, the CIB has been active in the development of standards for sustainable construction through the ISO.

Standards and codes have two functions. On one level they provide the designer with advice and guidance, on another they confer a certain amount of security on the specifier since they represent best practice. Thus in working to both relevant and current standards the designer will be safe in the knowledge that he or she is applying the most current knowledge, thus reducing risk for the design firm, those doing the construction, and the client. However, it should be remembered that many standards are developed in the light of failure and problems may, unfortunately, still arise. Structural codes are reassessed and usually revised in the event of a structural collapse (e.g. bridge design). Designers working at the cutting edge of technology are likely to be ahead of the relevant standards since they do take a long time to develop and/or revise. Specified and implemented correctly, standards and codes provide an important aspect of quality control and are linked back to national regulations.

6.3.1 British Standards Institution

Competition often leads individual manufacturers to develop their own system of sizes and grading which can be confusing. Nationally and internationally applied Standards help to address this problem. The BSI was formed in 1901 (as the Engineering Standards Committee) and the first British Standard (BS1) was published in 1903, concerned with standardising the size of rolled steel (Yeomans 1997). The BSI was the first national standards body in the world; now there are more than 100 similar organisations which belong to the ISO and the International Electrotechnical Committee (IEC). There are currently around 18,000 British Standards (BSI 1999). The first licence permitting a manufacturer to use the kitemark was issued in 1926 and the BSI was granted a Royal Charter in 1929, since which time BSs have become an essential tool for building designers. The Institution's objectives were set out in their charter of 1929 and are as follows (BSI 1999):

- to co-ordinate efforts for the improvement, standardisation and simplification of materials, products and process
- to promote the adoption and use of standards
- to certify comformity through the application of marks (kitemark)
- to deliver the services of systems assessment, product and materials inspection, testing and certification, training, consultancy and arbitration.

Concerned with establishing standards for manufacture, design and safety, they form a useful measure for ensuring QC and have become an integral part of the UK Building Regulations. The BSI is also involved in international standardisation work through CEN (European Committee for Standardisation), CENELEC (European Electrotechnical Standardisation Committee) and ISO.

6.3.2   Building codes

In 1942 the British Standards for Codes of Practice (CPs) for design were introduced to ensure a degree of uniformity. By designing in accordance with the CPs designers were 'deemed to satisfy' the legal requirements of the time and many CPs became standard works of reference (Yeomans 1997). CPs are based on a combination of practical experience and scientific investigation. They form an essential part of QA schemes and should be used by practitioners to demonstrate competence. Since the early 1990s Eurocodes have been published which establish standards for the design of structures across the European Union, examples being Eurocode 5 *Design of timber structures* (1994) and Eurocode 8 *Design provisions for earthquake resistance of structures* (1996).

6.3.3   International Organisation for Standardisation

With increased attention on the global economy and the world market has come a focus on international standards. The ISO was founded in 1947 with the aim of harmonising standards internationally. International standards aim to promote best practice through the culmination of world-wide experience in a particular area. As with national standards, such as BS and DIN standards, the ISO series serve as guidance. The standards do not have to be complied with, but it would be wise to do so. National standards are being replaced with European and international standards where appropriate, e.g. the ISO series on quality, BS EN ISO 9000–9004 which have superseded BS 5750. Likewise the codes of Australia and New Zealand are being replaced with ISOs.

Three ISO series that are closely linked and important to designers are the 9000, 14,000 and 15,000 series on quality systems and management, environmental management, and design life respectively. Combined they provide comprehensive guidance on important areas that building designers cannot afford to ignore.

6.4 Trade associations and independent standards organisations

In addition to the vast range of information contained in regulations and standards there is an even larger range of technical material produced by independent standards organisations and trade associations.

6.4.1 Trade associations

There are a number of self-regulating groups which influence building, notably the various trade associations. Just as architects and engineers may belong to their own respective institutions, so too do other distinct groups through organisations such as the National Federation of Roofing Contractors. Manufacturers of building materials and products also have active associations, well-known examples including the Brick Development Association, the British Cement Association, the Steel Construction Institute and the Timber Research and Development Association.

The trade associations exist for a variety of purposes, from the self-promotion of their members' interests, through the development of self-imposed regulations for members to ensure a degree of quality, to the development of industry standards to ensure quality. Some of the larger associations even publish their own guidance documents and trade journals, e.g. the publication of standard specifications and/or performance specifications as a means of setting standards. The larger trade associations are usually represented on standards committees and will have an input to changes to the Building Regulations. They also have an input to the development of the Eurocodes. In the UK the majority of house-builders belong to the NHBC which sets its own building standards (some of which are more stringent than the Building Regulations) and training standards for members. In recent years the organisation has made considerable progress in improving the quality of housing built by its members, for which new owners receive a guarantee.

Property is a major asset and it should come as little surprise to know that the major insurance companies have a say in building. In addition to the NHBC's insurance scheme many large building projects are vetted by insurance companies at the design stage to assess the amount of risk against their own guidelines for security and fire protection. Other organisations work to design guides such as the Housing Association Property Mutual *HAPM Component Life Manual* (HAPM 1991) which gives extensive information and benchmarking for component service lives of materials and some mechanical and electrical components.

6.4.2 The British Board of Agrément

An Agrément Board was set up in the UK in 1966, modelled on the French Government's Agrément system which already had an established track record. In 1982 the Agrément Board became the British Board of Agrément (BBA). The BBA is an independent organisation which is principally concerned with the assessment and certification of building materials, products, systems and techniques. The status of agrément certificates is defined in the *Manual to the Building Regulations* 1995. Certificates will give compliance with the regulations where health and safety, conservation of energy and access for disabled people are concerned. Specifying a product or system that carries an Agrément certificate will give assurance that the system or product, if used in accordance with the terms of the certificate, will meet the relevant requirements of the building regulations. Products assessed by the BBA are usually new to the market or are established products being used in a new, or innovative, way. For some products, such as thermal insulating materials, all new products must be certified by an independent organisation before they will be approved by a local authority. Thus an agrément certificate, BS kitemark and/or the CE Mark are essential for manufacturers hoping to sell their products to specifiers looking for some indication of quality.

6.4.3   Building Research Establishment

One of the most highly respected research organisations is the BRE located at Garston in Hertfordshire. Originally set up as the Building Research Station and government funded the BRE was recently privatised. The BRE publishes a range of informative material on a wide range of technical issues relating to construction. These include the BRE Digests, BRE Defects Action Sheets, BRE Good Building Guides, BRE Information Papers and BRE Reports. It also holds a significant amount of information relating to all issues of building in its library. It has been, and continues to be, a comprehensive and reliable source of information for designers. Unfortunately, much of this information which used to be provided free of charge now has to be paid for, one of the consequences of privatisation.

6.4.4   Manufacturers' own standards

Manufacturers set their own standards for production, delivery and after-sales service. The majority of manufacturers work to the current standards, simply because if their products do not comply they will not be specified by designers. Some manufacturers set higher standards than those set down in national and international standards, mainly because they have the manufacturing expertise to do so. Combined with installation by their approved fitters and fixers they can guarantee quality standards.

6.5   The Building Regulations – control and approval

For the vast majority of building operations permission is required to erect and make structural alterations. The Building Regulations (England and Wales) comprise a set of Approved Documents which indicate ways in which compliance can be achieved. It is a criminal offence to start building operations before planning consent has been granted. Once this is in place the next step is to gain approval for the detail of the building's assembly and layout. Plans or a building notice must be deposited with the relevant local authority giving at least 2 days' notice before work starts on site. In contrast to planning work can start on site before the approval is received. Whether the design team wait for approval before starting work on site or commence after 2 days' notice will depend upon the time constraints relating to a particular project.

6.5.1 The process

General arrangement plans, details and specifications (as appropriate to the size and complexity of the proposed work) must be submitted for certification. They must meet (or exceed) the minimum standards set down in the prevailing regulations. Approval is granted by the local authority or approved inspectors who also inspect the building work during construction and on completion to check for compliance. Changes in construction must be referred back to the certifying authority for approval prior to implementation. Inspectors are required to make few visits to the site during construction and rely on a degree of trust and co-operation between designer (contract administrator) and main contractor to ensure that the works are carried out as intended. Notification must be given to the local authority building control department before building work commences. Failure to comply with the relevant regulations and the approved drawings may result in the local authority serving notice on the building owner to remove and/or amend the work.

6.5.2 A word of caution

That a building project has got Building Regulation approval does not necessarily mean that it was constructed in the manner shown on the drawings. For designers involved in work to existing buildings experience has shown that when 'opening up' part of the building fabric there is no guarantee that what is exposed is the same as that shown on the construction drawings. This is one reason why invasive surveys are essential before work is detailed and costed, and also why contingencies are essential in work to existing buildings.

6.5.3 Manufacturers' input

Product manufacturers are happy to assist designers and provide detailed drawings and calculations for building regulation submission. For example, trussed roof manufacturers will provide designers with detailed roof plans, trussed rafter details and supporting structural calculations for approval by the building control officer. Other manufacturers, such as those of thermal insulation materials, will need to show evidence of agrément certification to ensure approval. More specialist systems, such as structural glazing or rainscreen cladding systems, could not receive approval without the specialist knowledge and supporting information provided by the manufacturing companies.

6.5.4 An unintended restraint

Emphasis on sustainable building practices has been made throughout this book and it is at this juncture where possible resistance to the adoption of such methods needs investigating. Building codes and regulations have developed over a long period of time and are based largely on responses to events and research findings. They are essential for safe building, but may form an unintended barrier to the adoption of more environmentally responsible practices.

Designing to ensure compliance with current regulations may conflict with a desire to design in a more environmentally friendly manner. Encompassing the philosophy of designing for disassembly is a case in point. The standard details used to illustrate conformity in the Building Regulations, although well intended, make no allowance for alternative approaches to construction, despite the performance method advocated. Because many designers simply copy the details to ensure compliance the opportunity to build a little differently is frequently missed. It takes time to get non-standard details approved, thus regulations can result in designers adopting the status quo, simply out of convenience.

6.6   Staying up to date

With legislation and guidance growing the need to control information within the office for currency is vital. Professionals have a duty to stay up to date with current developments and work to the prevailing codes and standards where appropriate. In the past, with the need to rely on paper information (hard copies), this was a task that had to be managed by a responsible member of the design office and/or sub-contracted to an appropriate independent organisation which was responsible for supplying updates on a regular basis. With the evolution of IT the task has been made easier for those companies who subscribe to an appropriate supplier. Subscription to on-line providers helps to ensure that information in the design office is current; indeed it is impossible on some systems to access superseded information, a problem for designers working on existing buildings (see below).

Regardless of the size or type of building project designers must ensure that the specification of building products, components and materials complies with current legislation. The legislation forms a very useful knowledge base in its own right, but one that is constantly changing as knowledge improves. The Approved Documents are updated and added to occasionally while standards and codes are constantly being added to, amended and in some cases withdrawn. To confirm the latest amendment see *Update* published monthly by the BSI. Other useful sources are the *Digests*, *Current Papers*, *Information Papers* and *Reports* listed in the *Construction Publications Catalogue* published annually by the BRE.

6.6.1   Old information

For designers involved with work to existing structures it is equally important to have access to the regulations and standards that applied at the time of construction. Another challenge is getting access to old trade literature. Some of the larger manufacturers have retained material relating to products which have been improved or superseded over the years, others have not. Furthermore, some companies may no longer be in business and their literature may be impossible to track down.

6.6.2 *More than a clause*

In stating that designers must stay up to date with developments, they must also know the implications of the standards they specify. It may seem a strange question, but do designers always know what they are referring to when they state that work should be in accordance with a particular standard? How many designers can put their hand up to reading, and understanding the implications, of every standard referred to in their specification? Very few. Furthermore, how many builders and tradespeople pay any attention to the specification? Again, very few until there is a problem. So what does a standard mean? A good example is that of clay bricks. British Standard BS 3921:1985 specifies the maximum and minimum dimensions for the cumulative length, width and height for a random sample of 24 bricks. This allows for a large variation in size which can cause problems on site. The majority of brick manufacturers are able to manufacture most of their bricks to tolerances much greater than the BS at no additional cost (all you have to do is ask). The point here is that not all standards are particularly useful. They need to be read and constantly re-read and reassessed against developments in manufacturing precision and the accuracy of the work required on site.

Further reading

Building Regulations Approved Documents (current editions).
Fitchen, J. (1986). *Building Construction before Mechanisation*, MIT Press, Cambridge, MA.

7 Healthy, safe and secure buildings

Closely linked to regulations, standards and codes are issues of health, safety and security, human factors affected by detail design decisions. This chapter attempts to pull together the pertinent issues concerning the detailing of healthy, safe and secure environments. These factors are often considered in isolation, but must be addressed concurrently if conflicting demands are to be resolved and anticipated risks kept to an acceptable level. How, for example, does the detailer resolve constraints imposed by fire safety and security? What effect have the CDM Regulations had on the detail design process? These are some of the questions addressed with the focus on building ecology and humane detailing.

7.1 Detail design and human factors

All human beings have a desire to live healthy lives in a safe, comfortable and secure environment. Our own health is influenced by our genetic make-up, lifestyle and socio-economic circumstances as well as the immediate built environments in which we work, relax and sleep. During the act of designing it is often difficult to separate out these issues because they tend to overlap, sometimes harmoniously, often conflicting. One of the skills of the designer and the design team is to resolve these apparent conflicts of interest during the detail design process. Another skill is to balance ecological concerns with other, more commercial interests. There is no doubt that architects, engineers, interior designers and technologists through their individual and collective decision-making affect the external and internal environment of our buildings. Design decisions, choices of materials and building products, the response to legislation and the preparation of specifications affect the usable life of a building, something that others have to live with, work and play in, long after the design team have moved on to other projects (Fig. 7.1).

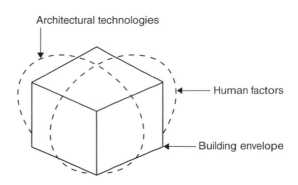

Figure 7.1 Design and human factors.

7.1.1 *An appreciation of the language of architecture*

Our perception of buildings comes from our senses: sight, scent, sound and touch – physical and psychological factors that influence whether or not we enjoy being within a building. Human beings do react to situations differently. Our ability to see, smell, hear and touch varies from one individual to another; sometimes the differences are small, sometimes significant. Designers, whatever the state of their own senses need to appreciate that users of their creation will perceive it differently because of their physical differences. Attention to detail is also important in aiding people with visual and hearing difficulties, where texture of surface finishes, sound, scent and colour are important attributes for the visually impaired and for those with hearing difficulties. How we perceive our built environment is crucial in terms of how we respond to it, issues explored in detail in Hesselgren's *The Language of Architecture* (1972) which concentrated on applied perception psychology, as summarised below.

(1) *Visual form.* Visual perceptions are formed from an integration of physical form, colour and light perceptions. Thus physical size of rooms and components (scale, proportion, rhythm and motion), colour differentiation, and contrasts between light and shade are important determinants. The experience of texture is a more complex perception that also relies on touch.
(2) *Texture and tactility.* When we touch things with our fingers we experience tactile surface sensation. Changes in materials, scale and surface texture combine and can be used effectively to signal changes between public, semi-public and private spaces.
(3) *Auditory sense.* Space is experienced through our auditory perception of it. Materials and their juxtaposition vary in their ability to absorb and reflect sound. Added sound, background music or the more natural sound of running water through a building interior can be very relaxing (or very irritating).
(4) *Smell and taste.* Smell and taste (the two are linked) may be more subtle influences on how we perceive the buildings around us, yet they are important. Materials, plants and the activities associated with building do give off a variety of smells, some of which may be pleasant, others less so.
(5) *Movement and time.* People move about within buildings, from one space to another, over time. As such they perceive spaces from different physical and mental perspectives.

7.1.2 *Ergonomics*

An appreciation of ergonomics is vital to the ability to design in detail for human comfort. This is perhaps an obvious statement, but one sometimes overlooked in preference for style. Human comfort should be interpreted as applying to all ages, religions, races and sex regardless of disability. Design guides such as the *Metric Handbook* provide vital anthropometric and ergonomic data to allow designers to make informed choices about space requirements.

Anthropometrics, the body and reach characteristics of people, affects design. With the growth of advertising and the constant bombardment of images of

Figure 7.2 Museum of Modern Art, Barcelona.

'perfect' people on our cinema and television screens one could be forgiven for thinking that everyone is good looking, has a perfect figure, and of course enjoys perfect health. At the risk of stating the obvious, human beings are incredibly diverse in their physical make-up, and whatever we would like to think, none of us is perfect – we all have imperfections. Although we may try and design for the average human, in reality few individuals meet the criteria of being 'average'. Extremes in height (short or tall), extremes in weight (fat or thin), and extremes in mobility (fast or slow) need to be considered by designers in order that buildings are accessible and enjoyable for all, regardless of our particular physical nuances, be it differences in mobility or hearing. Attention to detail is particularly important when it comes to ensuring equal physical access to all. Consideration of anthropometics is also required when detailing, because someone has to put the various parts in the correct positions on site.

Legislation exists to stop discrimination, in whatever form. Words such as 'handicapped' and 'disabled' are used in guides and in legislation, yet many find such terminology insulting. If designers are to detail in a humane manner, then they should be thinking about everyone who may use their buildings at some time in the future, regardless of their permanent or temporary disability. Selwyn Goldsmith's books *Designing for the Disabled* (1963) and *Designing for the Disabled: The New Paradigm* (1997) are essential reading for all building designers.

7.1.3   *Disability Discrimination Act*

Part I of the 1995 Disability Discrimination Act (DDA) came into force in July 1996 with enforcement covered in Part II, which came into force in December 1996. The DDA requires service providers to provide equal access for people with disabilities, in which the term 'disabled people' means people with impaired hearing, sight or mobility. Part III of the DDA came into force in October 1999 and requires service providers to make 'reasonable adjustments' in the form of providing extra help for those who may require it, such as induction loops and portable ramps. In 2004 the remainder of Part III will come into force and will require service providers to provide 'reasonable adjustments' to overcome physical barriers to access. In October 1999 Part M of the Building Regulations was extended from non-domestic buildings to cover all new housing (Access and Facilities for Disabled People: Building Regulations 1991, Approved Document M). Many responsible employers and designers have been providing for some time sensitive designs that are accessible to all, but now there is a statutory requirement. No longer is it acceptable to ignore access.

7.2   Healthy environments

Human beings spend a lot of time in and around buildings, be it their place of work, place of leisure or their home. As such the quality of the environment should enhance, not damage, our health. The link between the quality of the built environment and our health is well recognised, e.g. the *Black Report* (1980) made a positive correlation between poor quality housing and poor health. In a recent government publication, *Saving Lives: Our Healthier Nation* (1999), the point was made again that most people spend more time in their homes than anywhere else, and, therefore, 'good quality housing inevitably has an important impact on our health' (1999: 50). According to the report 1.5 million dwellings are not up to current standards of fitness, and, worse still, 2.5 million homes are cold and damp enough to cause ill health. Concern for healthy environments was the theme of the RIBA's publication *Buildings and Health* (Curwell *et al.* 1990), a collection of papers which sought to inform and guide all those involved in the building process with the aim of helping decision-makers to act in a more environmentally responsible manner.

7.2.1   *Indoor air quality*

One of the less desirable effects of our drive to make buildings more thermally efficient, combined with more tightly constructed buildings, is a generation of buildings that do not 'breathe'. Natural air flow from outside to in, and from inside to out, has been significantly reduced with the substitution of open fires by central heating, single glazing by double, and draft exclusion around door openings. One consequence of these 'improvements' to building design and construction has been the build-up of contaminants on the inside of buildings. Occupants may experience general discomfort, headaches, fatigue and illness leading to increased sick leave, discomfort, loss of productivity and disability. These health problems, perceived or real, have a financial cost in the loss of productivity, increased medical care costs and litigation.

This condition has been called sick building syndrome (SBS). While environmental attention has been turned to the cleaning up of our outdoor air quality following the Clean Air Act of 1956, our indoor air quality has, in many cases, been deteriorating. Air pollutants can occur within the building and/or may enter the building from external sources. Building materials, finishes and furnishings may give off volatile organic chemicals. Office equipment, such as copying machines, may give off ozone, and chemicals used for cleaning may emit a variety of toxic volatiles. Air conditioning systems can harbour a variety of microorganisms leading to Legionnaire's disease. Smoking tobacco is another, obvious, cause for concern for users as are the effect of passive smoking on other building users. Air pollution, e.g. from road traffic or nearby industries, can enter the building through window vents and poorly positioned air bricks.

Naturally occurring pollutants, such as radon, pose a serious threat to the health of occupants. Radon is a colourless and odourless radioactive gas produced as a by-product of radium-226 which is present in soils. Radon will enter the building through openings (cracks and joints) in the floor slab and build up inside the building unless adequate ventilation is provided. For new buildings a number of preventative measures can be taken. For existing buildings in areas where radon is known to be a threat to indoor air quality proprietary ventilation systems can be installed which draw the radon out of the building to the outside air. Local authorities are an excellent source of local knowledge and can give advice on what measures may be required, including monitoring to identify the scale of the problem. In the early 1990s the problem received widespread publicity and radon build-up in buildings is now recognised as a significant risk to health. Certain parts of the UK are more likely to experience radon ingress because of the local geology; local authority building control departments should be contacted if in doubt.

7.2.2   *Construction materials*

The products selected by designers to make up the overall building assembly and the manner in which they are detailed will affect the health, safety and security of the building users. Products now have to be labelled, clearly showing their toxicity, but this was not always the case and many toxic materials still exist within our building stock. Lead paint and asbestos are the most widely known but the variety of hazardous materials to be avoided is more extensive (see Curwell and March 1986). As designers we have a choice about the materials and manufactured products we specify, and awareness of the hazards posed to health during the whole life of a building should be borne in mind when specifying (see Chapter 9).

The Control of Substances Hazardous to Health Regulations 1988 (COSHH) imposes a number of duties on employers to protect their employees and others (e.g. visitors) from exposure to substances that may be hazardous to health. The regulations place a duty on employers to carry out assessments of risk to health created by work (e.g. construction activities) that may expose their employees to substances hazardous to health, and to consider steps to meet the requirements of the regulations. COSHH covers an extensive range of materials, exceptions being materials subject to their own regulatory codes, such as lead and asbestos.

7.3 Safe environments

Building is a hazardous activity and accidents during the construction phase do happen – some accidents result in minor injury, some lead to fatalities. In addition to accidents occurring during construction many accidents happen inside and around buildings during use, some of which could have been prevented through careful and sensitive detailed design. With the exception of fire safety, discussed below, there are three related safety areas to consider: safety during construction, safety of the building users, and the safety of those charged with recycling the building at a future, unspecified, date.

(1) *Safety on site.* By their very nature building sites are constantly changing in their physical structure and the type of activities being conducted. Constant vigilance and care are required from everyone on the site.
(2) *Safety in use.* Once the building is completed safety concerns shift to those using the building and those carrying out maintenance and repair activities. Consideration must be given to safe access to machinery for routine inspection and replacement at the design stage. This usually means allowing adequate space for access and in which to work comfortably.
(3) *Safety in recovery.* An area largely ignored by many designers is that of safety in recovery. Demolition of buildings is a particularly dangerous activity. With emphasis on the recovery and recycling of building materials there is, arguably, greater pressure on designers to consider the ease of disassembly and material recovery at a future date.

7.3.1 The Construction (Design and Management) Regulations

The CDM Regulations 1994 came into effect from 31 March 1995, were fully implemented from October 1995 and are legally binding. They set out defined roles, responsibilities and tasks that are applicable to the main contractor, subcontractors, designers and clients alike. In doing so they have emphasised the link between detail design decisions and safety. Here the designer's attention is concentrated on designing and planning for safe construction, operation, repair, routine maintenance and demolition. The regulations have contractual implications under criminal and civil law and failure to comply with the regulations can result in prosecutions, penalties and imprisonment.

Under the CDM Regulations specific duties have to be performed by the planning supervisor, essentially a management role responsible for ensuring safe systems of work through risk analysis and monitoring. The four key stages are as follows:

(1) concept and feasibility stages
(2) design stage
(3) construction stage
(4) commissioning and post-contract stages.

The planning supervisor is responsible for ensuring the preparation of the following:

■ the health and safety plan
■ the health and safety file

- risk assessment
- method statements.

Greater emphasis on safety is welcome in an industry with a poor record for health and safety. However, the CDM Regulations have resulted in yet another professional to be paid and added a further layer of bureaucracy and complexity to the building process. Critics of the regulations have argued that the whole exercise is little more than that of risk transfer, generating a lot of unnecessary paperwork. Advocates for the regulations have pointed to the increased awareness of health and safety issues brought about by their introduction. The majority of published sources concentrate on the mechanics of carrying out and implementing the CDM Regulations; there is little published evidence that addresses the effect the regulations have actually had on design and construction activities. However, as this book goes to press there is some evidence that since the regulations were introduced the number of accidents on site has increased, not decreased. This naturally raises questions about how the legislation is implemented and monitored on site.

Individuals interviewed for the purposes of this book were of the opinion that the regulations had improved their awareness of health and safety issues, but that they had made little difference to the way in which they worked: a view reinforced by the recent evidence noted above. Both designers and contractors complained about the 'form filling' and respondents were less than kind about the planning supervisor's role. All those interviewed claimed that few planning supervisors actually influenced the process because they were primarily concerned with the paperwork, not what was happening on site. Not surprisingly, this view was not shared by the planning supervisors who were quick to defend their position and their contribution to design and construction activities. However, when questioned further few could demonstrate concrete examples of their contribution. It is an important area in which further research is required.

7.3.2   Carrying out surveys and inspection duties

Another area of safety concerns the inspection of existing buildings. Professional consultants are often required to carry out condition surveys and inspections. It is important to consider individual safety first and then the safety of fellow professionals prior to and during any visits to buildings. Condition surveys are potentially dangerous, especially when inspecting redundant buildings. There are the physical dangers posed by the state of the building structure and also dangers posed by human activity such as drug and alcohol abuse. Hostile tenants are another source of danger. Guidance is published by RICS and companies have their own practices to ensure the safety of their employees when away from the office. Many of these policies require employees to take a mobile telephone and contact the office at predetermined times.

7.4   Secure environments

One of the primary reasons humans started to build was for protection from their immediate environment: the elements and other inhabitants of the earth. We need to feel safe in the buildings in which we work and reside, and thus designers should consider both the psychological and physical characteristics of their design intentions. Security is one of the fundamental aspects of building performance, so inherent security measures should be incorporated into the design process (Poyner and Fawcett 1995). Designing to accommodate security is not a new phenomenon, but one that grew in importance towards the end of the 20th century and is now a factor that can no longer be ignored in new build or refurbishment projects. Early guides on architecture dealt with the issues of security, with advice given by, e.g. Alberti (*The Ten Books of Architecture*, 1472) and Palladio (*Four Books on Architecture*, 1570). More recently three of the most well-known publications that have dealt with security in the urban environment are Jane Jacobs' *The Death and Life of Great American Cities* (1961), Oscar Newman's *Defensible Space: People and Design in the Violent City* (1972) and Alice Coleman's *Utopia on Trial* (1985). Jacobs made an attack on American city planning and argued for natural surveillance by residents (eyes on the street), a theme taken up and developed by Newman. His book was (essentially) a design guide which aimed to inhibit crime through design and building layout, creating a social fabric that would defend itself in the face of problems facing residential areas in the USA. *Defensible Space* was about empowering residents to take control of their immediate environments, aided and abetted by considerate design and planning. Coleman (1985) and her colleagues investigated the link between environmental neglect and building design. Her work concentrated on blocks of flats situated in Inner London and the resulting book *Utopia on Trial* was influential in shaping attitudes towards residential block housing. From a study of over 4000 residential flats she devised a 'design disadvantagement scale' and indices of environmental neglect based on the amount of litter, graffiti, vandalism and excrement. She found that poor building design was clearly related to social problems such as crime and safety. Despite the importance of security as a design generator it is not an area that has attracted a lot of research, a point noted by Poyner and Fawcettt (1995).

Design Against Crime: Beyond Defensible Space (Poyner 1983) brought together research published after Newman's book, concluding that the design and management of the built environment does influence the likelihood of crime. *Design for Inherent Security: Guidance for Non-residential Buildings* (Poyner and Fawcett 1995) takes this work further and applies the principles to non-domestic buildings. In this publication it is made very clear that the inherent security of a building and its occupants will be influenced by the site layout, the planning and detail design of the building – permanent features that cannot be rectified simply through the application of security devices. The authors also make the point that the cost of designing secure buildings can be minimised through consideration early in the design, an observation that is equally applicable to new build as it is to work to existing buildings (although the problems will be different). They also make the distinction between 'inherent' security issues (which are designed in) and security measures (which are an afterthought).

7.4.1   The 'Secure by Design' initiative

Security in design should be all pervasive (Poyner and Fawcett 1995). Detail design cannot solve all the problems associated with crime, but when used as a design generator, tried and tested design principles can be incorporated very successfully and enhance the completed scheme. The key to success is early consultation with the client and the relevant police authority who have first-hand experience of local crime patterns and can provide advice on ways of dealing with it. Architectural liaison officers are employed by some police authorities to provide important information to designers about security issues. The 'Secure by Design' initiative is a scheme that accredits professional design organisations, such as architects and technologists, who carry out research into crime patterns and consult with the local police force early in the design process. Accredited organisations are permitted to use the 'Secure by Design' logo.

Location is important. Urban, semi-urban and rural locations each have their own particular crime patterns and, therefore, it is important to discuss security measures with the owners (or users if different) to assess their requirements and to consult the crime prevention officer of the local police force. Planners will also need to be consulted and where sheltered housing or housing for the elderly is being considered the local authority often has some very knowledgeable people who are happy to advise and criticise plans and details from the viewpoint of security.

7.4.2   *Designing in security measures*

It would be easy to become paranoid if we took the headlines of newspapers, television and radio to heart and did not stop to consider the facts. We all have a built-in defence mechanism, expressed as a desire to protect our loved ones and our possessions. Our perceived fear of crime increases with darkness and with age as we become more vulnerable. Lighting levels and positioning of lighting are particularly important in public and private areas. We are all potential targets of crime, against either our person or our property. Vandalism, theft and damage caused by unlawful entry, and in some cases terrorism, need to be considered at all stages in the design process. Visual privacy, overlooking and natural surveillance have to be balanced bearing in mind the requirements of the user, site constraints and planning restrictions. There is a need to understand crime, i.e. how and where it is likely to occur and the possible design approaches to aid prevention. Building designers need to consider the following:

- location of the site and its immediate crime patterns
- building orientation – to provide natural surveillance
- elimination or strengthening of weak points, such as doors and windows
- sensitive positioning of lighting.

In addition to providing protection from the weather, through detailing a building to respond to a particular site's micro-climate, security of the building's contents is an important design generator. Doors and windows provide technical challenges, balancing the need to allow access, light and ventilation without compromising fire safety and security, and thus they may be a weak spot in the building's design from a security viewpoint. There is a problem with making buildings very difficult to get into since they also become difficult to get out of, so conflict can occur when detailing for crime prevention and fire escape. Prevailing social conditions will inevitably influence the way in which buildings are designed and used in terms of the threat to the building and its contents. For example, Georgian developments clearly differentiate between private space, semi-private space and public space, design measures that may deter some criminal activity.

Detailed design decisions are particularly important in trying to design out crime. Some materials and products are easier to get through or remove than others, roofs are particularly vulnerable and many commercial premises incorporate sturdy barriers to intrusion under tiles to prevent unlawful access. Doors and windows are vulnerable in houses, especially those concealed from neighbours and passers-by, while in commercial premises roofs and walls pose little resistance for the determined criminal. In some respects there is only so much the designer can do; some crime is opportunist, so the open window or the unlocked door is an easier target than closed and locked ones. Insurance companies provide an incentive to fit window locks and more substantial locks to doors through lower premiums for those who do. Manufacturers of doors and windows can, and do, make a contribution to issues of security.

(1) *A passive approach*. Adopting a passive approach to crime prevention is perhaps the most effective, yet one that requires a great deal of consideration at the design stage, i.e. inherent security measures. Building layout and the relationship between door positions, windows position, height and opening configuration, and footpaths are important elements. Designed in features tend to cost money up front, yet are cost-effective in the long run – many householder insurance policies offer discounts to policy holders whose doors and windows meet strict standards with regard to locking devices.

(2) *An active approach*. Alarms and monitoring devices may be employed in lieu of passive measures or in addition to inherent security measures. This approach is more common when considering the security of existing buildings.

Whether or not design or, more specifically, detail design can reduce crime is open to debate, after all inmates do escape from prisons and even the most secure buildings are still vulnerable to attack. In theory the likelihood of crime occurring can be reduced through careful detailing of buildings and their immediate environs. As noted above, we need to balance the perceived risk of crime against the measures that we may use to try and reduce our exposure to risk.

7.5   Fire protection

Fire has always posed a threat to life and to property, and attempts to resist the spread of fire have helped to shape regulatory frameworks throughout the world. Disasters caused by fire are a great concern to the public because of loss of life and damage to property. We should not overlook fires in domestic properties where most deaths from fire result. Buildings must be designed so as to limit the potential for a fire starting and spreading. Insurance companies looking to insure new buildings against damage or loss as a direct result of a fire may well insist on higher standards of fire protection than those required in the Building Regulations and associated standards. Such requirements need to be considered at the briefing stage and incorporated into the early scheme designs where structural systems and building siting can be addressed. A significant amount of damage can be caused by fires, from the burning of materials and the indirect effects of heat and smoke, in addition to the damage caused by water in an attempt to prevent the spread of the fire and to extinguish it. The detail design phase is where the majority of decisions that affect fire protection are taken.

7.5.1   *Combustible and non-combustible materials*

Ease of ignition, i.e. the combustibility of the materials used in buildings, is an important consideration when choosing materials and internal finishes for buildings. Choice may be limited by the use of rooms and/or buildings. In theory the choice is simply between combustible materials and non-combustible materials, but in practice the choice is rarely simple. Manufactured components and building products often combine a cocktail of materials and the designer has to look to manufacturers and their independent fire testing certificates for accurate information. A further complication is the combination of different materials and products that, in certain circumstances, may assist the rapid spread of a fire.

- *Combustible materials.* Generally speaking these are the organic materials, such as timber and timber products (e.g. plywood, paper), fabrics and petrochemical products, including plastics. Combustible materials can be and are used in buildings, but care is required.
- *Non-combustible materials.* Generally speaking these are the inorganic materials, such as brick, concrete, stone and steel.

7.5.2   *Fire resistance and spread of flame*

Fire resistance is a term used to describe the ability of building elements (floors, walls, doors, etc.) to resist the transfer of fire from one area to another for a stated time period. The period of fire resistance depends upon the function and volume of the space to be protected. Designated periods of fire resistance are 1/2, 1, 2, 3, 4, 5 and 6h, with the time representing the minimum length of time that the element can resist fire based on three performance criteria, namely stability, integrity and insulation.

The spread of fire within a building and from one building to another is a major concern of designers and the fire brigade. The Building Regulations Approved Document B 'Fire Spread' stipulates fire resisting periods and suggests appropriate construction techniques to ensure compliance. The document also provides guidance on the siting of windows and unprotected materials (e.g. timber cladding) to boundaries. The intention here is to prevent surface spread of flame to neighbouring properties. Within a building fire spread can be contained for a defined period through the use of compartmentation techniques, i.e. the division of large buildings into separate 'compartments' that are designed to contain the spread of fire for a defined period of time and thus allow safe evacuation from adjacent areas.

7.5.3   *Means of escape and fire fighting*

Means of escape and provision for adequate access for fire fighting are covered in legislation. That designers have exercised caution in the design, detailing and assembly of a building with regard to fire protection is only one part of the fire protection strategy. The use and misuse of buildings is a matter for those responsible for the safety of people within the building, the building owners and building managers, i.e. it is a management issue. Escape routes must be maintained, fire doors not locked and detection apparatus regularly checked and serviced.

7.5.4   *Fire protection as a design generator*

Fire precautions in buildings are an integral component of building quality and hopefully one that is not tested in practice. Fire safety covers many related factors, from the initial design of the building (such as the positioning of fire escapes and compartmentation) to the specification of materials and products which perform well in fires (non-combustible materials and materials with a low surface spread of flame classification), and the management of the building (to avoid fire hazards). One of many challenges facing the design team is that of designing a building to resist the spread of flame and retain its structural integrity in a fire for a certain period of time. Careful material selection is necessary, especially in situations where there is going to be a combination of materials.

7.6   Conflicting demands and risk limitation

At this juncture it may be worth pausing to consider the conflicting demands placed on the designer in the quest to satisfy all the relevant constraints. There are a number of areas which can, and often do, cause difficulties.

First, there is the constant challenge of balancing adequate escape in the event of a fire with that of trying to keep unwanted people out. Security of property and the building's occupants is a major problem in public buildings. Balance is perhaps the important word because it usually has to be met by the conflicting demands of security, preventing easy ingress, and fire safety, allowing easy egress. There are tragic examples where people have died in fires because they were unable to escape through doors that had been locked to prevent unlawful entry.

Second, there is the potential conflict between the desire to keep buildings air tight to reduce energy consumption, while allowing adequate air changes for the occupants to feel healthy without resorting to mechanical heating and ventilating systems (and stay connected with their natural environment). Passive ventilation measures are available, although they need careful detailing to be effective.

Third, there are financial considerations. Safety measures cost money and many owners will only do what is required by legislation, nothing more, nothing less. Thus designers have the task of educating their clients in order to achieve healthy and safe building environments.

Finally, there are aesthetic considerations, especially for existing buildings. Provision of ramps and improved circulation space may be desirable, indeed essential to meet new regulations, but care is needed to meet these provisions without compromising the character of the building. Another example is the fitting of security measures to historic buildings.

7.6.1 *Risk limitation*

Designers are no different to people working in other fields; they have to take risks in order to move forward. The extent of the risk will depend upon the culture of the design organisation and on the individual designer's propensity for taking risks. Risk taking will also be influenced by the individual client's own aims and aspirations. Design organisations will align themselves with a particular market sector and will develop an organisational culture which has a particular attitude to risk. For example, innovative organisations tend to take more risks than the more conservative ones, who are happy to follow the lead of the innovators once the route has been proven to be safe. Clients will select organisations because they have a reputation for taking risks, or, conversely, because they do not. Professionals have a duty of care to act responsibly and, therefore, a balance between what is deemed to be safe and what is deemed to be risky is required. Regulations and codes provide a degree of comfort to designers because they remove the risk. However, performance codes may increase the risk because they encourage (in theory) designers to innovate, i.e. take risks. Risk assessment is a relatively simple, three-stage process (Shillito 1990):

(1) *Hazard identification.* The first stage is to be aware of the existence of the potential hazard, and then to identify the extent and severity of the hazard.
(2) *Risk analysis.* The second stage involves analysis of the hazard, the chance of it occurring and the likely consequences that would result from it occurring.
(3) *Risk handling.* The third stage is to decide what to do about the risk. Options include risk avoidance, prevention, protection, insurance measures, or acceptance of the risk.

This process is carried out by individuals when dealing with everyday risks, such as crossing the road, and professionals in their everyday work activities. At this juncture it is worth remembering Murphy's Law.

Further reading

Adler, D. (ed.) (1999). *Metric Handbook: Planning and Design Data*, Architectural Press, Oxford.
Curwell, S. *et al.* (1990). *Buildings and Health: The Rosehaugh Guide to the Design, Construction, Use and Management of Buildings*, RIBA Publications, London.

8 The art of detailing

Detailing is an art. Detail design decisions affect the appearance, quality, cost, serviceability and durability of the building; they also affect the ease with which the building is assembled and eventually disassembled for recycling and disposal. Detailing is a critical part of the design process, and one which deserves more attention from researchers and practitioners. Here we take a brief look at detail design decision-making before considering typologies, typical details, manufacturers' details and office standards – important tools for professional design organisations, allowing quick and effective detailing, yet often criticised for hindering creativity. Criteria for detailing and critical intersections are also discussed before addressing the challenge of detailing for sustainable construction. The chapter concludes by looking at the cost and quality issues associated with the art of detailing.

8.1 Detail design decisions

When the project enters the detail design stage the decision-making process is different to the conceptual stage for a number of reasons. First, the designer will be constrained to a certain extent by the conceptual design, and thus the problems will be less ill defined. Second, many individuals will be involved in the development of the details: other consultants, manufacturers, contractors, cost consultants and project managers. Details of a building's assembly can be, and are, studied for their own sake, somehow isolated from the complex processes that led to the finished building. Details do not exist for their own sake – they form part of an interconnected whole. They also reflect the process by which they come about, reflecting the expressions of the designer, local traditions and culture, climate, design fashion and building techniques, i.e. they have their own language.

Underlying all issues concerned with design, manufacture and assembly is the need to solve problems, both large and small – essentially, the ability to make decisions in the available time. Design is a very particular type of decision-making activity, an activity on which there has been a lot of research and debate. Heath (1984) and Rowe (1987) provide useful, and critical, insights into design thinking. A slightly different perspective is that of design as an information processing activity (Akin 1986). This, and associated work, is based on the premise that designers, managers, and hence organisations, can be understood by observing their decision-making behaviour and then designing and implementing an information processing model (Simon 1969, Newell and Simon 1972). Heath (1984) concluded that the appropriate method is determined by the social nature of the task, with different methods employed to suit a particular situation. Through the use of models designers can select from a range of tactics to shorten the time required to produce the design and to reduce the potential for error. This observation is relevant to the conceptual and the detail design stages. Research into failures of detail design suggests that they arise because of an inability to conceive the building and its constituent parts as a dynamic system – not so much a case of ignorance, more an inability to apply the appropriate method (Heath 1984). John Wade described detail design as 'the selection of mutually compatible components to solve some specific defined standard problem or some specific unique problem within a larger consistent design context' (Wade 1977: 281). Whether the problem is 'standard' or 'unique' to the detailer is largely immaterial: there is rarely a right or wrong answer. Some solutions are merely better than others, although which was the better solution may only become evident as the building reacts to its environment through a process known as weathering.

8.1.1   *Group decision-making*

Much of the literature dedicated to design decision-making is centred on the actions of individuals, with less emphasis placed on the collective efforts of individual organisations and the building 'team'. Clearly, it is easier to observe the behaviour of individuals than it is a collection of individuals, so such bias is not unexpected. In practice, however, individuals are constrained and influenced by the behaviour of the group to which they belong, and by other groups party to the design process. Thus the behaviour of groups needs some consideration before proceeding further.

When groups make decisions on tasks where there is no one correct answer (a familiar state for design teams) the collective decision is nearly always more extreme than the average of individual opinions (Brown 1988). Groups are also prone to making bad decisions because they have failed to consider all the available information, and not appraised all of the possible outcomes before making the decision. Janis (1972) calls this 'groupthink' and studies suggest that it is a result of an over-directive leader. It would be easy to draw parallels here with construction.

8.1.2   *Decision-making*

When groups of people and individuals make decisions they tend to follow rules and/or procedures that they see as appropriate to the situation (March 1994). This is particularly so of professionals who are expected to act in a certain manner according to their particular professional background. Not only do designers have to satisfy their client, but they also have to satisfy different building users over time, and they have to satisfy their peers. Building designers are expected to act in a logical manner, assessing all the options against a background of legislation before making a rational choice. Research suggests this may not be the case. Much of the literature on decision-making makes assumptions based on rationality, assumptions often queried by actual studies carried out by behavioural scientists. Observational studies of decision-making behaviour suggest that individuals are not aware of all the alternatives, do not consider all of the consequences, and do not evoke all their preferences at the same time. Rather they consider only a few alternatives and look at them sequentially, often ignoring available information (March 1994). Decision-makers are constrained by incomplete information and their own cognitive limitations. Thus although decision-makers may set out to make rational decisions in reality they make decisions based on limited rationality: they search for a solution which is 'good enough', not the 'best possible' solution

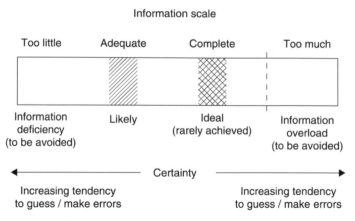

Figure 8.1 Information and effective decision-making.

(Fig. 8.1). A number of constraints on human decision-making are related to our individual characteristics, as follows.

(1) *Attention span.* It is impossible to deal with everything at once – too many messages, too many things to think about. Thus we tend to limit our attention to one task at a time, ignoring messages which are irrelevant to that particular task, engaging our selective exposure. Our attention span is also limited by time (a commodity none of us ever seems to have enough of).

(2) *Memory.* Individuals and organisations have limitations when it comes to memory. Memories are not always accurate; we tend to favour our constructive memory, remembering acts as we like to see them, rather than as they actually happened. Records are not kept, are inaccurate or are lost. Organisations and individuals are limited by their ability to retrieve information that has been stored. Lessons learned from previous experience are not reliably retrieved. Knowledge stored in one part of an organisation cannot be used easily by another part of that organisation (because of the format it is in, or simply because it takes too long to access).

(3) *Comprehension.* Individuals have difficulties in comprehending the relevance of information, despite having all the facts to hand. Failure to connect different parts of information will lead to incomprehension. Furthermore, individuals have different levels of comprehension, making it difficult to foresee how individuals will respond to the information before them. For example, the comprehension of an architect, a manufacturer and a contractor of the same piece of information is likely to differ simply because of the individuals' different backgrounds.

(4) *Communication problems.* Specialisation, fragmentation and differentiation of labour encourage language barriers and difficulties in the transfer of information and knowledge. Different groups of people develop their own frameworks and language for simplifying problems and so it becomes difficult to communicate across cultures and professional groups, a point taken up in Chapter 13.

One way of reducing these shortcomings, while at the same time reducing the amount of time required to make decisions, is to use familiar solutions. Solutions represented by office standard details and master specifications represent the expert knowledge of the organisation that produced them. Another solution is the careful selection and use of pertinent and current information. Both strategies attempt to reduce the effect of cognitive limitations and informational constraints – they help to simplify the process. In some of the design literature this process is described as questioning (e.g. Potter 1989). Because designers will face design problems that may be ill defined, misleading or diffuse in nature, attempts must be made to define the problem before it can be resolved. Definition of problems is made easier for the designer through the asking of questions of him or herself, and of others. The aim of this questioning process is to be able to take full account of information, explore possibilities and recognise limitations, essentially a process of simplification. According to psychological studies there are four general simplification stages undertaken by decision-makers.

(1) *Editing.* Information is discarded or ignored so that the problem is more manageable. This is especially so when time constraints are paramount.
(2) *Decomposition.* Decision-makers will break down problems into manageable parts. For example, designers decompose the building whole into manageable parts, an act that will take place in the mind and also through the act of doing the detailed drawings.
(3) *Heuristics.* Heuristics are familiar to building professionals: they are 'rules of thumb' for solving problems without resorting to complicated calculations or research. Experts tend to recognise patterns and relationships based on experience, essentially rule-following behaviour.
(4) *Framing.* Individuals frame problems to direct attention to different preferences and different options. Decisions will vary depending upon how they are framed by the decision-maker. Individuals copy frames used by others, their office colleagues for example. They also adopt frames proposed by consultants and fellow professionals.

8.1.3 *Vocabulary*

Hillier and Jones' (1977) article in the *New Scientist* has particular relevance to designers today. They argued that the difficulties being experienced in architecture at the time were related to changes in architectural vocabulary and building forms. This had 'stirred up a hornet's nest of technical problems which had been forgotten because their solution had become a matter of habit'. They made the distinction between information (that which we look up) and knowledge (what we learn) claiming a direct correlation between looking up, rather than learning, and the probability of failure. They suggested that what was needed (and still is needed) is knowledge of good ways of achieving objectives through the use of materials and details that can be handled competently by the construction skills available, i.e. an area of knowledge not well covered in textbooks, technical guides or manufacturers' literature, lying somewhere between technical knowledge and the repetition of standard solutions.

8.2   Typologies

Designers draw on experience (their own and that of others) to come up with
a particular design solution for a specific site and a particular client. Relying on personal experience requires a considerable amount of knowledge of various solutions to problems, a skill developed and honed over time. Young designers (with
limited knowledge) and older designers (with greater knowledge) will, to greater
or lesser extents, rely on solutions by others – building typologies. 'Typology' is
a model, impression or mould that is used as a base for developing other design
solutions. Typologies can be used to classify building types, e.g. Pevsner (1976)
History of Building Types, and hence are a valuable research tool, or they can be used
as a model (e.g. *Metric Handbook*) and hence are a valuable prototype for the busy
designer to develop into a new solution. Thus building typologies become a useful point of reference and design tool for both practitioners and researchers. Types
evolve over time (for better or worse) reflecting changes in culture and technologies, i.e. morphology.

Building typologies allow designers to apply knowledge to current problems
that are drawn from past solutions – solutions that they know will work, and can
be applied quickly. At the conceptual design stage the typologies are likely to be
drawn from the experience of other designers' buildings drawn from personal
experience or second hand from the images contained in the architectural journals.
It is unlikely that the typology will be applied in an identical fashion, but will be
used as a design generator, to save time 'reinventing the wheel'. At the detail
design stage the typologies are more detailed, again sometimes drawn from observations of other building design, but more often than not drawn from the firm's
collective experience of solutions that are known to work in practice: the 'standard' detail. Details are likely to be repeated from one building to the next simply because all buildings require foundations, walls, a roof, doors and windows.
It is common practice to apply these details with little or no modification from
job to job where appropriate. Changes to details tend to be made to suit site conditions, client requirements and architectural fashion. A design organisation's
collection of typologies encompasses their collective experience and knowledge,
a store of expert knowledge encoded in drawings and standard specifications. The
better the management of the organisation and ease of accessibility to these
typologies, the easier it is to manage the detail design process efficiently. The
tendency to draw on information (plans and details) that worked well previously
is not a new phenomenon. Before looking at standard details and their use in
practice it is useful to look at the precedents for using them.

8.2.1   *Precedent studies*

Many designers will embark on an information and knowledge gathering exercise
before starting to design, i.e. they embark on a research programme. This is especially important in situations where a design office is faced with a building type that
is new to them. Researching plans, details and materials of buildings completed by
other designers is a rich source of knowledge. Known as precedent studies, these
investigations help designers to identify both good and bad examples of particular
building types. Other designers' buildings may be a source of inspiration or may

help to limit the options by showing how not to do it. There is no substitute for visiting buildings and drawing our own conclusions, but often this is not possible (because of time and cost constraints) and we have to fall back on published material in journals and monographs. The importance of research into the use of materials and the detailing of components and junctions cannot be overstated. To see both where it has been done badly and where it has been done well is useful since both extremes are informative. For example, some designers are well known for their sensitive use of materials and their exquisite level of detailing, e.g. Carlo Scapa. Others are well known for using a limited palette of materials, e.g. Richard Meier. For established design organisations with a wealth of experience the tendency is to draw on their collective experience (and monitor the work of others).

8.2.2   Standard plans

The re-use of standard plans is not a new phenomenon, since clients and architects have been re-using over many years plans and details that worked well previously for their new projects. The small Fenland town of Wainfleet in Lincolnshire provides a striking example of the penchant for re-using a proven design. Barkham Street was built by the Trustees of Betham Hospital in the 1840s using the same design and architect's drawings used to build an identical terrace of town houses in the London Borough of Southwark. The terrace is beautifully proportioned and detailed, but a little out of place (and scale) in this Fenland town more famous for the beer made by George Bateman and Son. Mass housebuilders also utilise standard plans and standard details, with variations on housing estates created through a mix of a few standard plans with different detailing.

8.2.3   Pattern books

Manuals and pattern books started to become widely available in the 18th century. They represented a body of knowledge on architectural styles, plans and construction details, from which entire buildings could, and were, built. The repetition to be found in Georgian architecture was a direct result of the pattern books, with designers and builders selecting details from them (Cruickshank and Wyld 1975). Throughout the 18th century both builders and designers produced a multitude of books and manuals which others could and did use. Combined they assisted in the dissemination of knowledge from one to another and from one part of the country to another (Yeomans 1992). The publications ranged in content from the practical instruction of carpenters' manuals (e.g. Peter Nicholson's *The Carpenter's New Guide*, London, 1792), to the publications produced by architects whose aim was to draw attention to themselves in the hope of new commissions (e.g. James Gibbs's *A Book of Architecture, Containing Designs of Buildings and Ornaments*, London 1728), through to the sales brochures produced by the manufacturers of mass produced components, such as cast iron. Manufacturers were quick to exploit the sales potential offered by printing and started producing brochures of their designs (e.g. Elanor A. Coade's *A Descriptive Catalogue of Coade's Artificial Stone Manufactory ... with Prices Affixed*, London 1748). A more recent and well-known example is British Gypsum's *White Book*, a catalogue that designers and builders were quick to use.

On the one hand these publications assisted the handing down of knowledge from master craftsman to apprentice, and on the other they were an excellent source of expert knowledge from which many with little or no formal training were able to copy. Buildings built in the classical style were based on pattern books because few designers could afford to travel outside England to gain inspiration from the real thing. Now books on architectural style and information readily found on the internet provide a similar function, a source of visual stimulation without having to leave the office. A modern manifestation of the guides for craftsmen and designers can be found in the planning and design guides such as the *A.J. Metric Handbook* (Sliwa and Fairweather 1968) which has been updated and expanded through revised editions over the years. The most recent edition is the *Metric Handbook: Planning and Design Data* (Adler 1999) which provides an authoritative reference source for building designers. In response to the growth in the use of digital information the handbook can also be purchased on a CD ROM containing more than 1700 symbols for insertion into computer aided design (CAD) drawings, thus helping the designer to save time and money through the use and re-use of design data.

8.3 Typical details

Typical details are to be found in some building codes and in textbooks on construction technology. As noted earlier the Approved Documents contain typical details that will allow the designer to ensure compliance simply by copying the suggested solution. These and other typical details are copied and form the basis of many manufacturers' details (with their own product prominently featured) and design organisations' office standards. Typical details are at the heart of building technology education and form the basis of numerous books on building technology: Chudley, Mackay and the Mitchell's Series (all still in print) are good examples of the genre. Used by academics for teaching construction technology and by students to justify their designs, they encourage young practitioners to learn through copying. It is not surprising then that when students qualify and enter the design office that they instinctively reach for typical solutions to solve particular detailing challenges – represented in practice by the office standard details (discussed below).

The majority of construction textbooks tend to describe rather specific solutions (sometimes alongside general principles) and while they do provide useful guidance they date very quickly: some contain details that many would consider as inappropriate (or plain wrong) and some contain fundamental errors at the time of printing. The availability of a wide selection of materials, products and components, combined with designers' own aesthetic aims and project-specific constraints, mean that these solutions may not necessarily be appropriate in practice. Add changing levels of craftsmanship skills to be found on site, the amount of production off site (pre-fabrication), buildability issues and cost constraints and the picture becomes even more complex than might first be assumed from this genre of books.

In the 1970s the *Architects' Journal* ran a series of typical details culminating in the publication *Everyday Details* by Cecil Handisyde (1976), a book that sought to tackle the problems of detailing through the illustration of good (and bad) detailing.

Such publications are very useful, but they are in need of constant revision as practices change to meet changing regulations or experience (and the benefit of hindsight) shows that a particular detail was not such a sensible approach. One example is the concrete lintel detail which soon after Handisyde's publication became recognised as creating a thermal bridge in the construction and thus should not be used. It would appear that the message took some time to get through, since some construction books published as late as 1999 still showed this detail without highlighting the problem associated with it. The point is that not all typical details are correct, even at the time of publication, and caution should be exercised by the reader before applying them. Furthermore, the longer the book stays on the shelf without revision, the greater the likelihood that the typical details featured are no longer viable, because of changes in legislation, advances in technology and gradual innovation made in the light of experience of building and component failures. Although well intended and valuable, this genre of books should have a 'best before' date clearly marked on the front cover, after which time they should be archived as a record for repair and conservation work, and replaced by a revised edition. A different approach has been adopted by a few authors who have used an elemental method to realise architecture and technology. *Principles of Modern Building* (HMSO 1938) applied building science to architecture based on the functional characteristics of the elements, an approach adopted more recently by Rich and Dean (1999). Their book *Principles of Element Design* has attempted to address this issue by concentrating on the elements and providing a simple checklist of principles to be used.

Some building failures can be traced back to poor detailing, where an outdated detail and/or an inappropriate detail was used. This is often an office standard detail or a textbook solution applied without due consideration for the interaction between other materials and components, which, with the benefit of time and hindsight, is proven to be a bad decision. A more current source of details can be found in the product manufacturers' technical literature, although this too is not necessarily error free, and is prone to becoming superseded very quickly.

8.4   Manufacturers' details

In many respects the pattern books of the late 20th century have been replaced by manufacturers' own literature. Building product manufacturers' catalogues range from very simple and basic information to extensive information covering every product they manufacture, complete with standard details and specifications to assist the designer. Collectively, building product manufacturers produce a variety of information for a variety of uses, from promotional literature to technical literature. Promotional literature is principally designed to raise awareness of the company and its products to the specifier. Rarely does it provide enough information to allow the specifier actually to specify the product, rather the intention is that the specifier should make contact with the manufacturer to ask for further information. From here the manufacturer may choose to send technical literature, deal with enquiries by telephone and/or send a technical representative to the specifier's office to assist with the specification. Technical literature contains typical details and typical specification clauses which can be easily used by designers.

Manufacturers' details and specifications are an excellent source of detail design knowledge that busy designers can quickly import into their production information. Before the relatively recent advances in digital information and CAD these details were supplied on paper (hard copies) that could be traced by a draughtsman and hence incorporated into the detail design drawings. Hard copies are still supplied and still used by many design offices, either traced, photocopied or scanned into digital documents; however, with the widespread adoption of CAD the manufacturers are promoting their products using digital IT. Standard details featuring their own particular products are now available on computer disk, CD ROM, and may also be downloaded from their web sites in cyberspace. Manufacturers do this as an effective means of helping to secure the use of their products rather than those of their competitors. By making it easy and quick for the designer to import their standard details and standard specifications into project information they can find their products specified without even being contacted by the designer. This 'free' information has been carefully designed so that by selecting a particular manufacturer's detail the designer is also confirming his or her choice of product. The situation is a little more complex where performance related specifications are being used; however, manufacturers do provide performance specifications for their products that are so written as to confine the choice to their product only. Needless to say, in the longer term manufacturers hope that the designer, and hence the design office, will adopt their particular detail and their product as a standard detail. Many manufacturers will also employ technical staff who will provide bespoke details for a particular project. A feature of manufacturers' own details is that their details often contain errors. Manufacturers are concerned with the promotion of their own product range and thus other components may not necessarily be represented correctly. As with all 'typical' details, caution should be exercised when working such details into the overall detail design drawings, because once included they tend to stay.

In addition to providing detailed drawings of their products manufacturers also provide detailed specifications. These are product specific and, therefore, the performance specifications are written in such a way that only the particular manufacturer's product will fit the specification. As with the standard detail, supply of a product specification is an effective method in helping the designer to adopt a particular product over that of a rival manufacturer. This is true of proprietary specifications and performance specifications, the latter being written in such a fashion as to make the selection of a rival manufacturer's product impossible. For example, a performance specification for a particular product may specify a manufacturing tolerance that rivals cannot achieve.

8.4.1 Manufacturers' input

It would be misleading to give the impression that designers develop their detail designs in isolation. Successful design relies on co-operation between manufacturer and specifier. Manufacturers have a vital role to play in helping the designer to detail particular aspects of buildings, especially in circumstances where the detailing may be unfamiliar to the designer or to the design office. Many of the larger manufacturers employ technical representatives who visit design offices to assist specifiers and hence get the specification. Some manufacturers also employ technical staff to answer queries by telephone, fax or e-mail, in addition to, or instead of, trade representatives. On large projects and projects with unusual details many manufacturers will offer to provide the technical drawings and written specification clauses for the designers, e.g. cladding companies will provide a complete package. This saves the design team a lot of production work, shifting their emphasis to co-ordination and checking information from other sources.

8.5   Office standards – details and specifications

In the majority of design offices typical details and specifications are customised to suit the organisation and hence become 'office standards'. These standards are based on good practice and the collective experience of the office developed over many years. Some details and specification clauses will be unique to a particular design office, others will be amalgamations of typical details, typical specifications and manufacturers' details and specifications. Office standards must conform to current regulations, and some details will be copied from (or based very closely on) the illustrative diagrams in the Approved Documents. Together this collection of knowledge should represent good practice. Design offices operate procedures, sometimes formal, often informal, through which standard details are approved and adopted.

Through the organisation's collective experience some details will be discarded, others will be adopted for widespread use and re-used many times over. The use of office standards by design organisations is common practice, sometimes criticised for stifling innovative design, but used to save time and reduce the risk of failure. Not only do they save time in generating the same drawing or specification over and over again, they also encourage good practice because they are usually based on experience of detailing/materials that are known to perform, or more specifically known not to fail. As such, standards form an essential part of well-designed quality management systems. They form part of the organisation's collective knowledge (Fig. 8.2) and can be used by less experienced staff, as long as the process is monitored and checked by a more experienced colleague, or the design manager.

8.5.1   A 'standard' vocabulary of details

Much like handwriting, office standards are specific to individual design organisations, i.e. their own detailed design vocabulary. Given the same building to design, two different design offices will use different detailed vocabularies and the resultant building design will differ. In well-managed design organisations the vocabulary will form a vital component of their operating system, helping to ensure quality and consistency. Some designers become well known for their vocabulary of detail. One design approach is to detail using a limited range of materials, products and details as a standard palette from which to design. At the other end of the scale designers have been equally successful employing a large range of materials, products and details. For the sole practitioner and very small design firm a limited vocabulary is as much necessity as a design statement, simply because of the lack of resources to investigate alternatives adequately.

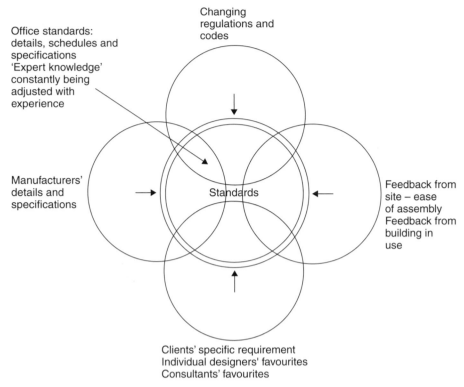

Office standards:
details, schedules and
specifications
'Expert knowledge'
constantly being
adjusted with
experience

Changing
regulations and
codes

Manufacturers'
details and
specifications

Standards

Feedback from
site – ease
of assembly
Feedback from
building in
use

Clients' specific requirement
Individual designers' favourites
Consultants' favourites

Figure 8.2 Office standards – expert knowledge.

8.5.2   *Standard specifications*

Graphic representations of architectural details are used to control the form and appearance of the building project. Written specifications are used to control the quality of the materials used and the quality of the work. It is the specification that controls quality, and the development of office standard specifications (the 'master' specification) is equally as important as the standard details. These office standards are frequently linked to national and international standard specifications. In the USA such a system has been developed by the Construction Specifications Institute (CSI). As with standard details, standard specifications are used by organisations to save time, merely adjusting the master document to be project specific. Given that many design offices tend to specialise to a certain extent, e.g. housing, offices, hospitals, etc., the development and maintenance of a carefully written master specification makes sense because of the major savings in time and the reduction in risk. Only the master document need be maintained on a regular basis to retain currency, with project-specific text added to suit particular circumstances. This means that someone in the office must be responsible for the upkeep of the master specification, responsible for its regular review and ensuring that all alterations are checked and recorded in accordance with the quality management system. In small offices an individual will do this in addition to his or her other work; in larger offices the task will be carried out by someone with responsibility for technical matters.

Care is required to distinguish the carefully and regularly updated 'master specification' from the 'rolling' specification. Rolling specifications are documents that have been used for a previous project and are simply rolled forward and adjusted to suit the next one. Their use should be avoided because there is serious danger of including text which is inappropriate and excluding that which is appropriate. Over time other dangers such as references to superseded standards and discontinued products are a real possibility. Because rolling specifications are often used when time is at a premium, i.e. they are rushed, the problem lies as much with ineffective checking of the text. Because of the inherent dangers of changes on site, inappropriate levels of quality, implications on cost and programme and the enhanced risk of claims being made against the design office their use is not recommended.

8.5.3   *Office standards – friend or foe?*

Standards represent an excellent knowledge base from which to detail familiar buildings and many organisations try and prevent departing employees from taking their 'knowledge' with them to a competitor. There are a number of advantages and disadvantages associated with office standards as discussed below:

(1) *Advantages*
  (a) *Quality control.* Because standard details and specifications have been tried and tested by the design office over a number of years they should be relatively error free. They will have evolved to suit changes in regulations and to accommodate feedback from site. Because they are familiar, tried and tested, standard details represent an effective means of QC when applied correctly. Checked and updated at regular intervals, standards may contribute to the quality management system of the office, reassuring clients and practice principals alike.
  (b) *Managerial control.* The use of standard details can save the design office time and money because common details do not need to be redrawn, merely selected from the design organisation's knowledge base. With increased downward pressure on professional fees, the use of office standards can help to ensure the commission is a profitable one. Indeed, there may be little time available to investigate alternatives.
  (c) *Risk management.* The use of tried and tested details helps to limit the organisation's exposure to risk, essentially a conservative, 'safe' approach to design.
  (d) *Benchmarking.* When faced with an unusual detailing problem the standards form a convenient benchmark from which to develop the detail and help to evaluate its anticipated performance in the completed building.
(2) *Disadvantages*
  (a) *Hinders innovation.* There is a school of thought which urges designers to start from scratch with each and every design, including the detailed element of it, through which action creativity is deemed to flourish. Standard solutions should be discarded and the detailer encouraged to develop an original solution to each specific problem. This is nice in

theory, but rarely practised because of time and financial pressures. Standard solutions can hinder creativity and prevent innovative solutions, but they also reduce an organisation's exposure to risk and keep the organisation competitive in the marketplace. There will be situations when standard solutions cannot solve a particular detailing problem, because the problem is unique and has not been experienced by the technologist and/or design office before. A balance is required between discarding valuable knowledge encapsulated in standard details and the search for new knowledge and new ways of tackling familiar intersections in the pursuit of constant improvement.

(b) *Perpetuates errors.* Where errors exist in standards details and specifications (and they do), the errors are perpetuated through re-use on many projects until such time that the error manifests itself, sometimes after a long period of time. Unless careful checking and updating is implemented the use of standards can prove a dangerous habit.

(c) *Incorrect application.* Inexperienced members of the design office are often left to apply standards with little or no supervision. There is a real risk that they may apply details incorrectly and managerial control is essential if costly errors are to be avoided.

(d) *Auditing.* Auditing the detail process is recommended, but rarely undertaken.

A word of caution: how do we know whether or not these details are correct? Do we really have the intellectual capacity to question them when we have been brought up in a culture of copying? It is essential that we gain and maintain a thorough understanding of the fundamental issues applied to building. Then we will be able to question and make informed judgements when confronted by a 'standard' detail, adopting, adjusting or rejecting it accordingly.

8.6 Detailing criteria

Drawings that describe the relationship between different building elements in minute detail are generally known as 'details', i.e. they deal with specific intersections. Details are necessary to illustrate the relationship between individual building components and changes in geometry. These drawings should clearly show those assembling the building the exact relationship between components, be clearly dimensioned and clearly annotated. Under the CI/SfB elemental system of drawing classification details are referred to as 'assembly' drawings (see Chapter 10). In many respects it is the details (the assembly drawings), together with the specification, that allow the designers to dictate, and hence control, the way in which the building is assembled. Given a free hand, the workers on site will exercise their own judgement; effective detailing prevents such action.

Details, along with specifications, schedules and other working drawings, constitute the contract documentation and hence form legal documents. In the event of a dispute the detail drawings will be examined to compare the designer's intent with the builder's action. Because the details occupy such an important place in the design and assembly of a building it follows that they deserve particular attention by designers. A number of questions need to be asked by the designer when working on the contract documentation. Questions such as:

- Is the detail necessary?
- Does the drawing communicate design intent effectively?
- Is there enough information on the drawing?
- Is there too much information?
- Do the details complement and enhance associated contract documentation (the layout drawings, specifications and schedules)?

These are questions that can only be answered through the actual process of detailing.

Detail design involves a mental process of trying to make the parts fit together harmoniously, often achieved by working through the details in sketch form (on paper or on the computer monitor) until the relationship between materials and planes is acceptable to the designer. To detail effectively and efficiently designers must first learn to see, i.e. observe others' detailing and visualise their own details before applying them. An ability to look at details and their relationship to the greater whole, analysing, questioning and selecting, will allow a better understanding of what can be achieved, a policy of continual education and improvement. It is all there, all one has to do is look (and know where to look). Rather than slavishly applying office standard solutions, designers should make time (programme permitting) to explore intersections with an open mind, for it is through such action that details can be improved.

Figure 8.3 Carved detail to timber entrance door.

8.6.1 *Towards harmonious detailing*

Detailing a building is a creative art. For sure, standard solutions will be used to save time, but the detail design process is much more than the tedious repetition of standard solutions, or for that matter the creation of new details just for the sake of it. The detailing process is a continual evolution of what the designer (and the design office) believes to be best practice, based on the sharing of information and knowledge culled from a wide variety of sources. It is also about the choice of the correct solution for a particular set of circumstances at a particular time, considering the benefits for clients, builders and users within a framework of limited resources and creative endeavour.

Details evolve, office standards over a long period of gradual improvement, specific details over a much shorter period, and their development requires a considerable amount of skill. Wakita and Linde (1999: 438) put it rather well: 'creativity, ingenuity, and craftsmanship are just as important in the design of a detail as they are in the overall design of a structure'. At the detail design stage the design team have a number of elements to balance if harmonious detailing is to be achieved. Individual designers are influenced by their own personality, their past professional experience and the collective experience of the office in which they work. They will have to deal with demands placed upon them by the client, their peers, current legislation, time constraints, cost constraints, buildability, aesthetics and proportion, and environmental issues as expressed in Fig. 8.4 and as follows.

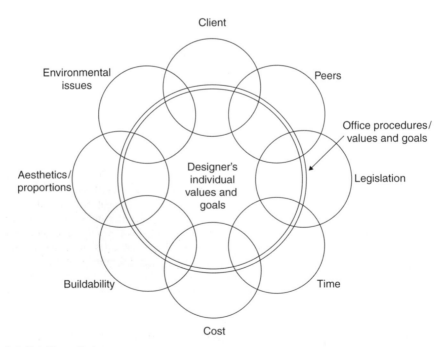

Figure 8.4 Detailing criteria.

- Client requirements – expressed through the design brief and the conceptual design.
- Legislation – current.
- Environmental considerations – weathering.
- Time constraints – legal and project.
- Cost constraints (these may vary as the scheme proceeds simply because as the drawings become more comprehensive so does the cost estimate).
- Buildability.
- Peer approval.
- Aesthetics and proportion. A fundamental concept of design is proportion: proportion of the steel section, solid to void, door knob to door, etc., all come back to an understanding of ergonomics.
- Sustainability.
- Synthesis.
- Fire.
- Material and product properties.

8.6.2   *Case study – Two different approaches to detailing*

The manner in which individuals deal with detail design decisions is influenced by their immediate office environment and their personal characteristics. In this example two designers working in the same design office were observed while engaged in detail design decisions for commercial projects: both were working on office developments, although on different projects.

The first designer's driver was the ceiling grid. Over a number of years he had gained experience of detailing and overseeing the erection of office buildings. He had come to the view that the easiest way to detail buildings was to start with the finishes and work outwards. His starting point from which all other decisions followed was the detailing and co-ordination of the suspended ceiling grid. It was the modular grid that determined the precise position of the partition walls. The designer claimed that this approach resulted in an aesthetically pleasing building interior and minimised cutting and waste on site.

The second designer's driver was the positioning of fire escapes. She always started with the positioning and sizing of the fire escapes to meet current regulations; then and only then did she proceed with the rest of the detail design – ceiling grids came towards the end of her priorities. Her view was that once the fire escapes had been positioned and sized, the remainder of the detail design could be fitted around them; they were seen to be too important to leave until later in the design process.

What is important is that both designers have an approach to detail design which works for them, and one would assume their employers. Neither approach could be described as right or wrong. Both designers have refined their approach over a period of practice in which they have adjusted and refined their decision-making process so that it results in effective decisions – decisions taken quickly and ones that they hope will not create further problems further down the line. Also, from a design manager's perspective the two designers worked very well together, their different approaches forming an effective cross-checking procedure when working on the same project.

8.6.3   *Golden rules of detailing*

Designers have their own way of working and many have 'golden' rules that they apply when detailing. In offices where managerial control is not particularly good this can and does lead to finished drawings taking a variety of slightly different forms, reflecting the idiosyncrasies of their authors. The end result can look unprofessional and can lead to confusion where, e.g. different approaches to dimensioning a drawing have been used. In the worst case this can lead to errors occurring on site. Professionally managed design offices take a much more considered and controlled approach. Designers work to office standards of graphic representation and to a standard approach to detailing and product selection, guidance for members of the design organisation being provided in the office quality manual. The end result may be a little sanitised for some tastes, but consistency will go a long way in improving communication and reducing errors on site, one of the primary aims of the design manager. Textbook authors are equally idiosyncratic in their recommendations for detailing. Some completely ignore the issue (relying on typical solutions) while others provide long checklists to be slavishly followed by the designer in practice. For example, Wakita and Linde (1999: 50–53) provide their American readers with 25 rules of detailing. In practice three 'golden rules' should suffice. They are as follows:

(1) *Compose and draw the detail as it is to be assembled on site.* Bear in mind that the detail has to be constructed or assembled by someone (with or without the assistance of tools and machinery) on a construction site, maintained and possibly replaced/dismantled by others at a future date. The sequence of assembly (and disassembly) must be understood. If you do not know how to assemble it, do not draw it. First, seek advice from more experienced colleagues in the design office and/or seek specialist knowledge from manufacturers and tradesmen.

(2) *Be consistent.* Whatever the approach adopted by the design office and the individuals within it, it is important to be consistent. If you do have an individual and different approach to detailing, those on the receiving end should be able to interpret instructions as long as the approach remains the same. Use of graphics, dimensions and annotation should be reassuringly consistent across the whole of the contract documentation. CAD packages and the use of the CI/SfB should both help to achieve this goal.

(3) *Check, and double check,* the detail for compliance with current codes and standards, manufacturers' recommendations, other consultants' details and compatibility with the overall design philosophy. It may be useful to remember that good designs can be rendered average simply through not constantly checking back to the brief and the conceptual design drawings. Common problems encountered by site personnel can be reduced significantly through a thorough check before information is issued to the contractor.

8.6.4 *Design considerations for achieving buildability*

In the light of the observations made above there are a number of factors for the design team to consider in order to achieve buildability. They are as follows:

(1) *Dimensional co-ordination.* Care needs to be taken to minimise cutting of materials such as timber and steel on site to avoid unnecessary labour costs and

waste. Materials are supplied in a range of standard sizes and the greater use of readily available materials which do not need to be altered on site not only minimises waste but also helps to ensure quality by limiting the amount of work which may be difficult to control on the site. Where difficulties are foreseen the cutting and fixing can often be transferred to the factory where it is easier to control quality. Structural solutions which rely on consistent structural grids and thus consistent column and beam sizes can reduce time and construction costs. A further consideration is that of dimensional tolerances – these need to be workable on-site – and an appreciation of the challenges of site assembly. Thus an appreciation of the labour skills and the tools available in a particular region, at a particular time, is paramount.

(2) *Use of familiar materials and construction techniques.* Such an approach relies on the use of standard details and tried and tested construction techniques; unique solutions and unfamiliar methods should be eliminated where possible. A counter argument would be for the use of innovative construction techniques and materials. That the construction method chosen should reflect the skills available locally is obvious, but is one aspect easily overlooked. For example, the adoption of vernacular building techniques may be a better approach than pre-fabrication in some locations, especially where sites are physically isolated. Economy of production will rely on how the work can be scheduled, and failure to take proper account of assembly sequences at the design stage can lead to inefficiency, especially where particular trades face discontinuity of work.

(3) *Design co-ordination of structure*, fabric and services to provide ease of installation and future access for maintenance and replacement. Service ducts, conduits and space for plant need careful consideration during the various design stages and demand extra consideration if design changes are required. For example, chasing out (cutting channels in concrete or masonry) conduits can be eliminated through careful detailing.

(4) *Appropriateness to the client's requirements and the ensuing conceptual design.* This requires appropriate personnel to deal with issues of detail design, structures, services, cost and time.

(5) *Accuracy of the information produced.* This covers checking for omissions and errors, accommodating design changes and auditing the process through quality management systems.

8.6.5   *Failure is inevitable*

All built structures will fail at some time in the future, some sooner than others. Eventual failure, the end of a building's design life, can be anticipated and often extended with sensitive and regular maintenance. It is the unexpected failures that cause the most concern for both designers (who may be liable) and owners (who face disruption and the cost of putting it right). Failures of materials and/or execution can never be entirely eliminated, even with mass production techniques and their associated QC procedures. Designers need to understand the limitations of the materials and manufactured products that they detail and specify, especially any changes in physical size due to moisture or temperature changes and the practicalities of working and/or fixing the materials on site if failure is to be minimised.

Ashby's Law of Requisite Variety – the complexity of the controlling body must equal the complexity of that being controlled – suggests that supervision and control of the assembly process on site can never be sufficient to ensure perfection (Heath 1984). Add in a liberal amount of human error during the design process, plus some ineffective communication, and failure is inevitable. Surveys by the BRE (1975) found that the main cause of construction problems could be traced back to poor detailing and associated breakdowns in communication. Poor detailing during design could be traced back to the designer's failure to consider adequately the assembly sequence. This was compounded by errors on drawings and amendments to drawings that had consequences for the assembly process which had not been adequately considered. Changes to details on site were another problem that needed to be addressed (see Chapter 11).

8.7   Critical intersections

Buildings are composed of a number of distinct architectural elements, the parts which collectively make up the whole. From an observer's perspective the combination of the wall, floor, roof, windows and doors results in the architectural quality of the building. That designers spend so much time agonising over the relationship of the main structural elements and the materials from which they are to be made should not surprise anyone because the intersections between materials and planes are always challenging. Any change in material, component or product will need to be detailed, as will any changes in geometry, especially between horizontal and vertical planes. There is always the potential for water penetration, air ingress and structural movement – factors which need to be accommodated in the form of special connections and joints (highlighted in Chapter 4). There are a number of critical intersections that, no matter how familiar they appear, or the type of construction employed, always cause designers and contractors difficulties.

(1) *Wall to ground*. Since every building sits in, on or sometimes above the ground one could be forgiven for thinking that the detailing of the intersection between the horizontal (ground) and the vertical (wall) would be simple, well understood and free from potential errors. Not so. Unusual designs, unfamiliar construction systems, sloping sites, etc., all have the potential to cause problems for the unsuspecting designer, especially in situations where the office standard cannot be applied without modification (or is applied inappropriately).

(2) *Wall to floor*. The junction of vertical and horizontal planes raises questions about how the two join, how forces are transferred from one plane to another and how movement is to be accommodated. Again standard solutions exist for standard situations.

(3) *Wall to roof*. Junction of vertical and angular planes raises similar problems for designers as horizontal to vertical junctions. Transfer of forces, fixing method and allowance for differential movement are prime concerns as is the ability

to make the junction weather-proof, yet at the same time allow adequate ventilation to the roof void.

(4) *Openings*. Providing doors, windows, service vents, rooflights, staircases, and elevators requires the formation of an opening in the building fabric, be it the floor, wall or roof. Potentially, the provision of openings in the external envelope will create a weak point for the ingress of water and wind and may compromise security. Thus careful detailing is necessary to maintain the building envelope's integrity. Internally, staircases often cause difficulties for designers.

8.8   Detailing for sustainability

When detailing and specifying, designers should be aware of issues affecting sustainability. Many designers have their own particular approach to ecological design principles which may vary from one extreme, not considering the issue at all, to modest ecological principles through to a kind of environmental evangelism. Strategies include using materials from sustainable sources, specifying low water use toilets and trying to minimise waste produced during construction through careful use of standard sizes of materials. Not only is this a personal issue for designers, but the team members need to have similar ideals if ecological design principles are to be translated into the finished product. These principles fall under four interrelated areas which should be considered, as described next.

8.8.1   *Detailing to conserve and re-use materials*

Recycling of materials has become a major design generator in many industries, including building. Social pressures and the concern of manufacturers for the environment have led to recycling programmes for glass bottles, beverage cans, paper and cardboard, and more latterly building components and materials. The manner in which a building is detailed will affect how it can be assembled; it will also determine the manner in which it can be dismantled at the end of its service life.

Limiting the use of finite materials and materials that may harm the environment during extraction, manufacturing and use is a responsible approach to adopt. Recycling materials can also help to limit further damage and also reduce energy consumption by maximising the embodied energy in the recovered material. These are principles at the heart of 'dematerialisation', essentially a philosophy of reducing consumption. Over the years concern has been raised over the destruction of the world's hardwood forests and specifiers have been given advice on specifying timber from managed and sustainable resources. Another example is the concern expressed over the use of aluminium because of the environmental damage caused when extracting it from bauxite found in the soil of rainforests throughout the world (Wakita and Linde 1999). Aluminium is widely used in the construction industry and ecologists and professional institutions (such as the AIA) have urged all parties to the building process to specify recycled aluminium. Aluminium also has a very high embodied energy and recycling it gives an energy saving of 80–95%

compared with using primary resources (Woolley *et al.* 1997). If in doubt as to whether a particular manufacturer uses recycled aluminium the designer should ask for clarification. Alternatively, the specification of materials with greener credentials should be tried. Recycling of construction materials makes sense for the environment and for commerce; however, there may be a premium to pay in terms of the cost of the recovered materials provided by architectural salvage organisations.

8.8.2   Detailing to conserve energy

As noted earlier, conservation of energy can be broken down into two areas: that taken to build the building and that taken to run it. Reduction in energy used to construct the building is something designers, given adequate information, can do something about. Reduction in the amount of energy required to heat and light the building can be addressed at the design stage, although the operation of the services is in the control of the building owners/users.

8.8.3   Detailing to minimise waste

The control of waste on building sites has become more important over recent years with increasing pressure on landfill sites. The imposition of landfill taxes has helped to highlight the issue, although the cost of disposal is passed onto the building sponsor – it is not borne by the design team or the contractor. Environmentally responsible designers and contractors can implement a variety of strategies to reduce the amount of waste created on site. Clearly, the conceptual design will have an influence on the detail decisions which follow, but it is in the detail design stage that a difference can be made through awareness and attention to the following issues:

■ *Component sizes.* A thorough knowledge of standard component sizes may help to reduce the extent of cutting on site and hence reduce waste. Working to standard timber sizes and standard sizes of plasterboard are familiar strategies. Constant monitoring and feedback from site can help to achieve gradual improvement in reducing waste on future projects.
■ *Co-ordination.* Co-ordination of different materials, components and systems should be considered.
■ *Error avoidance.* Avoiding errors on drawings and specifications will reduce the amount of unnecessary work on site (to correct mistakes).
■ *Control on site.* Control of materials on site to avoid damage combined with close control of work on site to avoid unnecessary reworking are important factors in reducing waste.

8.8.4   Detailing for durability

Designers need to design for today and have an eye on the future, since their buildings will still be around long after many of them have finished practising.

Durability and appropriateness to future use need to be borne in mind; however, the problem here is largely one of interpretation. What exactly do we mean by the word 'durability'? One interpretation is concerned entirely with the structure and its physical properties, e.g. the length of time the artefact is likely to remain weathertight, and hence useable. Another interpretation is that the building should remain weathertight for a long period but also incorporate the potential for a variety of uses, hence lengthening the potential functionality of the structure. Here durability would be interpreted as a robust structure (long design life) with a fully adaptable interior (to suit a series of shorter but successive service lives). In contrast, durability may also be interpreted as designing a short-term structure, but one built of durable materials and components that are easy to disassemble, recover and re-use in a new, more appropriate structure. Here emphasis is on the durability of individual components rather than the whole structure.

8.8.5   *Detailing for disassembly*

Early in this book the point was made about the similarity between buildability and disassembly principles. Detailing for disassembly is a very important and topical issue, and one those involved in renovation, alteration, demolition, salvage and re-use are particularly concerned with. Indeed, there appears to be a real need for those involved in the disassembly sector to share their knowledge with the designers and detailers thus helping to improve knowledge about this, often overlooked, area of detail design. The main principles of designing for disassembly, in addition to designing for versatility (flexibility) and simplicity are as follows:

- Provide easy access for inspection, maintenance, repair and replacement of individual components without damaging neighbouring assemblies.
- Position materials and components with the shortest service life so as to be more accessible than those expected to last for a longer period.
- Consider the independence (and inter-dependence) of assemblies to minimise damage when removing, replacing and disassembling.
- Specify materials with an inherent finish (thus making them easier to recover and re-use).
- Detail and position connections to be easily accessible, either through simple access panels or through exposing the connection.
- Use dry construction techniques and minimise the use of mastics, glues, etc.

8.9   The cost of detailing

It is one thing to talk about details in terms of their aesthetics or their durability, quite another to consider the cost implications associated with detailing a building. Traditionally the issue of costs associated with detail design, detailing, product selection and the production of information has not formed a central part of the education of building design professionals. We all marvel at the wonderful detailing of the latest fashionable building, captured in splendid photographic image and elegant prose, but apart from a list of building elements and their cost (if we are lucky) there is rarely any description of the 'real' cost of producing such details. There are two issues, first the 'cost of' the detailing and second the 'cost to' those involved in the process.

8.9.1   Cost of

(1) *Building elements*. These are often represented as a cost per square metre and including labour. It is less common to see the cost of individual products; indeed many manufacturers withhold this information in the hope of getting the specification first.

(2) *Time*. That is, the time required to produce the details, which includes the time required to select appropriate products and then incorporate them into the detailed drawings and describe them in the specification.

(3) *Managing the detail design stage, including QC and co-ordination*. For example, the process of checking cannot be rushed: consideration of design changes requires time so that all of the consequences of the change can be made.

(4) *Changes to the design*. Changes to a design can be expensive in terms of the amount of redrawing and rescheduling required. For example, the simple action of a client changing from timber cladding to brick cladding will affect the structural design and the detailing of the building, involving a considerable amount of redrawing work that someone has to pay for. Changes may come about through a variety of routes and must be anticipated. This can mean the difference between making a profit and making a loss on a project and needs careful managerial control.

(5) *Feedback*. Design professionals are constantly criticised for not returning to their buildings to gain feedback. A couple of points need to be addressed here. First, it costs money (largely time) to return to buildings and analyse them. It is not something a client will wish to pay for, unless the organisation is engaged in repeat business for the client, when feedback becomes far more prominent in the overall scheme of things, because without feedback it is difficult to improve the product constantly. Well-managed firms do engage in feedback and cost this as part of their overheads. Second, feedback is not just about returning to the building and looking at the finished artefact in use. It is also about analysing the details and information used, especially since the majority of firms will re-use information produced for previous jobs on current projects – it forms part of their expert knowledge system (office standards). So to a certain extent feedback is costed into the next project.

(6) *Getting it wrong*. Mistakes do happen and measures must be taken to keep them to a minimum, through both the use of management systems and the employment and utilisation of the best staff the firm can employ (and their constant motivation). At best mistakes will cost the firm time to put right, but in the litigious world of building it is more likely that the mistake may lead to some form of legal action against the design firm. Do not be fooled by the possession of PI insurance. The insurance company

may pick up the cost of putting a mistake right, but the design firm's premium will increase on renewal, as will the excess on the policy, and to make matters worse there may be new conditions attached to the policy which exclude cover for the organisation making the same mistake again. Furthermore, dispute resolution through, e.g. arbitration or alternative dispute resolution (ADR) costs everyone involved money, in terms of the time involved in preparing information to defend a case. Thus mistakes are more costly than they might first appear.

8.9.2 *Cost to*

(1) *The client*. Most clients are primarily concerned with the initial cost of the project which is easily quantifiable. They should also be concerned with the long-term cost of running and maintaining the building because mistakes made at the detail stage can have a significant effect on these costs. Thus changing details and materials to save money during the construction phase may well have an undesirable effect on running and maintenance costs.

(2) *The project participants*. Designer, contractor, consultants, etc., are all in business to make a profit. Professional service firms wish to stay in business and make a respectable return on their investment. Efficient detailing and preparation of contract documentation can form part of a design organisation's competitive advantage because it saves time and may well lead to repeat business with the client.

(3) *The building user*. Building users are often different to the client. They will be faced with the cost of running the building (energy consumption), maintenance costs and replacement costs. Detail design decisions, e.g. to add or remove solar shading, to specify the most energy efficient boiler or the cheapest available, will have a knock-on effect for the users.

(4) *The environment*. The environmental impact of the building, its energy consumption over a long period of time and recovery costs to future generations need to be addressed.

8.9.3 *Quality control*

Closely associated with the issue of cost is that of quality. QC should be foremost in the mind of the designer, an inherent part of the detailing process. With the exception of the aesthetics of the detail (assuming that there is an exposed surface) it is a relatively straightforward task to set parameters for achieving quality through the written specification. Drawings indicate the quantity of materials to be used and show their finished relationship. It is the specification that describes the quality of the work and the materials to be used, an argument developed further in Chapter 10. No matter how good the detail design process and how comprehensive the resulting information, the quality of the finished building depends upon those doing the assembly and those doing the on-site supervision. Designers specify the position, quantity and quality of the building work, they do not tell the builder 'how' to construct it – this is the contractor's responsibility (hence the need for method statements). Choice of procurement route is an important consideration because it will set the contractual obligations of the designers and the contractors with regard to site supervision, issues taken up in Chapters 9 and 11.

Further reading

Heath, T. (1984). *Method in Architecture*, John Wiley & Sons, Chichester.
Rowe, P.G. (1987). *Design Thinking*, MIT Press, Cambridge, MA.

9 Product selection

Perhaps product selection, above all else, is one of the most important consider-ations for the long-term durability of the completed building and an area in which building designers should excel. The selection and specification of build-ing products, however, has not attracted much attention from researchers or practition-ers. It is often seen as unglamorous and something that should be carried out as quickly as possible. With increased emphasis on sustainable design, detailing for durability and quality, has come fresh interest in product selection; a phase during which building product manufacturers, technologists and builders may interact to the benefit of the fin-ished building. The importance of correct product selection and the pressures that come to bear on product selections during the design process, including specification sub-stitution, is explored here. We conclude with an observation of a designer in the act of specification.

9.1   The specification of building products

At the heart of good architectural design lies the correct selection of materials, components and products that make up a building's assembly; they contribute to the aesthetics and durability of the completed building. However, despite the apparent familiarity of material selection to practitioners Leatherbarrow (1993) observed that the process of specification is rarely discussed and one that is difficult to describe simply and clearly; presumably because it is difficult to separate the designer's goals from building materials as entities in their own right (Patterson 1994).

The number of building products that are potentially available for selection by an architect is extensive. There are approximately 20,000 building product manu-facturers, many of whom offer more than one product for sale (Edmonds 1996). Every year new products are introduced by manufacturers in response to compe-tition, new regulations and changes in architectural fashion. In addition to these 'new' products, there are numerous minor product improvements that are con-stantly introduced by manufacturers to prolong their product's life on the mar-ket. But getting a new idea or product adopted is never easy as Rogers (1995) has pointed out, and this is especially true of building, where new products and prod-uct improvements, like the established products, are dependent upon decision-makers in the building industry for their selection – a process generally referred to in the building industry as 'specification' and carried out by 'specifiers'.

Traditionally architects have been the major specifiers, but with the introduc-tion of new procurement methods and the growth of other specialists, there has been a move to specification by a wide variety of building professionals. Although the architect's responsibility for building product selection has declined in recent years according to the Barbour Report (1993) architects are still the most influ-ential and important 'specifiers' of products in the British building industry. Architects have been described as 'licensed specifiers' (Pawley 1990), and their influence over the majority of product selection is well recognised by the building product manufacturers who bombard design offices with their trade literature in the hope of getting their products specified. Growing concern over environmental sustainability (e.g. Edwards 1996) combined with increased pressure to cut costs and improve efficiency (e.g. Latham 1994, Egan 1998) has placed additional pressures on specifiers and has started to focus attention on the area of detail design, an area largely ignored by the design methods authors in favour of the more creative conceptual phase. Writing about new materials and methods in 1933 the architect Chermayeff stated that 'it is essential to select for a specific purpose within the defined cost, the most adequate material and method; that is to say, that material which best solves the problems of purpose, money and time' (Chermayeff 1933), a sentiment that still holds true today. The challenge for the specifier, then, is to ensure correct specification.

Specification of building products is of great importance to the manufacturers and suppliers who do carry out a lot of commercial research into the adoption of their own, and their direct competitors', products. This research is not in the public domain simply because of its commercial sensitivity and helps to explain why published research is rare. Margaret Mackinder (1980) gathered information on product selection through diaries filled in by participating specifiers. She observed that designers frequently used 'short cuts' based on their own experience in order to save time, reporting a strong preference for certain materials and components that they had used previously, drawn from their personal collections of literature; this supported the earlier observations of Goodey and Matthew (1971) and Wade (1977). One-third of Mackinder's sample acknowledged that new materials and methods needed to be monitored but claimed it was office policy to avoid the use of anything new unless it was unavoidable, preferring to specify familiar products. Mackinder's study found that there had been very little research into how professionals actually selected building products, a situation that has changed little since 1980 (Emmitt 1997a). The majority of published literature that has investigated the way in which architects make decisions has concentrated on the 'design process' with emphasis on the resulting 'design' (Rowe 1987).

Mackinder also looked at the extent to which schools of architecture teach the selection of building products and found that they did not: the schools taught 'design' of which, it could be argued, material selection is a very important part. Failure to address such an important part of the design process has been described as a 'major weakness' in architectural education (Antoniades 1992, Crosbie 1995). One of the differences between the education of architects and that of technicians, and more latterly technologists, is the amount of time devoted to issues surrounding specification in their formative years. The technician has always had a more thorough education in writing specifications and with the recent introduction of the undergraduate degrees in architectural technology there has come greater attention to both specification writing and the product selection process that precedes it. However, there is still a shortage of literature that deals specifically with product selection. Textbooks deal with building technology, standard details and the process of physically writing the specification. None deals with the decision-making process we know as specifying, and, therefore, the young practitioner must learn the art of product selection when in practice, relying to a large extent on the experience of more experienced colleagues. Thus the tendency for specifiers to select products used by their colleagues and the office is strong.

Parallels can be seen in the prescription of drugs by medical practitioners where prescribing habits are known to form in early clinical practice and medical schools world-wide are starting to adopt a problem based approach to learning, so that medical students can develop the skills required to evaluate critically new drugs that come onto the market (MacLeod 1999). To encourage this approach the World Health Organisation has produced a teaching aid, *Guide to Good Prescribing* (WHO 1995), which is designed to help students develop a method for selecting appropriate drugs and be less susceptible to external pressures from drug companies. There is a clear need for a similar guide addressed at young specifiers, the nearest in philosophy being *Specifying Buildings: A Design Management Perspective* (Emmitt and Yeomans 2001).

9.2   Selling to specifiers

Building materials and products manufacturers are in business to sell their products to the industry's specifiers, and to do so they must make the specifier aware of their product range. From the earliest days of mass production manufacturers have advertised their products to potential specifiers, the designers, builders and tradesmen through trade literature and advertisements in the specialist journals. Trade literature is designed with the principal objective of helping manufacturers to increase their sales and the consistency and quality is as varied as the products on offer. Product catalogues were, and still are, an effective means of selling products because they are convenient for specifiers to use and order from, through the act of specifying them in the contract documentation. Provision of typical details and specifications on floppy disk which could be imported into the construction details was the first step towards the digital revolution – it was quicker than tracing them out of the technical literature. With the rapid advances in IT has come the CD ROM and the selection of details from cyberspace. In many respects digital information is not that different from that offered in printed form, the difference is the potential for interaction between specifier and manufacturer via the web. After all, there is only so much information a specifier needs to aid the selection process.

Manufacturers have also tempted designers to use their new products through advertising in the professional journals. The first and subsequent editions of journals such *The Builder* (1843) and *The Architects' Journal* (1895) have carried advertisements from a wide range of manufacturers selling an even wider range of products and services. Advertisements are important for the journals, since the revenue generated by them from the manufacturers helps to finance the production and distribution of the journal. Some of the 'product journals' that exclusively contain advertisements are distributed free of charge to specifiers' offices because the entire cost is borne by those advertising within the journal's covers. Specifiers should also exercise a degree of caution, because many technical features in journals are little more than a reworking of a press release sent to the journal by the manufacturer, usually evident by the lack of any critical debate about the components being described.

9.2.1   *Trade representatives*

Trade literature tends to describe and illustrate typical solutions, and in many circumstances the specifier is faced with anything but typical situations, so additional information has to be requested from the manufacturer and details may need to be discussed over the telephone or face to face with the manufacturer's trade representative. For the purposes of this book the term 'trade representative' is used to cover both sales representatives and technical representatives.

Representatives form an important link between manufacturers and potential specifiers of their products, but they are an expensive resource and not all manufacturers employ them. They have a dual role, employed both to raise the awareness of the specifier to their organisation's products (a marketing role) and to provide information and help to the specifier with the aim of getting the specification (a technical and sales role). Like designers, the quality of trade representatives does vary, from those with excellent technical knowledge of building and their organisation's product range through to those who have limited experience of building but are good at selling; the former are very useful to designers, the latter are usually a waste of time because they are unable to answer the questions asked of them (furthermore, many designers do not like being sold to). Specifiers require technical knowledge and technical information to be provided quickly and accurately for, usually, a very specific purpose and the trade representatives who have empathy with the designers' concerns and can answer their queries quickly will be influential in helping the specifier to choose their products over those of a rival manufacturer. Another strategy employed by manufacturing organisations is to provide a technical helpline to answer technical queries. Sometimes these are provided instead of trade representatives, sometimes in addition to them. Again, quick and accurate responses to specific technical questions will be expected by specifiers.

9.3   Selection criteria

Designers are perhaps better known for their creative endeavours than their practical abilities, yet when it comes to detailing and product selection clients expect their professionals to act in a dependable and above all practical manner. Professional designers, such as architects and technologists, are bound by professional ethics which prevent them from accepting any financial inducement for selecting a particular product, yet they are unique as consumers in that they have to select products that are the result of the design process, marketed through carefully designed advertising and technical literature. Therefore, the possibility exists that the specifier is more likely to select the products that he or she can empathise with, e.g. the product perceived as being most sympathetic to their individual design values (Grant and Fox 1992), thus competing products may not necessarily be analysed objectively, but subjectively. Traditionally, the factors affecting choice of building product have been the characteristics of the product (its properties, or 'fitness for purpose'), its cost and its availability. However, a number of other factors are beginning to influence choice, some of which are dependent upon legislation. Such factors include the safety of the product (both during construction and in use), its estimated durability in use, its embodied energy and its environmental impact, all of which are important points to consider when specifying.

At first glance the selection of materials and products to meet a specific purpose would appear to be a relatively straightforward activity, but on closer inspection the issues to be considered and the process are complex. Decisions are influenced by other parties to the design process, such as the client, other consultants, the quantity surveyor (QS), the contractor, sub-contractors, and by the government in the form of legislation (Mackinder 1980), areas which have been addressed more recently by the Barbour Index reports (1993, 1994, 1995, 1996) and the author (Emmitt 1997a).

Information provided by manufacturers, sometimes supplemented by verbal information from the trade representative, is used by specifiers to make an informed choice about which particular product to select. When asking designers what criteria they employ, they are likely to say that they are looking for products that are fit for purpose, i.e. suit their particular requirements at a particular time. Fitness for purpose can be broken down into a number of interrelated criteria for product selection. The most important criteria will be dependent on project-specific issues and the personal characteristics of the designer and/or the design office, as follows:

(1) *Aesthetics.* For designers the aesthetic appeal of a product is often top of the selection criteria, especially where it is to be seen and experienced when the building is complete. Internal and external finishes are dependent upon the materials used.
(2) *Cost.* The cost of proprietary products is not always known to the specifier when making the selection. There are a number of reasons for this. First, manufacturers are often reluctant to give the cost of their products to the design team, for fear that the specifier will choose simply on price and not on value. Second, in the UK and Commonwealth countries where it is common to employ a QS it is the QS who gets the cost information, not the specifier. The actual cost of the product to the main contractor will be determined by the relationship the contractor has with the supplier and/or builder's merchants and the level of discount provided by the merchant on certain materials.
(3) *Availability.* Availability should be checked directly with the manufacturer. This is especially important when materials, components or systems are being specified that take time to transport to the site or have to be manufactured to order. Checking availability at the specification stage can help to eliminate problems with delivery times when work is on site.
(4) *Health and safety.* With increased attention on health and safety in recent years the specification process has become more critical in helping to minimise risk at the assembly and maintenance stages in a building's life. Specifiers need to be aware of health and safety issues concerning individual products.
(5) *Durability and performance.* The physical characteristics of components will determine the durability and performance of the building. Design life and service life need to be considered at the specification stage, and since this information is usually provided by the supplier of the product the specifier has to place a certain amount of trust in the information provided.

(6) *Replacement and maintenance.* Frequency and ease of replacement is a consideration for items which have a limited service life. Frequency, ease and cost of maintenance should also be considered when selecting one product over another.

9.3.1   Underlying issues

There are a number of underlying issues that influence product selection which may not necessarily be expressed explicitly. They are liability, environmental issues and service provision by the manufacturer.

(1) *Liability (and evidence in disputes).* The specification of a building product that may fail in use is perceived as a major cause for concern by design practices, the majority of which go to great lengths to reduce their exposure by specifying products that are known to them. A topical example would be the selection of 'green products' which represents a change in existing behaviour for the majority of designers and hence higher perceived risk.

(2) *Environmental issues.* Many design organisations have long recognised the link between product selection and environmental issues (see Fig. 9.1). Consideration should be given to the following:

    (a) *Embodied energy.* It is particularly difficult to assess the embodied energy within a product, and furthermore, few manufacturers highlight such information on their product literature. This is an area being developed by the BRE through its construction profiles scheme which aims to provide the designer with an environmental rating for particular products.

    (b) *Pollution trail.* The transportation of building products from their source of manufacture to the building site has become something of a cause for concern in recent years. Until the advent of cheap and accessible transport systems (canals then railways then road networks), building materials were sourced locally, giving rise to the wide variety of vernacular architecture. In some instances, stone and timber were recycled from redundant buildings, seen by some as a sustainable building practice. Nowadays, it is not uncommon to specify products that have been manufactured in different parts of the country, not to mention different parts of the world, and regardless of their merits regarding embodied energy, their transportation to site leaves a pollution trail: timber from Scandinavia, marble from Italy, metal fixings from Germany, suspended ceilings from the USA, plant and machinery from Japan, etc.

On an individual level, some specifiers have always pursued a policy of trying to specify products that have been manufactured locally, but not just because of concerns for the environment. The reason for using local suppliers is that they can get to site quickly if there is a problem during the building's assembly; this goes some way to supporting the local economy and it reduces transportation costs (and, of course, reduces pollution from unnecessary transportation). Whilst such a policy is admirable, it is not always feasible. Clearly the specifier has a duty to specify the product that best suits the particular requirements at the time. If the local manufacturer of, say, bricks does not produce the colour required the specifier will have to look

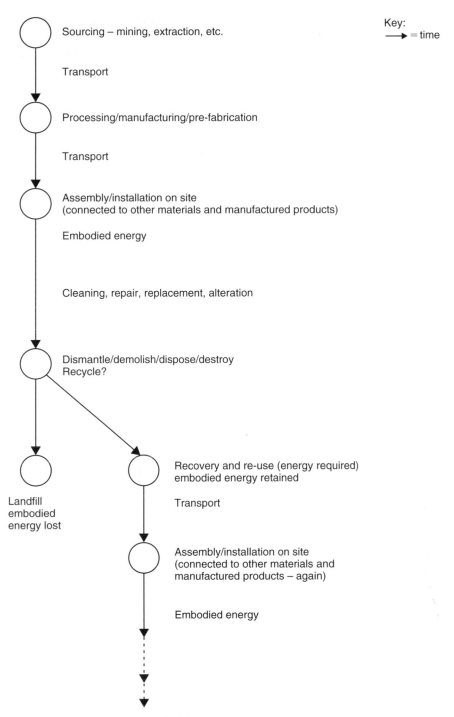

Figure 9.1   Life of a building component/building.

elsewhere. Furthermore, while some offices openly operate such a system of product selection, other offices leave it to the individual specifier to choose products, and still others have no policy on the matter.

(3) *Service provision.* For many specifiers the service provided by the manufacturing company and/or supplier may be equally as important as the characteristics of the product. Help with detailing difficult junctions and writing the specification may be welcomed by busy designers with a tight deadline to meet. Technical helplines and the prompt visit of a trade representative to assist and provide product-specific knowledge are important services that can give manufacturers competitive advantage over their immediate rivals. Typical services provided by manufacturers may include the following:

(a) Guaranteed response to technical queries (within 24 h).

(b) Bespoke design service and provision of free drawings, details, specifications and schedules.

(c) Provision of CAD files.

(d) Structural calculations for submission to building control.

(e) On-site technical support.

(f) Product-specific guarantees and warranties.

(g) Accredited installers.

Efforts to develop a working relationship between manufacturer, designer and contractor are a small investment for all parties to ensure a relatively trouble-free 'partnership'. Good working relationships help to ensure future specifications for the manufacturer, delivery of goods to site on time for the contractor and also peace of mind for the specifier, an ethos central to the development of a supply chain. There is of course, no such thing as a 'free lunch'. If drawings and specifications are provided free of charge by manufacturers then the cost of this service is built into that of individual products. Companies offering this service provide added value for specifiers, although the client and cost consultant may need some convincing. Guarantees and warranties offer a degree of comfort to the specifier, although such insurances are only valid whilst the company is still trading. Furthermore, they are only valid if the product has been installed as stated. Another service provided by some manufacturers covers accredited installers. Their product should only be installed by a number of specially trained and certified installers, which should help to ensure quality work. There may be an increase in cost for this service, but experience shows that the finished work is of a higher standard and there are fewer problems arising during the installation. Furthermore, product-specific guarantees may only be valid if the product has been installed by an accredited installer.

9.4   Searching for product information

As noted above, the volume of information available to building designers is vast. Each new project brings with it a new set of challenges and a fresh search for information to answer specific design problems. Consider a specifier working in a design office. He or she will be engaged in a whole raft of activities concerned with the design, detailing and production of a building project. In smaller offices specifiers may be working on two or more projects concurrently. Product selection is carried out within this environment, and thus the capacity to access relevant information quickly is important. There are problems with information acquisition, storage, etc., and the individual designer cannot, and should not be expected to, survey the whole body of literature available. Instead an easily accessible, accurate, concise but comprehensive body of information is required. A number of potential sources are summarised below.

(1) *Research and test reports.* Independent research and test reports published by recognised building research organisations and papers contained in peer reviewed academic journals are the best source of information.

(2) *Codes and standards.* Prescriptive and performance specifications both rely heavily on reference to current regulations, codes and standards.

(3) *Manufacturers' information.* From the manufacturers' perspective the primary aim is to raise the awareness of the specifier to their products, both those already established and those recently introduced to the market, and a number of ways in which this is achieved were discussed above.

(4) *Product catalogues.* Product catalogues such as the *Barbour Index* in the UK and *Sweets Catalog Files* in the USA provide a convenient and familiar point of reference for busy specifiers. Product catalogues are a compendium of manufacturers and their products listed under general subject headings. They do not cover all manufacturers, only those who pay to be in the compendium.

(5) *Client requirements and specifications.* Some clients, especially those who have a large portfolio of buildings, often develop their own requirements, expressed as a specification. Usually such specifications contain lists of products which the design team are forbidden to specify, usually because of concerns over health and safety issues and sometimes from bad experience of certain products by the client organisation.

(6) *Information contained in design office 'standards' and previous projects.* This information can be broken down into two categories, those products that are approved and those that are not:

    (a) *List of approved products and materials.* Most design offices maintain a list of approved products – products that are known to perform and have gone through rigorous research by the organisation to ensure quality and compliance with particular standards and regulations. Some clients insist that the design team use certain products or suppliers because they have good experience of using them, and when clients own two or more buildings the tendency to use the same products is strong simply because it makes routine cleaning, repair and replacement easier.

    (b) *List of prohibited materials and products.* Because of previous bad experience some products and/or manufacturers may get included on a prohibited list. This may because the product actually failed in use, was found to be of poor quality when delivered to site, was difficult to use on site or simply because the service provided by the manufacturer (e.g. failure to respond to technical queries on site, failure to deliver products to site to schedule) was found to be unacceptable.

(7) *The specifier's own favourite products.* In addition to the approved and prohibited lists many individual specifiers have their own personal favourites based on their individual experience, represented by a palettte of favourite products

from which they always choose unless forced to do otherwise (Mackinder 1980, Emmitt 1997a). Use of products from this personal collection reduces the amount of time spent searching for products to suit a particular situation and, because they are known to perform well (or more likely known not to fail), they offer the specifier a degree of comfort, essentially a knowledge base that is used to aid the specification process.

9.4.1   *Staying up to date and the need for comparative information*

Manufacturers are constantly seeking to improve their products and expand their market share, so products may be 'improved' or replaced as part of their strategy. Specifiers have to keep up to date with these developments in order to specify effectively. Publications found within the architects office, such as the *ASC Files*, *Barbour Compendium*, *RIBA Product Selector* and *Specification* are a compilation of individual manufacturer's building products and are published annually. The compendia, available in both paper and electronic formats, are not designed to offer advice on product selection, nor do they provide a comparative assessment of similar products; they merely list building products under separate subject headings and provide generic descriptions of materials.

There is no comparative advice on cost or performance. Thus the specifier cannot refer to a publication which provides comparative product assessment, unlike, e.g. the potential car purchaser, who can refer to specialist journals which provide comparative information about cost, performance and value for money. Although the industry journals include advertisements from building product manufacturers, they do not review the products for reliability, performance or value for money, and, therefore, specifiers can only rely on previous experience, peer group recommendation or their own judgement when selecting products. Furthermore, some of the technical articles are little more than a technical press release prepared by the manufacturer and so claims as to the product's performance need careful consideration.

9.5   Specifying design intent

Once a decision has been made to use a particular product the designer has to make reference to it in the contract documentation, i.e. it has to be 'specified'. This can be done by making reference to the product on the drawings, in schedules of work, and/or making reference to it in the written specification (see also Chapter 10). If design intent is to be translated into the assembled building then the specification must be well written, comprehensive and free of errors. The specification is an important document in ensuring a quality building for which adequate resources must be allocated. The biggest resource, and one frequently squeezed, is time – specification writing cannot be rushed. It is an essential part of the design process that requires particular skills in researching different product characteristics and being precise. In the USA it is a job carried out by qualified specification writers. In the UK the majority of design practices are small and so the specification is often written by the same person who carried out the design and detailing of the scheme, i.e. they only spend a small amount of their time dealing with specification writing.

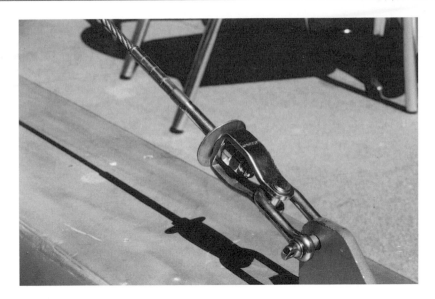

Figure 9.2 Steel anchor.

9.5.1   *Writing the specification*

Specification writing is a skill. In the USA the separate profession of specification writers carries greater importance than it does in the UK at present. In the UK, with the exception of the larger offices and as mentioned above, specification writing tends to be one of many diverse tasks expected of the professional designer – there are very few people who specialise in specification writing. Some large offices employ people to write and check specifications, leaving the designers to design and the managers to manage. Such an arrangement calls for close co-ordination between designer and specification writer. In smaller offices the designer has little option but to write his or her own specification. From experience of design management it is clear that some people are well suited to specification writing, while others are not.

Good specification writers tend to be individuals with very good technical ability and a vast amount of experience of both design and building operations. They should be precise and have an eye for minute detail. They also have to be exceptionally good at interpreting designers' drawings and communicating with people in writing. With the industry becoming increasingly litigious the specification has taken on a more important role than it had in the past. Like the drawings, the specification is a legal document and will be examined should a dispute arise. Help is to hand in the form of office policy and procedures and standard formats.

- *Office policy and procedure.* Individual organisations tend to have their own idiosyncrasies when it comes to specifications. In well-managed organisations the writing of the specification and any alterations to it are covered by QA and QC procedures which help to eliminate errors and omissions.

■ *Standard formats.* Over the years different countries have developed their own standard specifications. In the UK, the National Building Specification (NBS) is widely used. Available as computer software, it helps to make the writing of specifications a relatively straightforward affair because prompts are given to assist the writer's memory.

9.6   Specification substitution

An area of interest to manufacturers and specifiers alike is the problem of specification substitution or 'switch selling' – the substitution of a different brand product than that originally specified. It is not unusual for a contractor to propose alternative products to those specified by brand name under traditional forms of contract. In such situations the designer (or contract administrator) has to be certain that the substitution proposed is of equal quality to that originally selected because specification decisions are the responsibility of the design office, not the contractor. Because the original decision was often taken after an exhaustive search of similar products, specifiers are often reluctant to approve a contractor's request because of the time it takes to check the performance characteristics of the proposed alternative. In situations where the contract administrator is not the specifier, e.g. a project manager, the request should be referred back to the specifier for an accurate evaluation – it is unlikely that the project manager has the technical ability to make a decision to substitute.

The problem has been highlighted in the technical press (e.g. Hutchinson 1993) although with the exception of research by the Barbour Index (1993) there is little evidence to quantify the scale of the problem. Reasons for suggesting alternative products tend to be to overcome a problem with availability, to resolve a buildability problem that has arisen unexpectedly on site, or to save costs. As the case study below shows, it is worth checking the contractor's claims because they may not always be truthful. It is a well-known fact that many less reputable contractors propose alternatives simply because they can make more money on the contract – the true cost savings are rarely passed on to those funding the project. A particular 'trick' of contractors and sub-contractors is to wait until the last possible moment to request the change and to try and put the specifier under pressure to make a quick decision. Some designers do make snap decisions over the telephone and live to regret it, others refer the contractor back to the contract clauses – their QA procedures – and will not make a decision without the client's consent. Hutchinson's (1993) advice to specifiers is clear: stick to the specification at all costs.

9.6.1   *Substitution by contractors*

Another problem is that of products being substituted without the knowledge of the design team. The Barbour Index found that contractors were making changes without the knowledge of the contract administrator and sub-contractors were making changes without the knowledge of the contractor or the contract administrator. Motivation for such action is financial gain and because of this it is difficult to get quantitative evidence of the true extent of such action. Another reason why people are reluctant to discuss the extent of specification substitution is that it is an act of fraud – clients are paying for specified products and getting something else. In conversation with construction managers the extent of specification substitution would appear to be more common than suspected. Research in this area may help to shed light on its true extent and its effect on the quality and durability of the building.

In situations where the material is used externally the planning authority quite rightly takes a particular interest, but even so there are many examples of contractors changing products in order to save money which have backfired. A recent example taken from a design and build project concerns a 12-storey office building in a prominent city centre location. The contractor changed the stone cladding to the external columns of the building, substituting brickwork for the specified stonework in order to save money (the contract was running over budget). This decision was contrary to the planning approval in which the stone cladding was clearly stated. There was no discussion with the design team and the somewhat cavalier attitude adopted by the contracts manager was that the change would be made, and then the argument had with the planners (which of course he believed he would win). This considerable cost saving backfired when the planners noticed the change and served an enforcement notice, so making the contractor comply with the planning consent: an expensive mistake. The point being made here is that it is essential to check with the design team before any changes are made on site.

Manufacturers are concerned about the extent of specification substitution occurring at different points in the design and construction process. Many manufacturers invest a lot of resources in product development and marketing. They also spend a lot of time on 'getting' the specification through the action of their trade representatives. Once specified they have their work cut out to retain the specification until such time as their products are ordered, delivered to site and built into the building, highlighted in the case study below. For the manufacturers of cheaper products specification substitution is where they get a lot of their sales and they will expend considerable effort in trying to change the specification in their favour, i.e. getting the 'switch'. They know that the allure of cheaper products is often difficult to resist, especially if they can get the point across to the contractor and the client. As noted above, the product should be scrutinised on a wide range of characteristics, not just cost, before making any decision to change the original specification.

9.6.2   *Change of mind*

It is not all one-way traffic. Designers have been known to change their mind, usually because of time or cost pressures and brand name specifications are changed, sometimes before the job gets to the construction phase, sometimes when the job is in progress. Care needs to be taken that the change does not repudiate the contract. The contractor will want some form of compensation, usually in an extension of the contract period or costs for accelerating the work to accommodate the change if it is anything other than a very minor variation. Another issue concerns the time elapsed between the initial specification decision and commencement on site. In fast-track projects the time span from planning permission to commencement can be short; in other projects the time from specification to actual assembly of the product can be lengthy, during which time some products may change, circumstances may change and costs can vary dramatically, especially in periods of over- or undersupply, and so changes may be necessary.

9.6.3 Auditing the specification process

In line with a well-implemented and managed QA scheme there is a need to audit the specification process, both in the design office and during the contract stage to ensure compliance with the specification. In an attempt to control specification substitution some manufacturers and researchers are looking at the possibility of bar coding (electronically tagging) their products, for ease of identification during building and at any future date when the building may be remodelled and/or recycled and the materials recovered.

9.7 Over-specification?

With increased emphasis on cost and value for money comes the issue of 'over-specification'. Given the amount of cost associated with building components it comes as no surprise that product specification forms a major part of any value management exercise. As it is carried out before the drawings are sent out to tender there may be pressure to substitute products with cheaper ones. Sometimes over-specification is only evident when a building is finally demolished or substantially remodelled. Under-specification usually becomes evident when a component or system fails.

9.7.1 Three specification levels

Manufactured consumer products do not all occupy the same market segment. Some occupy the luxury end of the market and carry a high purchase cost to reflect their (alleged) quality. Other products occupy the middle ground and may be equally as long lasting but do not carry the same level of detail, etc. Third, there is the budget market, where products are not expected to be of the same quality as those with a high price tag. Putting aside environmental concerns for a minute, a similar argument could be made for buildings. They are not all expected to last for ever. All buildings are built with a design life, a figure that varies with the use and importance of the building. Design life needs to be stated and reflected in product selection and specification standards. Thus there is a need for different quality levels in specification instead of constantly trying to specify the 'best' product each time. Clients would need to sign up to such initiatives so that the designer is covered for using the 'budget' specification. There could be three levels of specification that exist for entire buildings and for generic product types. Combined with a policy on disposal and recycling to maximise embodied energy the clear stratification of product quality may help to address over-specification of products and hence reduce costs and waste.

■ *Premium.* The highest level of specification available covering top quality products from reputable manufacturers who also provide added value in the service to specifiers and builders. This would be used for prestigious buildings and those with a long design life.

■ *Standard.* Not the best available products, but those with an established pedigree from reputable manufacturers. This level of specification would be the most commonly used and would have a design life of, say, 50 years maximum.

■ *Budget.* Used for clients who (regardless of environmental impact) want a building to last for a short period of time, say 15 years, after which time it will be dismantled and (hopefully) recycled. In such situations the specification of durable products with a long design life would be wasteful. Cheap products with limited guarantees would be used here.

9.8 Case study – Observing the act of specification

This case study is based on the observation of a specifier in an architect's office. The specifier had 2 weeks to produce the working drawings for four single-storey retail units. Three of the four were to be built with timber rafters and concrete interlocking roof tiles, the fourth was to be detailed with a structural metal tray and a profiled steel roof to suit a particular client's requirements.

He first detailed the three units with the tiled roof, a task carried out quickly because he was familiar with this form of construction. He had used a very similar roof construction on a previous project, and the drawings produced for it were used to gain information for use here, thus reinforcing the tendency to use familiar products. When he attempted to detail the metal roof, a form of construction that was unfamiliar to him, he was unable to draw on his previous experience because he had not worked on any similar projects, although other specifiers in the office had. Since his personal collection of literature did not contain any information which could help him he was forced to look for products that might solve his particular need: he was forced to search for information about building products that would be new to him (see Fig. 9.3).

9.8.1 *Innovation A*

Rather than check the office library or the product compendia for suitable products his first action was to ask other specifiers in the office if they had experience of detailing such a roof; so drawing on the collective experience of the office, an action he later said was taken to save time. A colleague suggested a product that the office had used successfully before, Product A, but which was new to the specifier. He spent approximately 10 minutes talking to his colleague to gain more information and to establish whether or not the product was suitable for his particular requirements. Then he then sought further information about the product from the office library.

Because the trade literature was not comprehensive enough to solve all of his queries he telephoned the manufacturer to request additional literature. The manufacturer offered to send a trade representative (the change agent in Rogers' terms) to the office to assist with any queries: this was declined by the specifier who later said that he did not have sufficient time to see the representative. Information was received by post 3 days after the request (during which time the specifier had been working on another project). After reading the information he made a decision to specify Product A and continued with his detail design work.

(continued)

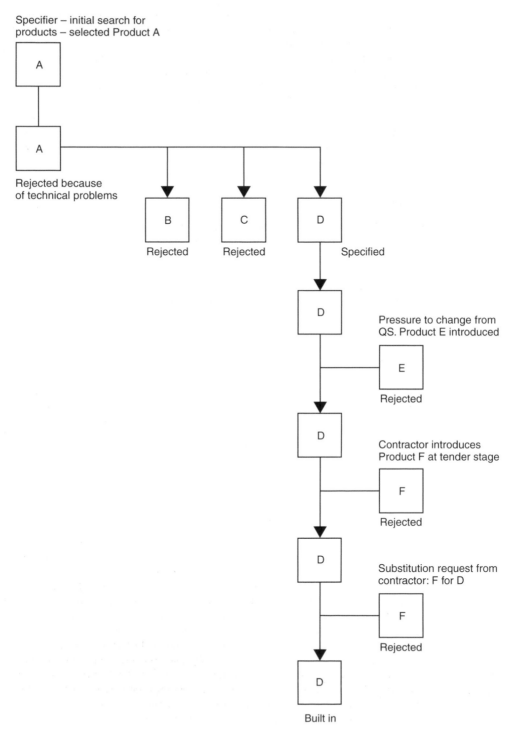

Specifier – initial search for
products – selected Product A

A

A

Rejected because
of technical problems

B

C

D

Rejected   Rejected   Specified

D

Pressure to change from
QS. Product E introduced

E

Rejected

D

Contractor introduces
Product F at tender stage

F

Rejected

D

Substitution request from
contractor: F for D

F

Rejected

D

Built in

Figure 9.3 Steps in the specification process (from Emmitt 1997a: 196, adapted).

While detailing the roof he discovered a technical problem that he could not resolve from the literature so he telephoned the manufacturer's technical department for clarification. During the telephone conversation it became clear that Product A would have to be modified to resolve his particular problem, but the manufacturer did not have a 'standard solution' simply because it had not considered such a possibility arising. This resulted in a state of dissatisfaction on behalf of the specifier, who immediately went to the office library to search out an alternative. He did not use the electronic database or the printed product compendia, he selected entirely from the trade literature on the shelf, a search pattern he later confirmed to be the quickest way of finding suitable products, further emphasising the time pressures exerted during the detail design stage.

9.8.2   Innovations B, C and D

From his search in the library a further three building product innovations were selected. The library contained trade literature from 10 manufacturers of similar metal roofing products, seven of which were rejected simply because their technical details in the literature were seen to be of 'poor quality' by the specifier. On returning to his work station the specifier telephoned all three manufacturers to question them about their products. Product B was discounted because the technical representative was perceived as not knowing his product well enough (described as a 'complete idiot' by the specifier). Product C was rejected because the company would only answer technical queries by sending a trade representative to the office; since the earliest appointment would be too late for the specifier to complete his task to programme the product was rejected. Product D was adopted because the technical representative 'knew his stuff' and had offered some additional practical advice to the specifier which helped him to complete his detailing quickly. In line with office policy the specifier went and spoke to the organisation's technical partner who was responsible for granting approval for the use of any product that was new to the office. Following a short discussion approval was granted and the specifier returned to his desk to resume his detailing of the roof. Product D was referred to by name on the drawings and later in the accompanying written specification.

9.8.3   Pressure to change – Innovation E

The production information was then sent to the QS for production of the bills of quantities and also for a cost check of the design against the original budget. During the 3 weeks that the QS took to complete this task he telephoned the specifier to suggest an alternative to that specified in order to save money. The alternative, Product E, was unknown to the specifier so it constituted a further building product innovation, one introduced to him by a contributor to the design process who was primarily concerned with the cost of the product, not its technical performance. This illustrated the contribution made from outside the architect's office during the specification process, with pressure to change the specified product and also the introduction of a product that was known to the QS but not the architectural office.

Product E was immediately rejected by the specifier simply because he had invested a lot of time in solving a particular problem and did not want to go through the process again with a different product and different fixing details. He made no attempt to analyse the information, despite the potential cost savings reported by the QS. As a result Product D survived this first attempt at specification substitution and was included in the

(continued)

documentation sent out to competitive tender. Again time pressures appeared to be of paramount importance to the specifier.

9.8.4 *A further innovation*

The lowest tenderer was accepted, but the contractor had also submitted a list of products he wished to substitute to save money. Twenty-three products had been identified, ranging from the facing bricks and cavity insulation to the ironmongery for the internal doors, plus the steel roofing system, Product D. Thus a further innovation had been introduced, Product F. The client asked the specifier to analyse the cheaper specification. Although the specifier wanted to reject the substituted products immediately, further information had to be sought so that a report could be made to the client. He telephoned the manufacturer and asked a number of questions about delivery and guarantees. The answers raised further issues to be investigated and since he did not have the time to pursue them he rejected all of the substituted products, including Product F, recommending to the client that the cheaper products were of insufficient quality. The contractor was appointed with no change to the original contract documents. Product D had survived.

9.8.5 *Adoption*

Further attempts to change a number of products, including Product D, were made by the contractor once the project had started on site, confirming evidence of specification substitution (Hutchinson 1993), although in the event all were refused. First the contractor claimed that the specified product could not be delivered to suit his programme and proposed Product F again. This was found to be untrue when the specifier checked with the manufacturer who confirmed that the contractor had made no attempt to place an order for Product D (presumably the contractor had hoped that the specifier would accede to his wishes without checking). The request was refused. After the first request had failed the contractor again proposed that Product F be substituted to save money (for whom was never made clear), but again this was refused by a specifier keen to see his design decision transferred from drawing board to finished building. Eventually Product D was delivered to site, to programme, and built into the building without any problems being reported from site. Thus, after a number of attempts to change it, it had finally been implemented. Towards the end of the project the specifier added Product D to his personal collection of literature for use at a future date. It had now become part of his personal inventory of products.

9.8.6 *Reflection on the act*

Although the specifier described himself as creative and always looking out for new products he was aware that his actual behaviour was contrary to this. He claimed that he was 'forced to be conservative' about product selection and detailing because of his, and the office's, concerns about building product failure. Products that were new to the office carried with them a perceived enhancement of risk. His risk management technique relied on the specification of products that he had used previously, or, failing that, those used by the office. His collection of literature had been assembled over a long period in the building industry from products that he said were 'known to perform', i.e. he was fairly confident that when detailed and implemented correctly these products

(continued)

would not fail. He also said that he tried to stick to products he had used previously because the time pressures imposed on him by both the design programme and the construction programme rarely allowed him any time to investigate alternatives.

At the time of the observation the specifier was working on three other jobs, all at different stages, and all with demanding programmes, and thus the potential for investigating manufacturers' claims as to the performance of their products was very limited, serving to reinforce the established products. Again there are parallels with medical research. Studies into repeat prescribing (Harris and Dajda 1996) found that medical drugs were prescribed without further reference to the doctor by the patient (primarily to save time), thus reinforcing the use of a familiar drug. Like the patient's drugs, the products have not been reassessed, merely applied because they worked successfully before. The danger is that the situation might not be the same and both the patient and the building might not be getting the correct prescription. In both cases any problems will only become evident with the passage of time.

One of the issues highlighted in this observation was the impact (and potential impact) of other parties to the design and assembly process. At different stages in the innovation–decision process contributions were made from outside the architect's office by individuals with different priorities to those of the specifier, and the pressure to change specifications is something a specifier has to deal with, not just during the design phase but during the assembly process as well. Interestingly, the external contributors to the specification process have the potential both to resist and to promote innovations, a complex issue that requires further investigation.

From the architectural firm's point of view, this behaviour could be seen as good practice, since it shows effective use of time and risk avoidance techniques. As pressure on time and resources increases there is likely to be greater reliance on standard details, products and design typologies – the tendency may be to reinforce conservative behaviour and reduce the potential for the specification of products new to the office unless absolutely necessary. On the other hand it could be argued that this is bad practice because the tendency to stick to familiar products stifles creativity. Furthermore, many standard details have design faults and many products prove to be less durable than the manufacturers claimed some time after they have been used in the building.

From the building product manufacturer's perspective, marketing strategies need to consider both the specifier and other members of the design and assembly team because of the many opportunities to change the original specification. For those manufacturers attempting to bring new products to market there will be little comfort in the specifier's behaviour because their products are only likely to be considered when the favoured products are not appropriate or a new situation arises. Once specified the trick is in keeping the product specified until the moment it is built into the building. For the manufacturer attempting to gain market share through specification substitution this case study has shown that many opportunities exist, although there may be resistance from the specifier, especially where time is at a premium.

9.8.7   Conclusion

Product selection, it would appear, is a very personal and individual act relying primarily on the specifier's inventory of favourite materials, yet influenced by other parties to the project. Furthermore, the specification process was shown to be as much concerned with managerial skills, to get design intent into the built product, as it was with technical skills, with the professional resisting more commercial pressures to protect the integrity of the

(continued)

finished building and to limit his firm's exposure to risk. The case study has shown that specifiers actively search out building product innovations only when the need arises, and not before. The implication is that the adoption of 'new' products may face considerable resistance, not just from the specifier, but also from the other contributors to the specification process. At different stages in a building's life cycle decisions regarding the selection of building products are made, both at design stage and during maintenance, repair and improvement programmes. At all of these stages the specifier will go through the innovation–decision stage and the long-term durability of the building will be reliant on, and affected by, the building products actually used. By gaining a fuller understanding of the individual's innovation–decision process, both professional design offices and building product manufacturers may be better equipped to consider the use of materials and products that can contribute to an environmentally responsible approach to building.

Further reading

Emmitt, S. and Yeomans, D.T. (2001). *Specifying Buildings: A Design Management Perspective*, Butterworth-Heinemann, Oxford.
Woolley, T., Kimmins, S., Harrison, P. and Harrison, R. (1997). *Green Building Handbook: A Guide to Building Products and Their Impact on the Environment*, E & FN Spon, London.

10 Communicating design intent

An essential requirement of the professional design firm is to be able to produce clear, concise production information that can be used to assemble the diverse range of materials and components into a high quality structure. This chapter looks at communication skills and the media used to convey information from designer to assembler. The media considered are drawings, models, schedules of work, specifications, reports and oral instructions, i.e. tools used to convey design intent. This is followed by an overview of IT and its potential for improving communication and information flow: CAD, knowledge bases and virtual details are discussed. Synthesis of disparate information through the effective co-ordination of information chains is explored, as are design changes and the challenge of producing timely information of sufficient quality.

10.1   Communication skills

With the exception of artisans and the designer-craftsman, designers work and communicate indirectly (Potter 1989). Their creative work is expressed in the form of instructions to manufacturers, other consultants, contractors and sub-contractors, usually in the form of drawings and written documents collectively known as 'production information' (see Fig. 10.1). It follows that manufacture, design and construction rely on effective communication to achieve quality artefacts. Instructions must be clear, concise, complete, free of errors, meaningful, relevant and timely to those receiving them. At every stage in the process the ability to communicate is essential. Designs need to be explained and defended to colleagues, consultants, planners and of course the client. Discussion, argument, compromise and (hopefully) agreement are integral parts of the whole; thus

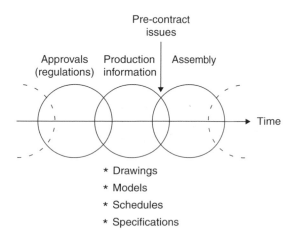

Figure 10.1   Production information.

communication media need very careful consideration – the selection of one medium over another chosen to satisfy a particular set of circumstances. Yet the ability to communicate design intent from client, through inception, detail, tendering and then assembly on site, is often taken for granted, especially the verbal and written elements. Professionals should get it right every time, but for a variety of reasons communication can be ineffective, leading to abortive work, increased costs and time overruns, and in the worst cases result in expensive and protracted disputes which few, other than the legal profession, benefit from. Mistakes can happen through misinterpretation, omission and error which often leads to disputes, and in the worst cases conflict (see Chapter 11).

Michael Brawne (1992), in his book *From Idea to Building*, makes the point that architectural ideas require considerable effort, discipline and commitment if they are to stand any chance of translation into buildings. Effort, discipline and commitment are all necessary if ideas, technical data and instructions are to be transferred to a diverse range of people effectively and efficiently. Sending all of the information to everyone involved in a particular project is now possible with electronic distribution through the internet or an intranet, but the issue of relevance and information overload needs very careful consideration. The tools of communication are oral, written or drawn, or physical models, video and physical gestures. All to lesser or greater extents will assist in the evolution of the design and the delivery of the building. Whatever the media being utilised, there are a number of 'golden rules' that need to be constantly borne in mind.

10.1.1   *Golden rules*

Designers and design offices have differing views of how information should be prepared and presented. However, the following golden rules should apply whatever the circumstances:

(1) *Clarity and brevity.* The most effective information has clarity and is concise. This is far easier to state than to achieve because it is impossible to represent everything in an individual's mind on a drawing or in text. The skill is to convey only what is perceived to have relevance and hence value to the intended receiver. This helps to avoid information overload on the part of the receiver and should allow the receiver time to look at relevant information only. Repetition should be avoided (see below).

(2) *Timeliness.* Good quality information received at the right time is valuable. Good quality information received late is, arguably, valueless (except for use in disputes!). Thus the timing of information issued needs careful consideration in relation to the various programmes that run during the design and assembly phases.

(3) *Repetition.* Repetition of information in different documents is unnecessary, is wasteful of resources and, when repeated slightly differently (which it invariably is), can lead to confusion. Repetition should be avoided and a good management system, with its checklists and controls, utilised to minimise repetition.

(4) *Check, double check and check again.* Not too long ago it was common for drawing offices to employ someone to check all drawings and specifications before

they were released from the office. In the constant drive for efficiency and ever tighter deadlines for the production of information such checks have been left to the individuals producing the information. Self-checking is suspect, and subject to error simply because of the originator's over-familiarity with the material.

10.1.2   Written instructions and reports

As part of day-to-day business there is a need to record matters in writing. Like drawings and specifications (discussed below) these are a record of decisions taken, are essential for the smooth running of projects, and will be used as evidence in the event of a dispute. Written communications should be more concise, more discrete (there is no guarantee who may read them), more accurate and free of ambiguity than oral communications. They need care and dedication in their composition, i.e. time is required to ensure that the message contained in the text is that intended. In contrast to oral communication the response and feedback will be less immediate (even with e-mail).

- *Letters.* Letters are important for requesting and confirming action or simply to bring someone's attention to a particular issue. Letter writing is a skill and one in decline with the use of e-mail, which has been criticised because users adopt a more casual (careless) form of writing. It should be remembered that e-mail can (and will) be used as evidence if required.
- *Reports.* Reports are read (as are drawings) by people at a time that suits them. They may be tired, short of time, impatient or disturbed when reading them, and the originator has no control over how receivers assimilate the material contained within the report. Misinterpretation can occur and the opportunity to ask questions may be limited.
- *Notes on drawings.* These should be legible (if hand drawn), concise, relevant and used sparingly to avoid any repetition with other written documents, such as the specification. Many design offices discourage notes on drawings, preferring to use the elemental drawing system (discussed below).
- *Variation orders and instructions.* Essentially these are a contractual way of confirming action and/or variations to contract documentation which can be costed.

10.1.3   Oral communication

Oral communication skills are essential for designers. At various stages in the life of a building project designers will have to explain their ideas and intentions verbally, usually with the use of written and graphical material. Designers have to communicate with one another within a design office, with other designers and consultants in other offices (by telephone), with those representing legislative bodies, with local interest groups, contractors, sub-contractors, building users and of course their clients. The different skills required are explored in Chapter 13 in more detail, but the point is worth making here that empathy with others in the communication channel is vital to getting the message across. There are a number of different situations where verbal communication is used, often aided by drawings and sketches, which need to be recorded in writing and distributed for information/action. Not only is it good practice to record oral communication, it is an essential requirement of quality management systems:

- *Formal meetings.* Design reviews, meetings with planning officers and site meetings will be necessary at different stages in the project to discuss and hopefully agree a way forward. They must be planned and structured in a professional manner and recorded (minuted) accurately with clear points of action and time frames in which to complete the tasks.
- *Informal site meetings/inspections.* Whether these are minuted or recorded in the job diary is a matter for the way in which organisations manage their jobs. Those using quality management schemes will be obliged to record a summary of such meetings as evidence of decisions made.
- *Design reviews.* Design reviews are an excellent tool to discuss and agree project-specific issues. Again the meeting should be minuted and any decisions made 'signed off' by the client for record purposes.
- *Client presentations.* The manner in which client presentations are made will, to a certain extent, vary depending upon the client (a householder or a multinational company) and the size of the project. Thus some will involve one-to-one communication during which informal presentation skills will be most effective, others will involve large scale presentations to a client panel, committee or even an audience and require different media and more formal presentation skills.
- *Telephone conversations.* Telephone conversations are an excellent way of solving minor queries and reporting issues quickly and cheaply. All conversations should be recorded in the designer's individual job diary for evidence in the event of any discrepancies or disputes arising.

10.1.4 Media and their different uses

Whatever combination of media is used to convey design intent from the mind of the designer to that of the individuals doing the assembly it must be remembered that this information has uses other than a set of instructions from which to build. Letters, reports, operating instructions, maintenance manuals, drawings, schedules and specifications may be used for one or more of the following purposes:

- *As an aid to the development of the detail design before it is finalised.* Media can be used as an aid to recall and decision-making, so drawings, notes and diagrams are important tools for developing design ideas.
- *As an aid to co-ordination.* During the detail design phase information is provided by a number of different providers, from manufacturers and specialist subcontractors, structural and services engineers, to design, etc., to aid co-ordination.
- *For contract documentation.* Arguably the main focus of the production information, this is used by a variety of individuals to assemble the building.
- *As a design record.* Drawings and specifications will form the main part of the 'as built' documentation. Combined with maintenance information, operating instructions, warranties and guarantees this should be handed over to the building owner on completion. It is important information for the effective

operation of the building and also for reference when considering alterations and/or improvements at a future date.

- *As evidence in disputes.* Should a dispute arise during or after construction then the production information and any project documentation, e.g. letters and file notes, will be required as evidence, either to support or to defend a particular claim.
- *For facilities (asset) management.* As an aid to making decisions, such as space planning, maintenance, remodelling, etc., during the life of the building.
- *For recycling and disposal.* As a record document to aid with the effective and safe recycling/disposal of an existing building that has exceeded its service life.

10.2   Drawings

At this point it is worth remembering that we are not producing drawings for art's sake, we are producing them so that we can communicate ideas from the mind of one individual to the mind of others. The poetry of an idea can be conveyed through simple line drawings, well-chosen words and/or models. An interesting couple of questions have been posed by Pye (1968) which, adapted to building, are: how far is it possible to prescribe the qualities of the building in words, figures and drawings so that the designer's intentions are fully obeyed? And, is it necessary to leave anything to the worker's discretion?

First, in principle, it is possible for the design team to prescribe fully all of the properties required and to provide a full description of the building, through the use of drawings, specifications and written instructions. In practice this information is often found to be inadequate when received on site, simply because users have interpreted the information differently to that which was intended. An appreciation of and empathy with the user's requirements will help. This allows an opportunity to answer the second question. Clearly, by providing incomplete, vague or confusing information the designer is providing an opportunity for the worker to use his or her discretion. Was this the intention? In some areas of work, e.g. in work to existing buildings, it is sometimes necessary to allow the craftsman a certain degree of latitude (some would argue that drawings are of little use; instead the tacit knowledge of the skilled craftsman is more useful, with drawings to record the finished work). These areas are explored more fully below.

Drawings are one of the most effective ways of communicating information between all members of the building team. Because there are so many different parties to a building project the complexity, style and type of drawing may vary considerably, ranging from simple freehand sketches to explain a concept, through to complex detail drawings with a specific purpose. Designers use drawings as an aid to the development of designs and details as well as for transmitting information to others. Perhaps it is because building designers spend so much time engaged in the act of drawing that they sometimes forget that reading a drawing and understanding it fully takes quite a lot of skill and experience. This is important to remember when using drawings to communicate with the uninitiated, clients and members of public, and sometimes the people on site. Committee members may have little or no experience of reading drawings – they will need some help. Another associated problem is that drawings are used by many different disciplines during the design process and during construction – what is clear to one person may not be to another. While there is no guarantee that a drawing will be clear to every viewer, the originator should constantly bear in mind the risk of confusion. Drawings are a means to an end for the recipient, their expressive content being strictly limited to the conveying of instructions; they are not the end product in the process (Potter 1989). It follows that drawings are used for a number of very different purposes during the design process.

10.2.1   Design development drawings

Design development drawings may take many forms, ranging from a few lines drawn on the 'back of an envelope' to explain a principle or idea, through sketches to aid an individual's design decision-making process, to more detailed representations for discussion by others. Drawing is a visible manifestation of part of the thinking process. Visualisation helps to develop ideas and hence aids the creative design decision-making process. Diagrams, plans, sections and three-dimensional sketches provide a glimpse into the mind of the designer, the black box. As an aid to design thinking drawings are particularly important. Architects are trained to develop designs from first principles, exploring possibilities and evolving the design through constant drawing and redrawing. Diagrams and patterns are important graphical tools in getting ideas over very quickly. The importance of graphical representation through diagrams is well established, a famous example being the London Underground map. Patterns are important to designers and have cultural importance in some societies, such as Islamic ones. Repetition of simple units to form patterns, either by hand or by machine, has long been recognised. Whatever the pattern, be it squares, triangles, octagons or circles and with or without the use of colour, the dominant feature is the line (Day 1903).

Because sketching and drawing is an aid to decision-making, a graphical record of part of the designer's thinking process; these design development drawings and any source documentation should be kept as a record of the design process, which alongside a well-managed quality management system, may be useful in the event of a dispute. They also provide an excellent source of reference when making changes to the design at a future date.

10.2.2   Presentation drawings

Presentation drawings have one aim, to help sell the scheme, whether it is to the client, funding agencies, local community groups or the local authority planning committee. However, commonly the drawings are supported by written information and are often presented at some form of presentation, during which verbal skills are particularly important in helping to put over the pertinent points. A careful and considered approach to presentation is key to success. An ability to put oneself in the position of the individuals receiving the information is crucial because it is necessary to appreciate different audiences' ability to comprehend different types of presentation. Getting the presentation at the right level will assist with audience comprehension and will (hopefully) result in support for the concepts being aired. Presentations should be prepared in advance and delivered with as much skill as that which went into the design. Presentations should have an introduction, main content and a conclusion.

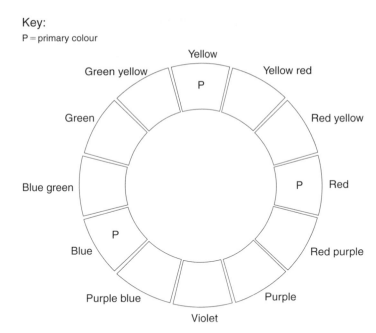

Key:
P = primary colour

Figure 10.2   Colour circle.

The amount of detail included on the set of presentation drawings will vary from office to office and with the complexity of the scheme. It is usual to include all elevations, all floor plans and roof plan along with a number of sections and three-dimensional drawings as appropriate. If submitting the drawings as part of a planning application it is necessary to indicate the type and colour of materials to be used on the building and its immediate environs. Usually planning officers request that samples of the materials to be used externally are also submitted for approval. Because of the complexity of many schemes and the complexity of the planning process it is also standard practice to support planning applications with written documents explaining the design philosophy and including any additional studies and reports which may be necessary to achieve consent. Colour is a further consideration (Fig. 10.2). Colour can be used very effectively for presentation purposes, especially for identifying different project phases and/or different room usage. Care is required because colour symbolism varies between different cultures.

10.2.3   *Production drawings*

Production drawings ('blueprints') are the main vehicle of communicating the physical layout of the design and the juxtaposition of components to those responsible for putting it all together on site. Referred to as contract information or production information, this set of drawings is usually complex and extensive. Not only does it take a great deal of time and skill to produce the drawings and co-ordinate them with those produced by other consultants, but also it is a skill to read all the information contained and encoded in lines, figures and symbols. It is this set of drawings that the main contractor will use to cost the building work and (subject to any revisions prior to starting work) will be the set of drawings from which the building will be assembled. At its most basic, the contract drawings will comprise drawings produced by the structural engineers, the designers and the mechanical and electrical consultants. Other contributors to this set of drawings may include interior designers, landscape designers, specialist sub-contractors, highway consultants, etc.

10.2.4 Dimensions on drawings and standard notations

Drawings should never be scaled to ascertain dimensions. Dimensions should be clearly shown so that there can be no ambiguity. If someone does scale a drawing, then it is a sure sign that the information provided is inadequate and a vital dimension is unclear or missing. One of the biggest complaints from site operatives of designers is that dimensions are missing, or that the drawing has been set out in such a way as to make the actual setting out on site impossible to complete from the information provided. Apart from the inconvenience caused to builder and designer there is always a danger that the dimension given (often verbally) is given incorrectly, or is interpreted incorrectly, resulting in abortive work on site that someone has to pay for. All drawings should be checked by someone other than the originator in the design office prior to issue. Standard notations are a useful shortcut for designers, ranging from north points, arrows (indicating the rise of a staircase), hatching on construction drawings to indicate the difference between brickwork and blockwork, electrical socket positions, etc. They help to save time and can help with consistency (assuming everyone is using the same notation).

10.2.5 The elemental drawing system

A drawing system which aims to reduce repetition and overcome defects in less well co-ordinated systems is the elemental method. The elemental method is based on a four-category system, starting with the location drawings, focusing on the assembly drawings, then the component drawings and finally the schedules. Each drawing has a code and a number relating to the CI/SfB construction classification system. There are four codes, namely 'L' for location, 'A' for assembly, 'C' for component, and 'S' for schedule.

(1) *Location drawings (Code L).* The purpose of this collection of drawings is primarily to serve as a reference guide to supporting drawings and schedules as well as providing essential setting out dimensions. They are used to identify, locate and dimension the design, using plans, sections and elevations. Sometimes described as layout drawings, they are specific to a particular site, comprising the site location plan (1:1250), the site layout (1:200 or 1:100), floor plans (1:100 or 1:50), elevations (1:100 or 1:50) and sections (1:50 or 1:20). They are also used for the location of services, e.g. the drainage layout.
(2) *Assembly drawings (Code A).* These drawings show how different parts of the building fit together, their juxtaposition within the assembly. They show the shape and dimensions of a particular part and how it relates to other parts of the assembly. References to these drawings will be found on the location

drawings. Typical scales used are $1:50$, $1:20$, $1:10$ and $1:5$. Many of these will be sourced from the office standard details and adjusted to suit the particular requirements of an individual design. A typical range of assembly drawings would cover junctions between elements, e.g. the wall to roof junction.

(3) *Component drawings (Code C)*. These drawings are used to show how component parts of a building are to be manufactured, usually off site. They show the geometry of the particular component and (finished) dimensions. Typical scales used are $1:5$, $1:2$ and full size $(1:1)$. Examples would be door and window assembly, special bricks, etc.

(4) *Schedules (Code S)*. Schedules are used to describe items of construction that cannot be dealt with in adequate detail on the assembly or component drawings. Items commonly scheduled include ironmongery, sanitary fittings, doors, windows, finishes, etc. These should be compiled as the drawings proceed and be cross-referenced to the specification to avoid the possibility of errors. As noted above, the drawing numbers are taken from Table 1 'Elements' of the CI/SfB construction classification system (see Chapter 13).

It is worth remembering that drawings and other media produced by the design organisation are an effective marketing tool. Accuracy and consistency indicate a well-managed organisation. Too much repetition and too many mistakes are indicative of sloppy procedures and poor managerial control. Clients are difficult to attract and retain; excellence is expected in everything a professional design organisation produces – a point just as relevant to the glossy brochure and client presentation as it is to the drainage layout or the ironmongery schedule.

10.3 Models

Architectural models have long been an effective way of communicating design ideas to people who are not familiar with the special language used in construction, and who may find drawings and specifications difficult to read, e.g. the general public and clients. Physical models have an advantage over drawings in that they represent space and form in three dimensions much more effectively than two-dimensional drawings. It is common practice for the modelling process (physical or computer generated) to run parallel with the sketching and drawing activities – another form of visualisation that assists the evolution of the design. With the uptake of computer based drawing packages the use of physical models has declined, simply because they are more time consuming and hence more expensive to produce than virtual models.

10.3.1 Design development models

Some designers use models in conjunction with drawings to develop their design at both the conceptual and design stages. Sometimes referred to as 'massing' models they help with spatial representation and rarely contain much detail. A variety of materials may be used, from modelling clay to recycled cardboard, i.e. cheap materials that can be adjusted quickly as the design develops and readily discarded. The use of three-dimensional modelling on computers has resulted in a decline in the use of design development models because the generation of a virtual model is usually quicker and cheaper than making a physical one. This is especially true of computer packages that are based on the development of the design in three dimensions (rather than two).

10.3.2 Presentation models

Drawings and computer simulations are very effective communication tools. So are physical scale models. The cost of producing them increases with the amount of detail required and specialist architectural model makers may be required. Clients, planning committees and local pressure groups like physical models because the concepts being presented are easier to grasp than in two dimensions. Many major schemes utilise models, in addition to computer generated graphics, to get the idea across to the many individuals likely to view the proposals.

10.3.3 Detailed mock-ups

Used in manufacturing and production, full scale models help to develop and hone the design before going into production. Again, mock-ups are being replaced by computer software packages.

10.3.4 Sample boards

Samples of finishes and colours are sometimes provided on a sample board to allow the client to get some idea of the overall scheme. They are an essential component of the designer's (especially interior designer's) presentation – materials and finishes can be touched and experienced. Colour, texture and scent can be experienced first hand, and, arguably, computer graphics and models fail in this regard. There can be no substitute for the real thing.

10.4 Schedules

Schedules are a useful tool when describing locations in buildings where there is a repetition of information that would be too cumbersome to put on drawings. Particularly well suited to computer software spreadsheets, a schedule is a written document that lists the position of repetitive elements, such as structural columns, windows, doors, drainage inspection chambers and room finishes. For example, rooms are given their individual code and listed on a finishes schedule which will relate room number, use and the finish to be applied to the ceiling, walls and floor. A finishes schedule and colour schedule provides an illustration as follows:

Room no.	Use	Ceiling	Walls	Floor	Woodwork
Finishes schedule					
202a	Reception	Plaster	Plaster	Tiles	MDF
203	Office	Suspended	Lining paper	Carpet	Timber
Colour schedule					
202a	Reception	White	Terracotta	–	White gloss
203	Office	White	Magnolia	–	White gloss

10.5   Specifications

Drawings, models and schedules cannot convey the whole message, so they have to be supplemented with descriptive information. On very small projects this information is often provided in the form of notes on drawings, but for the majority of projects the descriptive information is extensive and is contained in the specification. The word specification is used in two different ways in the building industry. On the one hand it is a term used to describe the selection of a product (as discussed in the previous chapter) and on the other it refers to a physical document which contains a written description of standards of work and the performance of materials and products. Discussion here is concerned with the written specification.

Specifications are written documents that describe the requirements with which the service or product has to conform, i.e. its defined quality. It is the specification (not the drawings) that determines the quality of building construction. Like drawings specifications do vary in their size, layout and complexity. In all but the smallest of design offices it is common for specifications to be written by someone other than the designer, so communication between designer and specification writer is particularly important. The majority of designers are visually orientated people whose skills are best employed in the conceptual and detailed design phases, and, therefore, few have time to be involved in the physical writing of the document: this task is usually undertaken by a technologist or construction project manager, someone with more technical and managerial skills. Specification writers require an appreciation of the designer's intention and the ability to write technical documents clearly, concisely and accurately. They also need to be able to cross-reference items without repetition. Standard formats form a useful template for designers and help to ensure a degree of consistency. In the UK the National Building Specification (NBS) is widely used because it helps to save time and is familiar to other parties to the design and assembly process.

Responsibility for the written specification is the architect's, although in the UK it is not uncommon for the QS to contribute to the process of its preparation. In Mackinder's survey of practices it was common practice to use a *standard specification* where possible to save time. There are two types of specification, performance and prescriptive. A performance specification is a description of the attributes required. A prescriptive specification is a statement of the proprietary building product to be used. In practice it is common for both types of specification to be used, albeit for different purposes.

10.5.1   *Prescriptive specifications*

A prescriptive specification describes a product by its brand name. A facing brick would be specified as, e.g. Ibstock Red Rustic. This automatically gives the performance of the brick in terms of size, colour, texture, durability, water absorption and frost resistance (compare this with the performance method described below). In specifying proprietary products the designer has made a choice and given the contractor precise instructions. Changes cannot be made by the contractor without the permission of the contract administrator. Given that a lot of time and effort will have gone into choosing a particular product in the first place many specifiers are reluctant to change their specification without very good reason. Some designers, for reasons best known to themselves, specify proprietary products and use a clause 'or similar'. This invites the contractor to suggest alternatives and is not good practice – if in doubt then a performance specification may be a better alternative. A degree of caution is required because it does not necessarily follow that the prescribed product has been used on site (as discussed in the previous chapter).

10.5.2   *Performance specifications*

Unlike prescriptive specifications, performance specifications do not identify particular products by brand name, instead a series of performance characteristics are listed (essentially a technical brief) which must be met. Performance based specifications do vary in their scope: they can be used to describe a complete project, one or more systems, or individual components. For example, clients may produce a performance specification for a design and construct project, engineers may produce a performance specification for the mechanical and electrical specification, and designers may specify components such as facing bricks by the performance required. Continuing with the example of the brick, a performance specification would identify the required size, colour, texture, durability, water absorption and frost resistance, and depending upon the standards set a range of different manufacturers' bricks may satisfy the performance required. This leaves the choice of product to the contractor and is popular in contractor led procurement routes. With performance specifications it is not uncommon for the contractor to make last minute changes to products in order to save money or meet programme deadlines. It is important that the final product choice is recorded, both as evidence in the event of a claim and for reference as and when alterations are made to the building. It is also important to check that the product selected complies with the performance specification required.

Performance specifications were pioneered in the USA through their use in a school building programme in California in 1961 and started being used in the UK at a similar time (Cox 1994). Performance specifications are generally regarded as being more difficult and time consuming to write than prescriptive specifications, but they are used for complete buildings (e.g. design and build contracts) and for sub-systems (especially building services). They tend to be used by client organisations keen to leave the choice open (in the hope of getting the same performance cheaper than if a proprietary product was used).

10.5.3   *Schedules of work*

It is common practice in repair and alteration works to use a schedule of works. This document describes a list of work items to be done, a list that the contractor can also use for costing the work. It is common practice to append the schedule of works to the specification, but it must not be confused with the specification or for that matter schedules (as described above).

10.6   **Digital information and virtual details**

Powerful computers and computer software are now affordable for even the smallest of design offices, providing the opportunity for networking, sharing of information and the handling of vast quantities of information. There is a tendency to take such technological advances for granted and overlook the fact that the ability to communicate in digital format is a relatively recent phenomenon. Charles Babbage is widely acknowledged as being the first person to try and build a machine that we now call a computer. The design of his Analytical Engine (*c.* 1832) embodied many of the logical features to be found in modern digital computers, namely the store, arithmetic unit, control unit, input and output devices. Yet despite his independent wealth and years of research and development Babbage failed to build a complete engine. A number of mechanical devices which used punched cards were tried up until the 1940s. It was not until 1946 that Eckert and Mauchly invented the electronic analogue computer, the Electronic Numerical Integrator and Calculator (ENIAC). Early computers, the mainframes, followed which were physically very large and slow by comparison with today's machines. The smaller mini-computers led subsequently to the personal computers (PCs) of IBM and Apple in the 1980s and then to the mobility and power of laptops and palmtops. Of course this selection of hardware would not have caught on without the development of software. With the development of the PC, rapid reductions in purchase cost and equally dramatic improvements in processing power the software applications followed.

10.6.1   *Computer aided design*

In its widest sense CAD includes any part of the design activity that is assisted by computers. Designers use CAD and associated software to model designs in three dimensions, to simulate environments, provide walk-throughs for presentation purposes and to test ideas quickly and relatively inexpensively before going to production. Until relatively recently the term 'computer aided design' was something of a misnomer, with the majority of CAD packages being little more than drafting tools. CAD has been, and continues to be, used as an aid for the more efficient production of working drawings, making repetitive tasks much easier, quicker and less tedious: more a case of computer aided draughting than computer aided design. The ability to import standard details held in the organisation's database or those provided by manufacturing companies has been vastly improved. Before computers standard details had to be traced or copied onto negatives, a time consuming process which provided very little job satisfaction for the creative individual. CAD heralded the end of the tracer or draftsman in the traditional sense. These roles have been re-defined as CAD operators and designers with proficient computer skills are highly sought after within the industry. Computer software continues to develop at a rapid pace, making the designer's job much easier and at the same time providing the opportunity to produce better drawings more quickly and cheaply. To use software packages as a true design tool the three-dimensional object based modelling systems provide a more user friendly design tool than do the two-dimensional ones which are essentially a drafting tool. With the recent development of the computer aided virtual environments (CAVE) has come the ability to test and experiment in a 'safe' environment. This has implications for health and safety as well as the detailing of buildings which can be developed in virtual reality and 'tested' before being used on site.

10.6.2   *Networking*

With the growth of cheap, powerful computers and more compatible software packages the possibility of integrating production information and co-ordinating complex information is now easy to achieve. With digital information exchange production drawing co-ordination is quicker, cheaper and with the right software considerably easier to avoid clashes between information on drawings from different consultants. Perhaps one of the greatest benefits of digital information is the ability to network from remote locations. No longer is it necessary for design teams to share the same office space when they can be working on the same project from different locations, linked through an intranet or the internet. The integrated service digital network (ISDN) comprises recent technological developments in such areas as fibre optics, satellite communications, broadcasting and digital transmission. Combined they form the electronic superhighways that offer instantaneous communication with high quality visual and audio resolution, ideally suited for the transmission of architectural images. For small design organisations the potential of networking to form a larger, more experienced, network of individuals with different skills and experiences is considerable. No longer do the large architectural practices have a monopoly on the large schemes. Indeed, many of the larger design organisations have embraced the opportunity to network and have outsourced much of their work to individuals who work from remote locations, home, factory or building site, thus reducing their space requirements and saving money on office rentals (and essentially becoming a network of small organisations). With these arrangements it is becoming increasingly difficult for a client to differentiate between large and small organisations.

10.6.3   *Case study – Outsourcing technical design*

With the widespread use of computers in construction has come a real opportunity to transfer information in digital format, quickly, effectively and cheaply. Not only may this provide an opportunity to improve the flow and co-ordination of information, but also it provides an opportunity to outsource non-core services to others. The case study organisation is a firm of designers who took a decision to retain conceptual design, space planning and information co-ordination functions, but outsource all the 'production' work to others. They no longer do the detail design, merely co-ordinate it – designers as signature architects and information managers. It is a strategy that works well for this design organisation (and others). Production information is carried out by separate production information organisations and product manufacturers (details and product-specific specifications). Outsourcing the detailing for this organisation gives it a competitive advantage over other design organisations because it can deliver the contract documents quickly and more cheaply than its competitors. It is an interesting strategy, and one that raises a number of questions about quality, knowledge retention and the transfer of risk.

10.6.4   *CAD or manual drafting?*

There has been considerable debate as to the advantages of CAD systems over the traditional manual one, with strong arguments put in defence of both systems.

Although it is largely a matter of personal preference as to which is preferred, with significant developments in CAD systems (and reduction in costs) many design offices have thrown out their drawing boards and become fully digital. The advantages and disadvantages of each system are summarised below:

CAD – advantages:
- Consistent drawing style where more than one designer is contributing to the drawing.
- Elimination of repetition, monotonous drafting reduced (if not eliminated).
- Alterations easy to accommodate.
- Easy co-ordination and automatic drawing register (assuming the software is compatible).
- Rapid distribution via e-mail.
- Quicker than manual techniques (in the majority of cases).
- Rapid access to previous projects and details.
- Storage of drawings does not take up a lot of space.

CAD – disadvantages:
- Initial cost of hardware and software.
- Maintenance costs, upgrades and training costs for operatives.
- Drawings can lack character.
- Operators can become bored.
- Greater health and safety considerations.
- Software compatibility problems.
- Still need to print drawings (most screens are small compared with an A0 or A1 drawing).
- Not all software is effective as a design tool.
- System may 'crash'.

Manual drafting – advantages:
- Cheap equipment and negligible running costs.
- Quicker for small projects/one-off drawings.
- Drawings have more character than digital ones.
- Higher level of satisfaction for the drawer than operating a computer.
- Sketches can be done anywhere with very simple tools, pen and paper.

Manual drafting – disadvantages:
- The majority of drawings take longer to produce than they do with CAD.
- Alterations to drawings often involve a complete redraw and can take a lot of time.
- Consistency and style is difficult to control.
- Difficult for two or more people to work on a drawing at once.
- Co-ordination is time consuming.
- Storage of drawings takes up a lot of space.
- Have to rely on physical conveyance of drawings from originator to receiver(s).

10.7   Co-ordinating production information

Co-ordinated project information (CPI) is a system that categorises drawings and written information (specifications) and is used in British standards and in the measurement of building works, the Standard Method of Measurement (SMM7). This relates directly to the classification system used in the NBS. One of the conventions of CPI is the 'common arrangement of work sections' (CAWS). This lists around 300 different classes of work according to the operatives who will do the work. This allows bills of quantities to be arranged according to CAWS and items coded on drawings, in schedules and bills of quantities can be annotated with reference back to the specification. It is not unusual to find that this system is adhered to in part, and rarely by all participants in a particular project.

10.7.1   Drawing registers

In addition to the challenge of co-ordinating the vast quantities of information, itself a major management task for which someone has to take responsibility, there is the task of managing the production of detail design information within a particular design office. Drawings, schedules and specifications coming into and going out of the office need very careful consideration, whether on paper or in digital format. The process needs to be audited to enable those managing the process to be aware of the status of information at any particular time. Drawing registers are an effective tool (can be automated on some CAD systems) and should contain the following information:

- All information issued must be recorded and a copy retained in the office. Date sent, drawing number and who it has been distributed to will need to be recorded.
- All information received must also be recorded, distributed to those who require the information, and retained as a copy for future reference. The date received, drawing number and who sent it will need to be logged.

10.7.2   Time and cost of producing information

Regardless of whether information is provided on paper or in digital form, time and resources are required to complete the task in a professional manner: time to research possible solutions, time to think about the consequences of designers' decisions, time to produce the drawings and schedules, time to check individual drawings, time to co-ordinate individual drawings with others, time for other consultants to integrate information with their own, time to record and manage the process and, last but not least, time to make changes (because there will be some).

The cost of producing information is often underestimated, nor is it particularly well controlled in many design practices. Given the vast quantity of drawings which have to be produced during the detail design stage the careful management of their production and especially the time spent in producing the information is critical to the profitability of individual jobs and will influence the long-term viability of the business. Each and every drawing, schedule and specification should be costed as a percentage of the job and allowances must be made for unforeseen changes which can easily eat into a job's profitability. There are a number of costs associated with each and every document which need to be recognised in order to cost and manage the process efficiently:

(1) *Cost of producing the drawing.*
(2) *Cost of checking the document.* Often included in the cost above, but by separating this function the task of carrying it out is explicit and there is less likelihood of forgetting to do it (until it is too late of course).
(3) *Cost of co-ordinating the documents.* Co-ordination of information produced by the professional service firm should be relatively straightforward, but time must be allocated so that the task can be completed as part of the overall programme. Co-ordination of other consultants' work is more challenging, especially if some are working in different formats (paper or digital).
(4) *Cost of altering the drawings.*

In very small organisations the tasks listed above may be carried out by the same person, but in the majority of organisations some of these tasks will be allocated to people with different skills and responsibilities.

10.7.3   *Co-ordination and checking for compatibility*

Information will come from a variety of sources and will be contained in a variety of different media, thus making the co-ordination of this diffuse information a challenging and interesting task. As noted earlier information is required for many different purposes, for developing the design, approvals, for building and for record purposes. To be effective it should have three important characteristics, namely: clarity, brevity and timeliness.

No matter how good the members of the design team, no matter how effective the QC and quality management system, discrepancies, errors and omissions do occur. Such errors are frequently related to time pressures and changes made on site without adequate thought of the consequences for other information (decisions made without adequate information). Many faults in buildings can be traced back to incomplete and inaccurate information and also the inability to use the information that has been provided. Discrepancies between drawings, specifications and bills of quantities can and do lead to conflict. Some of these can be avoided, e.g. not rolling a specification from one project to another, but some slip through the net. Mention was made earlier in the book about the importance of design reviews and their contribution to improving communication and helping to check information before proceeding to the next stage. Figure 10.3 illustrates a number of junctures where design reviews act as QC checks in the production and transmission of production information. An effective check for completeness of the information is carried out when the bills of quantities are produced (usually by a QS in the UK). Although this is not a checking service it does serve as a secondary check, usually by someone new to the information, prior to issue for contractual purposes. Discrepancies and omissions may be spotted by the contractor and reported during the tendering procedure. Regardless of the sophistication of the technologies employed to minimise mistakes and ensure co-ordination it should be remembered that people make the decisions and input the information. Thus errors may occur.

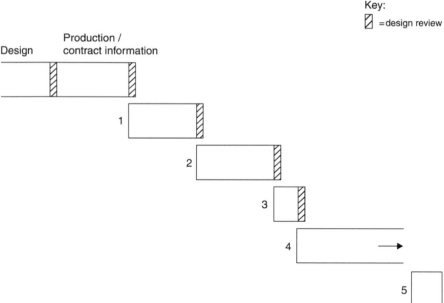

Key:

◨ = design review

1. Cost consultant.
   Preparation of bills of quantities
   Check for completeness – omissions highlighted
2. Tender.
   Contractors may highlight errors
   Contractors may suggest alternative details, products, etc.
3. Information revised and re-checked prior to issue as contract information
4. Assembly.
   Changes may be required. New information issued/revisions made
5. As-built drawings.
   Required for record purposes. Must reflect all changes made and thus
   be an accurate record of the building's construction

Figure 10.3   Information flows and checks.

10.7.4   *Accommodating changes during the production information stage*

In an ideal world the process of producing the production information would be a smooth affair with everyone contributing their information on time, with the information received being complete, cogent, error free and sympathetic to other contributors' aims, objectives and constraints. In reality this is rarely the case, regardless of how good the managerial systems and the effectiveness of information co-ordination. Project teams are often assembled for one job and the participants may not have worked together previously. As it is towards the end of the project that teams start to gel and communicate effectively, there is the potential for many errors to occur along the way simply because empathy has not been achieved, so the possibility of design changes should be expected and allowed for in any programming. Changes to the design can come from a variety of sources: from the client, the design team and/or the contractor if involved early in the process. All changes need to be approved by the client before they are implemented, costed, their consequences fully considered and the change recorded.

(1) *Client approval.* All changes, no matter why they are needed, must be approved by the client, preferably before they are actioned.
(2) *Costing.* Costing the implications of design changes can take time, but the costing exercise is necessary to allow decisions to be made. Changes made to try and save money need to be considered and any knock-on affects anticipated.
(3) *Implications and consequences.* Changes may have implications for the long-term performance of the building. They may also affect previously approved documentation, such as planning consent and building regulation approval.
(4) *Recording.* Perhaps an obvious statement, but it is essential that design changes are recorded (many are not).

10.7.5   *Quality matters*

Information for building design is produced and consumed by organisations which are in business to make a profit. Organisations, regardless of size or market orientation, must give their clients (customers) confidence in the service that they provide. Those involved in construction related activities must also

Figure 10.4   Finlandia Hall, Helsinki, column and light detail.

satisfy their clients about the quality of the finished building. Here QC and QA are essential tools.

Whatever format detailed design information is held in, on paper or in digital format, the issue of QC must be paramount. No matter how perfect we would like to think we are, we all make mistakes, some more often than others, some more disastrous than others. Because of our inability to avoid mistakes there needs to be some form of formal checking system in place to ensure information is both correct and complete. To do so requires some secondary checkpoint. In some design offices individuals are employed solely to check information for omissions and errors prior to issue, although this is less common than it used to be. With the downward pressure on professional fees and time to produce information the trend has been towards individuals checking their own work, and hence being responsible for any errors. This has potential pitfalls, although a secondary check is available to those working in offices with QA procedures. Indeed, quality management systems provide an important tool for helping to record and monitor information as it comes into, and flows out of, organisations.

At the risk of labouring the point about QC and information flow this is an area that many organisations have experienced increased difficulties with since the adoption of CAD and IT. The problem would appear to be ineffective managerial control, of both individuals and the networks in place. Quite simply, it is far too easy to press the 'send' button without first pausing to consider the consequences. There is plenty of anecdotal evidence to suggest that the information management role needs far more attention than it is currently receiving, both in education and in practice.

Further reading

Cooper, D. (1992). *Drawing and Perceiving* (Second Edition), Van Nostrand Reinhold, New York.

11 Assembling the parts

Few designers build in a physical manner. Instead, the buildings they design, detail and schedule are assembled by others from the information contained in the contract documentation. Design and production drawings are a means to an end, with information converted into physical artefact by contractors and sub-contractors, using labour and machinery to assemble a multitude of different components that have been produced by manufacturers. Here we provide a brief overview of the different methods of procurement, QC on site and the sources of design changes. We conclude by addressing practical completion and user information, disputes and how to avoid them, and the issue of feedback.

11.1 Different methods

How the building will be constructed, maintained and eventually recycled should be discussed and agreed at the briefing stage. It is here also that the benefits of different procurement methods can be discussed, analysed and agreed against the client's requirements and objectives. Foremost in the mind of the client should be the quality of the building, although other concerns such as cost, time and risk transfer also have a part to play in the final choice of procurement route. This decision needs to be made early because the decisions that follow will be influenced by the type of development 'team' assembled, as discussed in Chapter 3. Essentially, the choice is between a route that is design led or contractor led.

Traditional routes tend to leave the choice of contractor until the production information and contract documentation is complete. There are essentially two methods of appointing a contractor, either by competitive tendering or by negotiation. With competitive tendering a select number of contractors are invited to prepare competitive tenders for the work, with the contract normally going to the lowest bidder. In this case the main contractor will be faced with a large amount of information that it has had no involvement in prior to being invited to tender. Alternatively, the work may be negotiated with a contractor (or two contractors), to agree a fixed sum for the work. This may also be carried out after the completion of the contract documentation, although negotiation does allow the opportunity for earlier involvement of the main contractor and thus the opportunity to agree how the building may be best assembled. There is a very convincing argument for involving the main contractor (and specialist sub-contractors) at an earlier stage so that their experience and knowledge can be used to assist with the detailing with a view to improving buildability and lowering costs. Taking this argument a little further, it could be argued that a contractor led procurement route offers a better option in terms of buildability. With contractor led routes production information may have been produced by the contractor 'in-house' or outsourced to a variety of consultants; so there is still the need to co-ordinate the information and check for accuracy before starting to build. Whatever route chosen, time, cost and expected level of quality will be the determining factors.

However, once the work starts on site it is all too easy to become absorbed in the mechanics of the project, sometimes at the expense of the finished quality of the building.

11.2   Pre-contract issues

The creative phase quickly moves into the tangible – the assembly phase. At this juncture in a project's life the designer becomes known as the 'contract administrator'. This may be the same person who did the design and production information in small offices and on small projects. In larger offices the contract administrator will be different to the designer, requiring different skills and abilities. Thus communication between the contract administrator, designer and builder (Fig. 11.1) is important throughout the contract period, especially when changes to the design and construction of the building are being contemplated. After the appointment of the main contractor it is necessary to have a pre-contract meeting to discuss issues that need to be resolved prior to the contractor taking possession of the site and starting work. This is an important meeting whatever procurement route is used because it gives all those involved the chance to discuss any problems and discrepancies in production information before work starts – the how, why and when questions.

11.2.1   *Method statements and risk assessment*

It will be necessary for the contractor to produce method statements and risk assessments based on the contract documentation (it is a requirement of the CDM Regulations). Method statements are a detailed assessment and description of the construction methods to be used. A well-written method statement should be able to outline clearly how the work is to be carried out and contain all the relevant information relating to the work stage, method of construction, plant to be used, personnel required, duration, quality of work and safety measures to be adopted. Risk assessment is inherent in method statements. As such it provides a very useful tool for planning and managing the programme of work on site.

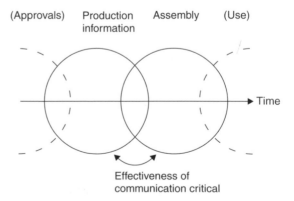

Figure 11.1 From information to artefact.

11.2.2   *Programme of works*

An indication of the time scale for a particular project is usually stipulated by the design team in the tender documentation. It is for the contractor to confirm that critical dates can be met and the building completed on time. Simple bar charts and critical path diagrams are useful tools for identifying time frames and critical operations/dates that must be achieved if the work is to be completed on time. Good designers have a clear understanding of site management issues such as storage of materials on site, phasing of the work and safe working practices. They also understand the requirements for site facilities, responsibilities, roadworks, protection of trees and neighbouring properties, contractor's plant, materials, and the need for temporary protection and temporary structures – factors that need building into programmes so that work can proceed safely.

11.2.3   *Contingencies*

A contingency fund is provided so that there is money within the agreed contract sum to cover any unplanned events. Clients do not like contingencies, but even on new build projects they are required to cover (as an absolute minimum) work in the ground. This is because even with extensive ground investigation there may be the discovery of an old basement or foundations that were not expected, and these will have to be dealt with. This is additional work that has to be paid for – hence the contingency fund. For work to existing buildings where there may be a high level of uncertainty about what lies beneath the surface of the existing structure; here contingencies will be required to cover additional work found to be necessary after opening up the structure.

11.3   Project information

From the main contractor's viewpoint the information provided in the contract documentation must be complete if the project is to be constructed to programme and to the agreed cost. Given an adequate design programme there is no reason why the information provided cannot be complete, free of errors and omissions and easy to understand – with a number of exceptions. First, it is impossible to know what will be encountered when excavating ground, especially where the site has had previous uses, no matter how much has been spent on site investigation pre-contract. Second, on work to existing buildings there is always the possibility that the 'as-built' information (if it is available) is not entirely correct because designers and/or builders made changes on site that were not recorded. Thus it is only on opening up the work that anyone can be sure exactly how the building was constructed and what materials were used. On work to existing buildings contingencies are provided in contract documentation for these very issues.

11.3.1   *Adequacy of contract documentation*

Adequacy of contract documentation is not just about being complete and free from errors. It is also about being easy to understand. As discussed earlier, information only has value if it is of use to the recipient. Thus in situations where information has been prepared for contractors and sub-contractors who have not worked with a particular design team before the scope for misinterpretation may be enhanced.

11.3.2   Information flow

In an ideal world the contract documentation should be complete before the main contractor is appointed and work started on site. In reality, because of commercial pressures to start on site as soon as planning consent is received, many projects start without full contract documentation. Sometimes this is due to poor planning or increased pressure from the client to start on site too early, thus putting pressures on the programme that usually come back to haunt the team and, in the long run, can cost the client more money. Alternatively this is deliberate and part of a fast-track policy. Fast-tracking of projects allows for information to be supplied in packages at certain intervals in the programme, intervals agreed by those producing the information and those who need it (Fig. 11.2). Additional care is required here to ensure co-ordination and avoid unnecessary changes on site to rectify errors. Such a strategy is also used on work to existing buildings, where information is provided in stages as part of a deliberate and planned strategy, responding to the existing fabric as it is opened up.

11.3.3   Information requests

Requests for information should be made in accordance with the contract and the design team given time to respond without making a hasty decision. In practice requests are often made at the last minute, putting pressure on everyone in the process. Formal communication channels should be adhered to. In practice many contractors will try and bypass the contract administrator and talk directly to consultants and the client (or the client's representative). This may be seen as a deliberate policy of trying to confuse the issue, although in fairness to contractors this is often done because of their frustration with designers and their failure to deliver information in time.

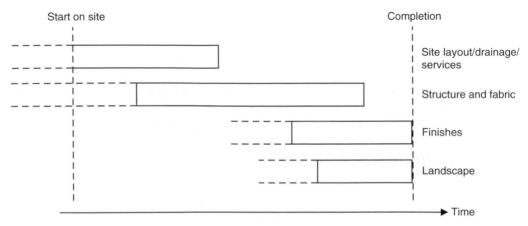

Figure 11.2 Phased information flow (a simplistic model).

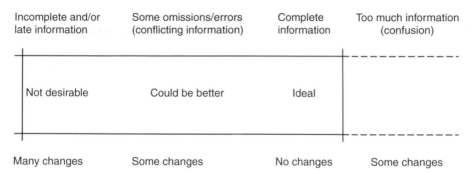

Figure 11.3 Relationship between information and changes.

11.3.4   *Information and changes*

Changes on site are often brought about because of problems with the information provided, or not, as the case may be and associated problems with communication. The most likely outcome of ineffective communication and/or inadequate information is unnecessary changes and additional work, resulting in additional costs. Changes and additional work are likely to increase in relation to the completeness and timeliness of information (Fig. 11.3), as discussed below.

11.4   Quality control on site

The various individuals on a building site are trained in their own area of specialism, for which they have responsibility for achieving the stated quality level. They work on clearly identified works packages and often have little more than a general knowledge of others' areas of specialism, of which they are tolerant. Achieving the specified standard of quality on site is the responsibility of the contractor through the co-ordination and control of sub-contractors' work. It is the main contractor's responsibility under the contract to ensure the building is built as shown and described in the contract documentation. Designers have no power to dictate how the work is to be carried out; indeed, this should be resisted because such action would transfer liability from contractor to designer. Rather, the designer has indicated the position and relationship of component parts, and has specified their quality in the contract documentation. It is for the main contractor to tell the contract administrator how the work is to be done through method statements and the respective health and safety documentation, and then to inspect and supervise the work to ensure the predefined quality standards are met. Quality work is dependent upon the use of suitably skilled site operatives and the close supervision of their work by the contractor's site manager.

11.4.1   *Inspection/supervision of the works*

The main contractor is responsible for ensuring the work conforms to the determined quality standards and thus from the client's perspective it is necessary to have some form of inspection that is not controlled by the contractor. If there is any doubt reference should be made to Schaffer's site guide for architects which

Figure 11.4 Concrete framed building under construction.

provides some illuminating examples of the tricks contractors get up to (Schaffer 1983). The clerk of works is usually employed by the client to look after the client's interests. However, under the majority of contracts the clerk of works can only give 'directions' which need to be confirmed by the contract administrator.

The most reliable way of controlling the quality of work is to inspect the work in progress – trying to put right errors after the event is more expensive and will inevitably result in conflict and dispute. Having a site architect and/or clerk of works on site every day will help to raise standards, simply by their presence, but this has to be paid for and may not be an option on smaller projects. Another method is to inspect at predetermined stages of construction which, depending upon the size and complexity of the project, may be on a daily basis by a clerk of works and weekly by the contract administrator. Periodic inspections will take place from others who have an interest in the project, namely planning officers, building control inspectors, the health and safety planning supervisor and the health and safety inspectorate.

11.4.2   Samples of work

Samples of work are an excellent means of establishing acceptable standards of work, quality and aesthetic standards, before work starts on the building. It is good practice to include for samples and tests in the bills of quantities so that the extent of the samples and panels is clearly identified. Samples form an important benchmark from which the quality of the building work can be assessed as it proceeds. It is through constant reference to the approved sample that it is possible to determine in an objective manner whether work is good, bad or indifferent. In some cases local authority planning officers may well wish to approve external materials, especially in situations where work is taking place on existing buildings which are listed or in conservation areas. These cost money and some clients need to be persuaded that expenditure on samples is worthwhile in the long run. Samples and tests form a very small percentage of the total contract sum and are worth the small investment.

11.4.3   *Compliance with the contract documentation*

British standards can be useful here. For example, monitoring and controlling work during construction to achieve the specified level of accuracy is covered by *BS 5606: 1990 (1998) Guide to Accuracy in Building*. Different materials are covered by a variety of standards and the reader should consult the necessary standards. As noted earlier, it is important that the designer reads the relevant standards before citing them in the specification and that the site operatives read them before starting work. Unfortunately, experience suggests that few people actually read the standards unless something goes wrong, which defeats the objective somewhat. They are an essential tool in ensuring quality, not just a document to help in disputes.

11.4.4   *The 'Considerate Constructors Scheme'*

Over the years site operatives have earned themselves a bad reputation for their inappropriate behaviour on site. Only too aware of the stereotypical image of the builder, the industry has made an attempt to improve the image of the building site and those working on it. The Considerate Constructors Scheme (promoted by the Construction Industry Board) is a national initiative to improve the image of builders through better management and presentation of construction sites. It seeks to minimise disturbance to immediate neighbours, eradicate offensive behaviour and language from the site, and to recognise constructors' commitment to raise standards with regard to site management, safety and environmental awareness beyond statutory duties. Constructors who sign up to the scheme must adhere to an eight-point Code of Considerate Practice, namely to be

- considerate
- environmentally aware
- clean
- a good neighbour
- respectful
- safe
- responsible
- accountable.

All participating building sites will be monitored to check for adherence to the code. Although one might argue that such an initiative should not be necessary at the start of the 21st century, the fact that it is being done should be applauded. Clients and designers should consider including an appropriate clause in the contract preliminaries to ensure the main contractor registers with the scheme. Obvious benefits are the business reputation of those following the code and improved public relations. Less obvious, but equally important, is the manner in which consultants are treated on site and the commitment to environmental awareness, especially a commitment to sourcing materials and products locally and addressing waste on site.

11.5   Design changes during the contract period

Changes can be made for two reasons: to put right errors in the contract documentation (which is different to putting right errors made by the contractor) and because people have changed their mind. It is the second category that may affect the durability and quality of the finished building because changes may be made hurriedly without due consideration for other aspects of the building's assembly and integrity.

11.5.1   *Changes during construction*

In many respects one of the most difficult issues to deal with concerns changes to the design during the construction phase. On new build projects the number of changes should be minimal, although experience shows that this is an ideal situation. Clients do change their minds and request changes, unforeseen difficulties may arise on site that relate to a particular detail and/or difficulties with delivery of components to suit the project, all of which may necessitate changes to the contract documentation. Omissions, errors and discrepancies in the contract documentation will result in the need to issue instructions to clarify matters and may well have cost implications. Changes may also be requested by the main contractor and sub-contractors, hoping to change specified products to those more familiar to the builders and assemblers (see Chapter 9). As noted earlier, care should be taken here because the responsibility for product selection, and hence liability, lies with the designers, not the contractor in designer-led procurement routes.

Work to existing buildings is far more challenging because in many situations it is impossible to guess with any accuracy what lies behind surface finishes. Even if the as-built drawings are to hand for reference purposes there is no guarantee that the building was built as illustrated. Once the structure has been 'opened up' there is a real possibility that the work is different to the record drawings, necessitating changes to intended details. Careful and considerate investigations of the built fabric at the design and detailing stages can save expensive changes later in the contract, but not all clients are prepared to pay for investigations. Consideration is needed as to the age and architectural importance of the building and its fabric. Respect for the fabric, original design ideals and original construction methods is required by those administering the project as well as those doing the work on site.

11.5.2   *Client requests*

Assuming for one moment that the briefing and design development has been carried out with the client's involvement and approval throughout, then changes to the contract documentation should be minimal. Changes of mind are often expensive, especially when requested late in the programme of works, and should be avoided. To a certain extent the tendency of the client to make changes will be determined by his or her personality and (where appropriate) the culture of the organisation he or she represents. There is little the designers or contractor can do about this other than to try and predict events. More important is for the designer to explore all of the possibilities at the briefing and feasibility stage and educate the client about the pitfalls of making changes after the design has been approved. This is a two-way process, dependent upon the communication skills of both designer and client; the better it is done the less likely the possibility of late changes (and potential for conflict and disputes).

11.5.3   *Design team instructions*

Some designers are notorious for changing their minds and requesting changes once the building work has commenced. Not only is this unprofessional behaviour but also it reinforces the stereotypical image of designers as undisciplined individuals who have difficulty in adhering to protocols and frameworks. Clients can minimise the tendency for designers to change their minds by careful vetting at the appointment stage and appointing designers with good reputations for contract administration. References from previous clients should be taken up. During the contract period there may be a number of areas where further information is required and/or where errors or omissions come to light, where changes may be necessary. When information has been supplied late such changes can be expensive.

11.5.4   *Contractor requests*

With contractual methods that are contractor led any changes to the contract documentation will need to be agreed between the contractor and the client's representative – the designers may have limited say in any changes. There is much more latitude here for the contractor than is possible under traditional methods. Under traditional forms of contract the main contractor must make any requests to deviate from the contract documentation to the contract administrator. Changes may be requested for a variety of reasons: to assist with the practical buildability of the details, because of problems with delivery dates of materials and components, or in response to conditions found when opening up existing work. Whatever the reason behind requests to change details it should be borne in mind that the changes requested may have consequences that extend beyond the area of immediate concern. So called 'improvements' implemented on site may well cause difficulties further along the assembly process, especially when decisions are made hurriedly and without due consideration for the larger picture. A cautious and considered approach is both sensible and professional, but that is not to say that changes on site should be rejected out of hand. Many skilled operatives are only too willing to give advice based on their experience if asked – the trick is being able to accommodate such comments with (only) positive consequences.

(1) *Changes in physical layout.* Requests for changes to the physical layout of elements on site need very careful consideration before they are granted. Design solutions take a long time to create and making piecemeal, often hurried, changes may be detrimental to the building as a whole. Again, the tendency to make changes may be greater on work to existing buildings.

(2) *Changes to details.* Changes to details may be requested for a number of reasons. First, the contractor may experience unforeseen difficulties with a particular area of the construction. On new build projects this may be down to inconsiderate detailing, inexperienced site operatives or a combination of both. Second, difficulties may arise due to unforeseen problems in the ground or with existing structures. Third, the contractor may know a better way of doing it. Designers' response to requests to change details will be influenced as much by their personality as the policy of the design organisation. Some designers positively refuse to alter details unless they have no other option, others positively encourage contractors to give them feedback on their detailing and invite requests to make the detail easier (and possibly cheaper) to build. Depending upon the type of contract being used the legal implications of such action need careful consideration.

(3) *Changes to materials and products.* Requests to change specified materials and products were discussed in Chapter 9. The main reasons are because of problems with delivery dates, in order to save money and in order to use a product that is familiar to the builder. Again the response to such requests will vary, as noted above.

11.5.5   *Case study – The sources of design changes*

A small commercial development was monitored during the construction phase to look at design changes in more detail. The project was a steel frame, brick clad building in an urban area, cost approximately 1 million pounds, new build. The contract documentation was particularly thorough. The design phases had been well managed and errors in the documentation corrected before tendering. Extensive site investigation had been carried out, the contractor and nominated sub-contractors carefully vetted. Yet still there were changes, noted below, with cost implications for the contract shown.

(1) *Changes initiated by the design team:*
  (a) Revised details required to the steel frame by the structural engineers after queries raised by the steel fabricators prior to fabrication (minor additional cost).
  (b) Specification for tarmac car park downgraded to save money.
  (c) Ironmongery and internal doors substituted with cheaper range to save money.
  (d) Roof vent tile changed because architect did not like its appearance (minor additional cost).

(continued)

(2) *Changes initiated by site topography:*
    (a) Minor alteration to foundation design because of unforeseen site conditions (additional cost).
    (b) Soft landscaping scheme re-designed to save money.

(3) *Changes initiated by client:*
    (a) Revised colour schedule to interior walls after decorating had commenced (additional cost).
    (b) Lighting positions adjusted after installation (additional cost).
    (A request to change the facing brickwork had to be rejected because the planning authority would not approve the change.)

(4) *Changes initiated by contractor and sub-contractors:*
    (a) Change made to a column/wall detail by the contractor to make assembly easier (no cost implication).
    (b) Changes made to drainage layout, agreed with clerk of works and local authority building control officer on site. Necessitated some re-design by architects (minor additional cost).
    (c) Cavity wall insulation substituted (minor cost saving).
    (d) Roof tiles substituted with alternative because of delivery problems (no effect on cost or appearance).
    (e) Air handling unit specification altered to allow contractor greater choice (minor cost saving).
    (f) Suspended ceiling grid adjusted on site to help buildability (no cost implication).

(5) *Changes by others:*
    (a) Minor changes to highway access requested by highway engineers on site, despite previously agreeing the drawings prepared by the architects (minor additional costs).

(6) *Changes after practical completion:*
    Within the first 12 months of building handover a number of design changes were requested by the client and carried out by the main contractor at additional cost. None of these were design faults, merely a case of the building users wanting something different to the client. They were as follows:
    (a) Additional security grilles to a number of ground floor windows.
    (b) Two rooms re-decorated with a colour to suit the building users.
    (c) Additional wall lights added to a number of rooms.

11.6   Practical completion and user information

Practical completion of the building work signals the end of the building work and handover to the client. Emphasis is given to the words 'practical completion' because the building should be fit for handover to the client but there may well be a number of outstanding items still to be completed. Prior to practical completion the contract administrator will inspect the building and produce a list of outstanding items to be completed, a 'snagging' list. The majority of these defects (which should be minor in nature) should be completed before practical completion.

Most forms of building contract stipulate a period of time after practical completion during which the contractor will be liable for putting right any defects that occur, the 'defects liability period'. Common time scales are 6 months for the building and 12 months for the mechanical services, although 12 months defects liability for the building as a whole is also widely stipulated.

11.6.1   *User information*

On contract completion a new set of people become involved in the building. Building owners and building users will need a comprehensive set of information in order to use the building to its maximum potential and also to keep its fabric and services in good condition. Traditionally referred to as a 'maintenance manual', this information is also known as the owner's and/or users' manual. Prepared by the design team, the manual has the same function as, e.g. the owner's manual supplied with a new car, which contains technical specifications and maintenance requirements. Although much of the information to be included in the manual will have been produced before the construction phase, the manual cannot be completed until the construction contract is complete – this is to allow for any changes made to be incorporated in the as-built drawings. Format and content will vary depending upon the complexity of the building, although user manuals should include the following as an absolute minimum:

- design and technical information
- planning and building control consents
- as-built drawings
- mechanical and electrical services information
- health and safety information
- operating manuals
- product and systems guarantees
- routine maintenance guidance
- recycling information.

11.7   Disputes – avoidance and resolution

An area which many project participants would like to avoid, but invariably get caught up in at some time or another, is that of contract law and arbitration. That disputes do occur in construction is as much a reflection of the complexity of the task as it is of the rather convoluted procurement systems and resultant ineffective communication. Disputes and conflict are not a particularly pleasant area for designers and technologists to become involved in; the process is time consuming, stressful and definitely not creative. The only real winners are the legal profession, and thus care should be taken throughout the development process to avoid (or at least reduce the chances of) disputes occurring. Design organisations with effective office management practices and/or effective quality management systems have in place a system for ensuring consistent quality and for helping to reduce errors in their own work. If things do go astray it is important that lessons are learned and acted on in the future, through feedback into new projects and office procedures.

11.7.1   *Causes of disputes*

Disputes may arise on construction projects for a variety of reasons. Some are easily resolved, some have consequences for the project, and in the worst cases the parties may end up in the courts. A combination of experience and research has shown that disputes tend to be centred around well-known themes. Communication breakdown, inadequate information and quality of work all have a number of root causes. One might be forgiven for assuming that the greater the technical complexity the greater the possibility for disputes, but there is little evidence to support such a view. Indeed, the opposite is sometimes true. There are a number of common causes of disputes:

(1) *Communication breakdown.* Construction projects involve many different people, drawn from many social backgrounds, and who have different agendas. The concept of the development 'team' does not translate in reality, it is more a collection of groups which are brought together, often for the first (and only) time, for a specific purpose. That many projects run smoothly is a testament to the skills of construction managers, designers and project administrators who manage to keep everybody on speaking terms and produce good quality buildings. Yet even the best managers experience difficulties and sometimes fail to ensure effective communication between all the parties all the time.

(2) *Inadequate information.* Inadequate information may be a direct result of poor communication and ineffective management during the design process which can lead to communication breakdown and disputes. Equally, communication difficulties can result in a situation where the information provided is deemed to be inadequate by those who are expected to use it.

(3) *Quality of work.* On the surface the quality of work on site should be exemplary, given the extent of the details, specifications, standards and knowledge brought to bear on a construction project. Unfortunately the quality produced is sometimes below that required, or expected.

(4) *Quality of supervision on site.* Regardless of the contractual arrangement agreed at the start of a project, the extent to which supervision is carried out on site may well vary. No matter how good the individuals on site, or how well the works are monitored, there are times when the standard of supervision may drop, and some individuals may be quick to exploit the situation. Selecting reputable contractors and taking care with the use of sub-contracting and sub-sub-contracting can help to minimise the risk.

11.7.2   Avoiding disputes

Identifying the causes of disputes (listed above) and taking preventative action to limit the possibility of their occurring is arguably the best approach. Different approaches to avoiding and limiting risk are taken by different organisations and individuals. Strategies include limiting the details and materials used on building projects to those used previously and known not to fail, limiting the choice of contractors to those known to produce good quality work on time, using risk assessment strategies, etc.

11.7.3   Resolving disputes

In situations where communication has broken down or a situation has been reached where there is no consensus, then the dispute will have to be resolved via another method. A number of different approaches are available and the benefits of one over another will depend on the particular issues being fought over:

(1) *ADR.* Advocates of ADR claim that this method of dispute resolution is less stressful, faster, more effective and cheaper than arbitration or litigation. ADR is a non-confrontational technique which has been successfully employed to resolve disputes on construction projects around the world. The technique does, however, rely on parties being willing to negotiate to arrive at a mutually acceptable standard and to do so there must be some trust between these conflicting parties.
(2) *Arbitration.* An impartial third party, an arbitrator, is chosen by those in dispute (the litigants) to resolve their dispute.
(3) *Adjudication.* Adjudication uses a third party to decide on a dispute judicially. Early involvement of the adjudicator can prevent the dispute getting out of hand and going to litigation.
(4) *Litigation.* Litigation involves the resolution of disputes in a court of law with a third party (trained and qualified in law) and a judge. It can be a lengthy process and hence expensive; thus it is only recommended for resolving complex cases.

11.8   Feedback

Buildings do affect people. We live in, use, visit and study buildings on a daily basis, and as such we are influenced by designers' efforts, a fact often overshadowed by the attention afforded to the programme and financial matters. On completion of a project many project participants may well let out a sigh of relief and vow never to do it again (they do). Many designers will already be working on new projects and so the tendency to forget about the important matter of feedback (or debriefing) can be overlooked as new, seemingly more important and urgent issues take centre stage. It may strike some people as odd, but many designers never go back to visit their completed projects unless they have to, i.e. because of contractual commitments or to investigate a latent defect. In part this is due to other demands and hence the lack of time to carry out this important function, often the designer's budget has been exceeded and so it costs the organisation money to send people back to the project, and sometimes clients and new building owners are not prepared to let the designers back into the building (especially if the project ended less than amicably). So excuses for not engaging in feedback are easy to find, but there should be a strong desire to follow such activities as part of the desire for constant improvement. Designers can and do learn from reflecting on the process and the product of that process. What went well? What could have been better? How is the building weathering? How is it standing up to daily use and abuse? Is it a delight to use? Is it easy to service? These are questions that can only be answered by going back to the building and looking.

During the life of the project the design and assembly team will have gained valuable experience of the process of design and assembly. Good, bad and indifferent experiences need to be aired, analysed and incorporated into ongoing work and office knowledge systems. The sooner this process is undertaken after project completion the better. Feedback is essential to the concept of TQM and is also an essential characteristic of professional organisations, since it is through feedback that the firm can increase its knowledge base and be in a better position to compete. Feedback takes time and the cost associated with it needs to be built into the project costs or overheads – it should not come out of profits. In situations where the design firm has run over budget and the profits are below those anticipated the tendency tends to be to limit the feedback exercise and/or forget about it, yet it is this very process which should help to identify the reason why things did not go to plan and help to eliminate such errors in the future. As with other surveys, the use of a checklist will serve as a useful *aide-mémoire* and will help with the carrying out of the survey in a systematic manner.

11.8.1   *Feedback at project completion*

At project completion, client handover, it is necessary to evaluate the completed building against the original brief and design concept. The four factors considered at the outset, namely budget, aesthetics, buildability and functionality, need to be evaluated (Fig. 11.5).

The client's involvement here is crucial: is the client happy? Objective evaluation, the measuring of the tangible against the initial goals, is easier for some issues than others.

- *Budget.* Easy to determine and measure against the initial cost estimates.
- *Aesthetics.* Difficult to determine through objective means.
- *Buildability.* Experience of the assembly process will be fresh in everyone's mind and objective evaluation is possible if careful records have been kept of the work.

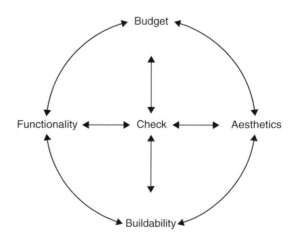

Figure 11.5 Feedback at project completion – quality loop.

■ *Functionality.* Whether the building is functional from the viewpoint of the client is quickly established; whether or not it is functional for the building users will take a little longer to establish.

11.8.2 Feedback at 12 months

Contractually there is a requirement for a visit to the building 12 months after completion, the end of the defects liability period. Focus is likely to be on dealing with complaints, problem rectification, checking that the contractor has dealt with all outstanding items – essentially getting the project 'signed off', so that the file can be closed. Analysis carried out after 12 months tends to be more concerned with product than process. How is the building responding to its environment? Are all the services working correctly? Is the client still happy? Are the building users content with their new environment? These are just a small sample of the questions to be asked at this juncture.

11.8.3 User feedback

Building users will, very quickly, judge the quality of the environment provided for them. If asked, many will claim they would done it differently if they were the designers or builders – this is human nature. Few will be concerned with the technologies employed to create and maintain the building in the condition they find it (until something goes wrong), instead they will be primarily concerned with the environment created by the juxtaposition of materials. There are a number of well-established tools and techniques for evaluating users' experiences, which fall under the facilities management (or asset management) umbrella and are known as post-occupancy evaluation (POE). User feedback is discussed

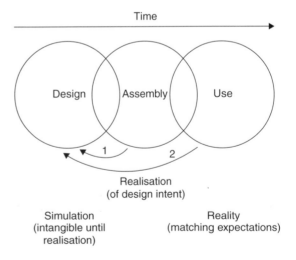

Figure 11.6 Incorporating feedback.

in greater detail in Chapter 12; however, it is necessary to make a couple of points here. First, user feedback may be too late for a particular building project (unless modifications are planned), but it can be added to the design organisation's knowledge base for consideration on similar future projects. Second, designers hone their design skills through the act of reflection, observation, analysis and synthesis – user feedback is essential in this regard.

11.8.4   *Incorporating feedback*

Feedback and user surveys are not done for fun. The results of the feedback process need careful consideration and incorporation of the new knowledge into the designer's working practices. This is usually through the adjustment of standard details and specifications, revising tender lists, revising management procedures, etc.

Figure 11.6 shows two learning loops for designers. First, designers can learn from the act of construction. Second, designers can learn from evaluation of the building in use. Both are important because designers need knowledge about construction and building use in order to develop realistic concepts for future projects, closing the loop from inception to use and back again.

Further reading

Kwakye, A.A. (1997). *Construction Project Administration in Practice*, Longman, Harlow.

12 Building performance and durability

Decay is inevitable, unavoidable and costly. Closely associated with issues of performance are the evaluation and monitoring of both services and fabric, with early repair and replacement crucial to serviceability. When problems occur building pathology can help to identify the factors that led to the failure and provide solutions to prevent it happening again. This leads into a discussion about re-use and recovery of scarce resources locked into the building fabric, raising issues that naturally return to a focus on architectural decision-making and the detail.

12.1 Decay is inevitable

Buildings are an embodiment of the design thinking process. Buildings represent the physical trace of specific decisions and actions started long before the building was constructed and extending long after its completion (Fig. 12.1). Entropy is a rule of nature that states that as soon as something reaches its desired state, i.e. maturity, it starts to decay. It is easy to think of buildings starting to decay at some fixed point in the future, and certainly many building owners find it convenient to ignore routine maintenance and minor repairs, dealing with them only when absolutely necessary. But buildings are starting to decay even before they are commenced on site. For example, stacks of brickwork in the producer's

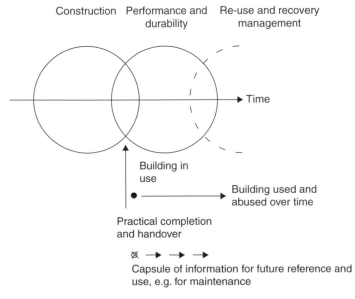

Figure 12.1 Building in use.

or merchant's yard will be exposed to the elements and will be starting to weather long before they arrive on site.

All building materials and services are finite in their life span. Just as materials have unique coefficients of expansion they also have unique coefficients of decay, and thus elements of the building will be decaying at different rates. The effect of weathering is to erode, dissolve and discolour the designer's 'perfect' building, often resulting in staining and eventually in the need for repair. Some materials are enhanced by weathering, e.g. stone, seasoned timber such as oak and moss covered roof tiles. Weathering can give otherwise quite ordinary buildings a romantic feel. Other materials may fare less well when exposed to the elements. Even the best designs may look drab when the wrong choice of material, poor detailing and insensitivity to a building's micro-climate combine. The point is that buildings are not static, they will weather and if detailed correctly they may well be enhanced through the passage of time, an ever changing facade. Sensitive, strategically planned and monitored maintenance programmes are required to maintain the weathered (yet weather-proof) building. Those responsible for implementing and overseeing the maintenance programme must have empathy with the materials they are charged with maintaining. There is a need to understand how materials are likely to behave – the more materials employed the greater the challenge, especially where different materials interact.

12.1.1 *Agents of decay*

Over time buildings are subjected to attack from a number of different sources. Sometimes these agents of decay act independently although it is more common that they act in conjunction with one another. Designers and users of buildings need to be aware of these agents of decay and to try and minimise, or at least delay, the rate of decay through sensitive detailing and materials selection, competent construction and proactive management of the building during its life. Agents of decay may be classified under the following headings:

- biological agents – vegetable and microbiological, animal
- chemical agents – water and solvents, acids and salts
- electromagnetic agents – solar radiation and lightning
- mechanical agents – snow and water loading, ice pressure, wind loading
- thermal agents – heat, frost and thermal shock.

12.1.2 *Damage*

In addition to the natural tendency to decay over time, a building may also be subject to damage through everyday use and misuse. General use will result in 'wear and tear'. Such damage can be anticipated and planned for with relative accuracy. Damage can also be caused through accidents, none of which can be anticipated, merely allowed for in some form of contingency fund. Malicious damage to property, such as theft and vandalism, is less easy to foresee and can have a long-term effect if not rectified promptly. For example, the theft of lead flashings from the roof of existing buildings can lead to a rapid deterioration of the property through water ingress. Left unchecked damage will occur directly from the water penetration and indirectly through the possible development of wet and/or dry rot given the right conditions. Vandalism can leave buildings vulnerable to damage from the environment and can leave unsightly scars on buildings. Removing graffiti from stonework is a specialist job and there is always a danger that chemical residues are left within the stone that will show through at some later stage. Arson is potentially the most dangerous act of malicious damage which leads to serious damage through the fire and in its containment and extinguishment.

12.1.3 Defects

The majority of building defects and failures tend to be caused by design and/or work errors, with a few attributable to faulty materials and errors of procedure and even fewer to poor maintenance (Crocker 1990). Defects may manifest themselves in the structure, fabric, services or other facilities of the building and may not become apparent for some time after the building has been completed and occupied. Sometimes many years pass before the defect becomes apparent, especially where it is 'hidden' within the structure. The root cause may often be difficult to assess without a thorough investigation of the building and the process by which it was designed and constructed. Good conceptual designs can be upset by poor and poorly supervised detailing during the production drawing stage and many buildings fail prematurely because knowledge of good detailing principles was poor and choices of materials were not given due consideration (Crocker 1990, Gumpertz and Rutila 1999). In situations where the conceptual designer is different to the detailer(s) then it is very important that the detailers have an ability to understand the philosophy behind the conceptual design and be able to retain it through competent detailing and material selection. The most common types of defect are ones we know how to deal with – rain penetration, condensation and cracking of the fabric – yet they still occur far too frequently. Defects can usually be traced back to one or more of the following:

- an inability to apply technical knowledge
- inappropriate detailing and specification
- non-compliance with regulations and codes
- incomplete information
- late information
- poor work
- inadequate site supervision
- inappropriate alterations rendering an otherwise good detail ineffective
- insufficient maintenance.

One might be forgiven for assuming that given the appointment of a competent designer and an able contractor defects would not occur. The reality is less clear cut. Pressure on time and cost can often lead the most careful designer and the most fastidious contractor to cut corners and make mistakes. Once a defect has become evident the tendency is to apportion blame, simply because someone has to pay for the defect. Accurate identification of the cause (or causes) of decay is necessary before any remedial work can be carried out. A professionally

conducted condition survey is essential as a first step to providing some information about the cause and extent of the problem. Building 'pathology' is a term
borrowed from medicine and one used to encompass the field of building defect
identification, diagnosis and recommended action to correct the error. Deterioration cannot be prevented, but it can be retarded through a combination of good
detailing, good building and regular maintenance.

12.2   Durable assets?

There is a tendency to build structures that require less frequent maintenance, i.e.
that are more durable. Recurrent repair costs are a financial drain, have not always
been anticipated and are often delayed as long as possible before action is taken.
For the building owner maintenance is a chore, can be disruptive and costs money.
Permanence without maintenance is an illusive ideal. Reduction of maintenance
can be addressed at the briefing stage and through sensitive selection of good
quality products with an 'in-use' pedigree, usually resulting in a higher initial
financial cost, but reduced running cost. This is an issue dealt with through life
cycle costing techniques and assisted through the use of feedback into the design
decision-making process.

Re-use of our existing building stock is essential to current urban design thinking and sustainable design philosophy. With a more sensitive and politically aware
approach to design in the light of *Agenda 21* the emphasis is on brown-field development and the revitalisation of our existing buildings through creative design.
Durability has become an important concept, one that was familiar to past generations but one that is almost lost in our consumer driven, throw-away society.
Much of the literature concerned with sustainable design and development has
tended to concentrate on new developments. Yet only 1% of the building stock
turns over each year, so our attention should be on alterations and extensions to
existing buildings.

12.2.1   *Durability*

Durability should be a preoccupation of every designer and builder. It all fails,
either sooner or (one hopes) later. Tried and tested construction methods tend to
endure, not so much because they are particularly good, more because they have
proven to be durable over time. John Ruskin's much cited comment 'If we build,
let us think that we build forever' is an enduring one simply because it makes economic and environmental sense. The present trend of designing for short design
lives and service lives is at odds with Ruskin's sentiment and also at odds with a
desire to minimise the impact of building on our natural environment. Our
materialistic, throw-away culture is the antithesis of durability – products are
designed to fail after a short period of time, thus requiring the owner to buy
another, 'better' product. This philosophy has spread to building and is not
particularly helpful in an age when efforts to reduce waste are needed.

Creative design solutions and detail design decisions will be influenced by the
existing building and its context, each providing limitations and opportunities in
equal measure. Designers need to work with the existing palette, not against it, if
successful design solutions are to be found. New uses for redundant buildings

require a complete understanding of the building's construction, structural system, material content and service provision, as well as the cultural and historical context in which it is set. A checklist would need to cover the following issues:

■ historical context
■ social context
■ condition of fabric
■ condition of services
■ stability of the structure
■ potential for re-use and recovery of materials
■ assessment of embodied energy
■ scope for new use
■ access limitations
■ health and safety
■ economic constraints and potential
■ LCA
■ re-use or demolish.

These factors need to be considered before the brief is finalised and should form an essential part of the critical condition survey and feasibility study.

Alterations to facilitate disabled access are a major challenge for many custodians of existing buildings. While different changes in level and various widths of access may contribute to the character of a particular building, equally these are factors which can and often do create barriers to access. Providing equal access for all often requires structural alterations and careful detail design which must be done sensitively if the character of the building is not to be unduly affected. Equally the implementation of successful (non-intrusive) fire strategies is a constant challenge which must be addressed. Buildings must be seen in the context of the society and the people who interact with them. Alterations and extensions, no matter how minor, will affect the building's character. The desire of building owners to upgrade their buildings leads to the need for more design activity: extensions, alterations and upgrading. We are far more flexible and adaptable than the buildings that we build to house our activities; therefore, the desire to alter, extend and upgrade buildings is ever present. The majority of buildings are designed for a specific function and that function may alter (with new technologies) or cease and be replaced by other uses. Successful remodelling of buildings is usually achieved by employing one of two design strategies:

(1) *Match existing*. Use of materials and building techniques to match those used previously, a continuation of tradition through colour, texture, application, scale and design philosophy. Specialist publications and design guides are essential reference tools.
(2) *Contrast existing*. Use of materials and building techniques to contrast with those used previously, a break with tradition, through use of new materials, contrasting textures, new techniques, different scale and new design philosophy.

Both are sympathetic approaches which are usually successful, the philosophy adopted depending upon the wishes of the client, planners, designer, context and resources available. Done well the building will outlive its custodians and probably be remodelled again in the future. Done badly and the value of the structure can be affected negatively and future alterations will be more costly, not to mention maintenance. It is surprising how many building owners entrust such work to less reputable companies ('cowboys') with, unfortunately, predictable results.

12.2.2   Case study – Upgrading domestic properties

To reveal the true extent of upgrading we need to research the work actually done to buildings. A modest housing development built in a small town in 1970 was evaluated in an attempt to see what changes had been made to the 15 houses over a 30-year period. The houses were all detached, two-storey, four-bedroom properties built to a relatively high specification. A condition survey was carried out externally and one house studied in further detail internally.

(1) *External survey*
   (a) *Roof.* Thirteen of the houses had some repair work done to the roof. Three had added tiled entrance porches over the front door. Eight had replaced timber eaves boards with uPVC.
   (b) *Walls.* Evidence of injected thermal insulation to cavity walls in three properties.
   (c) *Windows.* Two properties retained the original single glazed windows. Four had upgraded half of their windows to double glazed units, nine had replaced all of their windows with double glazed units (uPVC).
   (d) *Doors.* All 15 front doors had been replaced (eight with timber, seven with uPVC doors). Three rear doors had been replaced. Two garage doors had been replaced.
   (e) *Drives.* Four of the concrete drives had been upgraded, two with brick pavers, two in tarmacadam.
   (f) *Conservatories.* Three properties had added large conservatories to the rear of the property (one built in timber, two in uPVC).
(2) *Internal survey*
   By focusing on one of these houses the scale of the upgrading internally becomes apparent. In just over 30 years the kitchen had been upgraded (replaced) twice, the bathroom once, and a separate shower room created. The extent of decorating and replacement of carpets could not be established from the current owners. Additional upgrading comprised the following:
   (a) Door opening repositioned.
   (b) First-floor bedroom and bathroom doors replaced.
   (c) Additional electrical points had been added in all rooms and wall lights added in three rooms.
   (d) The hot water system had been replaced by an instantaneous gas hot water boiler. The wall mounted gas fire in the living room had been replaced twice.
   (e) Thermal insulation (100 mm thick) had been added in the roof.

12.2.3   The challenge of accessing relevant information

When dealing with any aspect of an existing building there will undoubtedly be a problem with accessing information about the building's construction. In the study reported above it proved a fruitless task trying to get information about the construction of the building and exact dates when repairs and alterations were undertaken. Work had been carried out on an ad hoc basis by a variety of local builders and tradesmen and there was no recorded evidence of the extent of the work carried out. Evidence was gathered from a visual inspection and in conversation with building owners.

12.3   Building conservation

Conservation of our built environment is a relatively new preoccupation for many countries. France was one of the first to compose lists of historic buildings from the 1840s. In the UK ancient monuments have been scheduled since 1882, but it was not until 1944 that lists of historic buildings were produced under the Town and Country Planning Act, and designation of whole areas as conservation areas was introduced as recently as 1967. Since these early legislative acts the power of local authorities to protect buildings and structures of architectural or historic interest has grown, as has the number of buildings listed and the number of conservation areas. Views on the importance of conserving our built environment vary, although most would agree that some preservation and conservation is important. Whether there is too much emphasis on the retention of the past is open to debate.

Protectionist legislation and pressure groups aiming to protect and conserve our architectural heritage grew rapidly towards the end of the 20th century. In part, this may be seen as a backlash to the insensitive post-war redevelopment which replaced slums and bomb damaged structures. It may also be a reflection of society trying to hang onto the familiar in a time of rapid change and increased uncertainty. What is certain is that we are surrounded by contradictions. We may be interested in steam trains and even enjoy a ride on one in our leisure time, but to commute by steam on a daily basis is quite another matter – modern, quick and clean trains are preferable. Architects renowned for their innovative approach to design choose to reside in Georgian buildings, planners opposed to modern developments choosing to live in a new house. The point is that conservation is a personal issue and one that people tend to have a strong view on. A balance between retention and progress is required.

There is a difference between 'building preservation' and 'building conservation'. Building preservation is concerned with the retention (or reinstatement to its original form) of an important structure. For example, a preserved Georgian town house would not have many of the modern technologies, such as electricity, that we take for granted. Few people would want to live in such a building, but many are interested in visiting one. It is not surprising, then, that many cases of 'preservation' result in a building becoming a museum, somewhat sterile and not in line with modern standards. There is, however, a limit to the number of buildings which may be preserved that are only used as visitor attractions. It is far better to find a new use for them – this makes economic and environmental sense. Conservation enshrines the idea that buildings are used by people and thus make up part of the living tapestry of the built environment, so alterations, improvements and change of use are to be expected. A conserved Georgian town house may resemble the preserved one from the outside, but inside the picture would be very different: electricity, insulation, internal bathroom and toilet, telecommunications and modern domestic appliances would be commonplace.

Many of the arguments about the extent of preservation and conservation can be traced back to the current owner's intentions for the property and the designer's brief. Legislation relating to conservation areas and listing impose restraints on the owner's rights to do what he or she likes with the property without first obtaining consent from the local authority planning department. While some owners are happy to work within the current legislation, others may wish to develop the site in a manner deemed to be unsuitable in a conservation area and conflict is sure to follow.

12.3.1   *Listing*

There are approximately 400,000 buildings in England that are listed as having architectural and historical importance. The infamous demolition of the art deco Firestone factory in west London led to a major relisting in the 1980s in an attempt to protect important buildings from demolition or insensitive remodelling. Originally the cut-off date for possible consideration was for buildings constructed before 1840. In 1970 the cut-off date was extended to those built before 1939 and in 1987 a 30-year limit was introduced. Buildings, ranging from industrial buildings to pubs and post-war schools, may be surveyed and considered for listing once they are 30 years old. There is an additional rule which allows exceptional buildings between 10 and 30 years old to be considered for listing if they are threatened with demolition or alteration. The first building to join this category was the Willis Faber Building in Ipswich, designed by Foster Associates in 1972. It was listed Grade I in 1991. New additions to the list are proposed by English Heritage to the Department of Culture for their possible approval and listing. In 1998–1999 the vast majority of English Heritage's 1258 recommendations were accepted (Cadogan 2000). The listing grades are as follows:

Grade I – exceptional. Covers buildings of national importance and some of international importance.
Grade II ★ – unusual. Of significant regional importance and some of national importance.
Grade II – still valuable. Of significant local importance.

There is also a non-statutory Grade III list used by local planning authorities. This is an advisory list and the local authority may seek to upgrade the building to Grade II if it is threatened with demolition. Listings and further information can be obtained from the local authority responsible for a particular geographical area. Once buildings are listed, alterations or demolition cannot be undertaken without first applying for and receiving listed building consent from the local authority planning department. Listing does not mean that buildings cannot be altered, but any proposed alterations will receive rigorous scrutiny to make sure they are sympathetic to the existing character of the building. The listings provide greater protection to buildings than a local authority declared conservation area does. Routine maintenance does not need consent but such work is subject to value added tax at the full rate of 17.5% and this tax may well hinder important work, thus affecting a building's long-term durability. In the majority of cases listing will improve the financial value of a property.

12.3.2 Conservation areas

Designated conservation areas aim to maintain the overall character and architectural quality of an area via additional planning restrictions. New buildings may be built, but they should enhance, not detract from, the character of the conservation area. Establishment of conservation areas came with the Civic Amenities Act 1967 which gave powers to local authorities to designate and control them. Additional powers of control came with the Town and Country Amenities Act 1974 with consolidation of conservation legislation in the Planning (Listed Building and Conservation Areas) Act 1990 (Greed 1996). The growth of planning legislation and the extension of conservation areas has resulted in some peculiar architectural styles. Developers, designers and planners alike have been guilty of misinterpreting the spirit of conservation and many towns and cities have got their share of mock Georgian and mock Victorian buildings, the majority of which are completely out of scale with the period they have attempted to ape.

12.3.3 Facade retention

Erecting new buildings behind existing (historic) facades is known as facadism or facade retention. In essence the historic facade is retained and supported in place by a temporary structure while a new shell is built behind to replace that which was no longer functional. Opinion differs as to whether this is an 'honest' design approach, but it is a viable option for building developers where the total demolition of a building would be unacceptable, because of the impact on the existing urban character. On the one hand, some would argue that buildings should be retained in their entirety, exterior and interior in harmony. On the other hand, others would argue that a modern interior behind an old facade is both realistic and exciting. In practice there is usually a certain amount of conflict between the wants of the planning authority and the developer, and thus facade retention is sometimes a compromise, although few would admit to this.

Buildings most affected are those in towns and cities, generally medium to large buildings in commercial use and dating from around 1850 to 1940 (Highfield 1991). Demolishing everything but the facade and building new structures and interiors behind the wall (usually traditional load bearing construction) brings with it very specific technical challenges for designer and builder. These challenges are technically different from both new build and more usual work to existing buildings simply because of the rather extreme treatment of the existing building. Experienced designers and contractors are required if a successful outcome is to be achieved. A number of different techniques may be employed, but whatever the approach, skill is required by the contractor to retain the facade safely and complete technically challenging work behind it without causing damage to the fabric to be retained. Temporary support needs very careful design, assembly and disassembly. Connecting the new structure to the existing facade is not without its challenges: the different rates of thermal movement, differential settlement, etc., must be correct if future problems are to be avoided. 'Retention' of the facade will also involve a certain amount of conservation work, such as cleaning, redecorating, repair and replacement of weathered materials, which also needs sensitive treatment.

12.3.4   Urban renewal

Go to any town or city and look at the number of empty houses, flats, commercial and industrial buildings. Not only do these redundant structures blight our townscape, they are also an indication of the way in which society neglects its assets. As a rule of thumb the development of brown-field sites is more expensive and often technically more challenging than development on virgin ground. Incentives are often required. Financial incentives to retain and revitalise redundant buildings on brown-field sites could be improved in the UK. New buildings, including new homes on greenfield sites, are currently exempt from VAT; redevelopment of redundant buildings is not. The issue has been raised with the Treasury on many occasions but to date with no effect. Conservation bodies are still applying pressure to the Treasury for change. *VAT and the Built Heritage* published in October 1999 argued for a harmonisation of VAT at 5% on repairs to listed buildings and alterations to listed buildings.

12.4   Principles of conservation, repair and maintenance

There are a number of well-established principles that should be applied to the conservation, repair and maintenance of historic buildings. These principles are also relevant to recently constructed buildings. Perhaps the biggest challenge in appraising existing buildings is to understand the thought process of the original designers and builders. Did the designers use the most up-to-date guidance? Did they use the most modern detailing techniques or rely on more traditional methods? Did the builders put it together as indicated on the designer's drawings or were (unrecorded) alterations made during the building process? Did the builder have to innovate to achieve the designer's objectives? Documents available at the time may show how it should (or could) have been done, not necessarily how it was done. So to answer these questions it is vital to carry out research and recording before any work to the fabric is considered.

12.4.1   Research and recording

Before any work is carried out those involved need to have a full understanding of the building's history, both social and technical. Information may be collected from a wide variety of sources. Measured survey drawings, as-built drawings, written descriptions, specifications and photographs will be useful. So too will local government records for planning and building regulation control and other documentary sources such as insurance records. In attempting to gather information about buildings it is essential that the search is methodical and critical. All sources should be accurately recorded (even those which are negative) and an accurate record built up through constant cross-checking of different information. A good starting point is with the original date of the building, if this can be established quickly, e.g. from a date stone in the fabric or through local records. Since the late 19th century architects and builders have been required to submit copies of their plans and proposed construction details to the local authority building control department for approval. This body of information can provide an important source of material, the date of design, construction details, survey drawings, etc. Plans are indexed chronologically and searching can take a long time. Unlike planning records, permission to access the drawings will be required for security purposes. Information sources may comprise some or all of the following:

■ maps and plans
■ title deeds
■ newspapers and journals
■ planning records
■ building control records
■ records held by local builders, etc.
■ local knowledge
■ specialist publications and books.

Whether this exercise is conducted before, after or concurrently with an assessment of the building's condition will depend upon circumstances relating to a particular building. However, the on-site assessment is often easier if it is carried out after the data collecting stage. The important point is that it must be done before any objectives, design work or building work are carried out.

12.4.2   Analysis of condition

On-site investigation and analysis should, time permitting, not be carried out until at least some of the information required has been found; this knowledge helps to focus the attention of the site survey. There are two surveys to be done. The first is an accurate measured survey of the building from which plans, elevations and sections can be drawn. This may differ from historical data because of inaccuracies in recording and/or because of unrecorded changes made since its original construction. The resulting scaled drawings show the building plans, elevations, sections and finishes as they exist at present. The second survey is an analysis of the building's condition, a 'condition survey' during which the building fabric is assessed to ascertain its current physical condition. One of the most effective means of assessing the condition of a building is to carry out survey to observe and record its current state. Architects and building surveyors need to draw on a number of different skills when carrying out a survey or inspection, but first and foremost they need to be rigorous in their observation and recording of what they find. Photographs and video can supplement this exercise. To support the data collected by a physical survey it is usually necessary to consult historical sources, as noted above. Condition reports serve two purposes. First, they should provide an accurate and comprehensive description of the condition of the building fabric and services as observed at a particular point in time. Second, the report should act as an information source on which decisions can be made. Thus the

Figure 12.2 Stone replacement and restoration in progress, Harewood House, Yorkshire.

report must be well structured and clearly written, and contain clear conclusions and recommendations.

12.4.3   *Objectives and damage avoidance*

The main objective will be to conserve the building through stabilisation of the fabric and structure. Sensitive repair work will help to extend the serviceable life of the building. The manner in which this is achieved will depend upon the importance of the building and its intended use. A key principle of conservation work is 'minimum intervention'. Combined with a strategic maintenance and repair plan, repairs can be undertaken only when deemed necessary to secure the long-term serviceability of the building. With a well-maintained building repairs should be minimal.

12.5   Asset management

Buildings are an asset. For home owners their property is first and foremost their home, complete with emotional baggage, and second a financial asset. For commercial properties the effective utilisation of the built asset should be part of the strategic business plan. Effective utilisation is subject to the effective management of three core areas: the building, the people using it and the commercial goals of the owners. Co-ordinating the physical workplace with an organisation's people underlies much of the growing literature on asset (or facilities) management.

Definitions of facilities management vary widely, though it would be fair to say that it is the facilities management discipline above all others that espouses a total build approach to construction. There has been, and continues to be, considerable criticism of the development team for not considering the needs of the building users in as much detail as they should. With increased emphasis on saving money on running costs has come additional emphasis on getting the detail design and servicing requirements right before construction.

12.5.1 Maintenance as a ritual

Maintenance must be fully anticipated by client and designer and conveyed to the building owner. Strategically planned periodic maintenance should be a ritual; just like servicing an aeroplane or a car, buildings should also undergo the same checks for safety and performance with the obligatory owner's handbook. Maintenance should be carried out every 12 months, or more frequently depending on the complexity of the building and its services, e.g. cleaning of gutters, checking the roof for loose tiles, etc. Rarely is this the case. It is more common to wait until a fault develops.

12.5.2 Repair

Maintenance and repair should benefit the building, not hinder its aesthetic appeal of technical performance. For example, inappropriate pointing to stonework may accelerate future decay and be visually incorrect. Again, such a statement is easy to make, but in practice the repair of buildings tends to be undertaken in an ad hoc manner, in stark contrast to the time and effort spent on the original building project. Inconsistency will devalue a property.

12.5.3 A case for more adaptable buildings

Worthington (1994) has made the point that the emphasis should be on 'total organisational effectiveness' through the integration of business concerns, buildings and space. To achieve this requires a certain amount of change to achieve better user briefs, better use of performance data and a better understanding of user and building interactions. The challenge for facilities managers is to match the available assets to constantly changing organisational goals.

12.5.4 Evaluation and monitoring

In addition to condition surveys, noted above, it may be sensible to monitor buildings and how they are used over time, a field of study known as POE. This is an important consideration for commercial and public buildings that have to be managed cost-effectively. Evaluation and monitoring of an existing building are usually done for one or more of the following reasons. To evaluate and monitor the

- performance of the building against specified criteria (e.g. energy consumption)

■ functionality of the building against its current (and proposed) use
■ behaviour of building users with a view to improving working conditions.

There are a number of research techniques that may be used to gather information on which informed decisions can be taken with regard to the building's functionality, as follows:

(1) Asking building users about their internal environment, through the use of questionnaires and interviews. This should be carried out strategically, to gather information over a long period so that trends can be established and reaction to any changes clearly recorded for analysis.
(2) Encouraging users to give feedback on their working environment, through the use of a feedback system and user groups (quality circles).
(3) Monitoring how people use the building through observation, e.g. monitoring room usage.
(4) Monitoring how people use the building through the use of IT based 'expert' systems, e.g. monitoring room and equipment use electronically.

Whatever method is used, the data recorded should be used to aid decision-making and utilise the building asset effectively. It is only through monitoring, data collection and analysis that decisions to improve, increase or decrease the space of the working environment can be made with any confidence.

12.6 Re-use and recovery management

Because the land buildings are assembled on is usually more valuable than the materials that form the building resting on it, few structures are allowed to decay gracefully and eventually fall down. Instead they are remodelled or removed and a new structure is put in their place. Recent emphasis on recycling and recovery of materials from redundant structures (recovery management) is welcome, although adopting a recycling culture may not be the long-term answer to our immediate challenges. We tend to see property as belonging to us, i.e. property ownership. Instead it may be useful to think of ourselves as custodians of our buildings, responsible for their upkeep and enhancement, and passed on to future custodians in at least as good a condition as that inherited. Upgrading a building's environmental performance before passing it on to the next custodian would be admirable policy.

One reason why life cycle design was largely neglected in the past lies in the inaccessibility of information – information that exists in the form of specialised knowledge and which is held by a number of poorly linked players in the temporary project network. Progress may be achieved through improved ITs making access to information easier and quicker; however, the number of individuals involved in building continues to increase with the potential to hinder progress. Thus both ITs, such as computer-based expert systems, and the number of people contributing and drawing on the information within the system need to be managed. Whatever strategies are evolved to secure sustainable building they must embrace all of the contributors to the building process, in both the project and the product phases (Emmitt and Wyatt 1998). Thus building product manufacturers and suppliers as well as the disassembly sector must be included within the whole life appraisal if an individual development's environmental impact is to be reduced. So while we must understand the temporary networks and the challenge posed by an information driven environment, we must recognise that the role of the designer is changing.

12.6.1 Return to detail

Earlier in this book the point was made about the importance of staying up to date and the need to incorporate feedback into the design process, especially at the briefing stage. Many of the issues addressed above are influenced by decisions made at the briefing stage and during the detailed development of the design. Experience of buildings in use, such as how they weather and how they are used by people, is important information that should, somehow, be incorporated into the briefing and design stages. By observing and questioning how buildings have fared over time designers are adding and adjusting their practical knowledge base with a view to doing it better next time for the benefit of all those party to the process and all those who use the building. It is essential that a strategic plan is formulated at the briefing stage that incorporates time to revisit the building and carry out any research into its functionality. Left to one's own devices more pressing issues will prevail and the opportunity to incorporate essential experience will be lost.

Further reading

Cook, G.K. and Hinks, A.J. (1992). *Appraising Building Defects: Perspectives on Stability and Hygrothermal Performance*, Longman Scientific and Technical, Harlow.

Mostafavi, M. and Leatherbarrow, D. (1993). *On Weathering: The Life of Buildings in Time*, MIT Press, Cambridge, MA.

Watt, D.S. (1998). *Building Pathology: Principles & Practice*, Blackwell Science, Oxford.

Yeomans, D. (1997). *Construction Since 1900: Materials*, BT Batsford, London.

PART III: SYNTHESIS

Previous page shows flood defence barrier, Rotterdam

13 The language of detail

Regardless of how good we are at detailing buildings, if we cannot communicate our intentions to the building site clearly and concisely, with the minimum amount of ambiguity, we are unlikely to achieve the level of detail intended, despite everyone's best intentions. In this chapter we consider the language of detail, the media used to convey the thoughts from the mind of the designer to the mind of the builder. We consider codification, language barriers and detail as a special language before concluding with a plea for a common medium.

13.1   Building communication

Within the field of building, communication as a process has been neglected. Yet everyone concerned with the design, erection, use and eventual recycling of a building relies on communication, or more specifically effective communication, to get things done. Initiators and sponsors of building projects must communicate their thoughts and aspirations to designer, designer to contracts manager, and contracts manager to tradesmen. The greater the empathy between individuals the better the communication and the greater the client satisfaction with the finished building. Conversely, less effective communication usually results in the potential for dissatisfaction and conflict. Having just stated that communication has been ignored as a process, it has nevertheless received a great deal of attention in other areas where it is tackled implicitly rather than explicitly. Reports urging greater efficiency in building (mentioned above) have tilted at communication and the interaction of people, the root cause of inefficiency. Furthermore, research into the effectiveness of architectural practices has concluded that greater management skills are required if they are to maximise their potential, again implying an emphasis on communication.

One of the most cited studies into communication within the building industry is that published by the Tavistock Institute in 1965, a pilot study by Higgin and Jessop, who concluded that communication was ineffective at all levels within the building industry. They also drew attention to the lack of effective communication and commented on the gulf between the designers and the producers, a situation that has not improved much over the years. A recently published paper by the Cabinet Office on sustainable living and working (*RIBA Journal* 1997) expressed concern about the fragmented approach of the building process and suggested that there were missed opportunities with regard to the adoption of ecologically sound ideas and technologies resulting from professionals' inability to work as a team. Perhaps we should not be surprised by this given the enormity of the task facing anyone charged with managing building projects; relationships in this inhomogeneous, volatile industry are often adversarial in nature and convoluted because of the procurement routes used, resulting in complex (and arguably ineffective) communication routes. As discussed earlier, the response to problems in the building industry has been to add further complexity in the form of new management disciplines. Unfortunately these new intermediaries add a further stratum, or another link to the chain through which information will pass, thus increasing the potential for greater complexity and misuse of information.

13.1.1 Communication in building

The building process relies on a vast quantity of information to enable a project to be built, maintained, re-used and eventually recycled. Building projects require information in the form of drawings, specifications, schedules, calculations and written instructions. Not only do they have different purposes but also they are usually prepared by individuals from different backgrounds, such as architects, engineers, sub-contractors and specialist suppliers, often using different terms and graphical representation. Thus verbal communication between two or more individuals is often concerned with resolving queries over the interpretation of the information provided. Drawings are used to transmit the designer's intent to the contractor. However, it is widely accepted that the format and intent of the drawing is far more apparent to the originator than it is to the receiver, and as such it is not uncommon for the receiver to request clarification or even misread the originator's intentions, sometimes with costly consequences if it happens on site. The effect is magnified when several drawings from different originators are being referred to at the same time: it is rare, even with the use of electronically generated drawing systems, for architects, structural engineers, electrical and mechanical engineers to use the same symbols and terminology, so co-ordination is a challenge for the user and especially the co-ordinator, the project manager, whatever his or her background happens to be. The generation of drawings with the originating office is a process that relies on the use of information and knowledge, much of which will not be included in the finished drawing. Such information must be managed within the office and the quality of the resultant document checked and controlled before it is issued. Building is about information transfer, exchange and use.

The two reports published by the Tavistock Institute, *Communications in the Building Industry: A Pilot Study* (Higgin and Jessop 1965), along with the less well-cited *Interdependence and Uncertainty* (Building Industry Communications 1966), helped to highlight the increase in specialisms and the fact that each specialism had developed its own 'language'. We were left to ponder how anyone managed to build given the difficulties identified by the Tavistock Institute's publications. Since the 1960s the number of specialisms has increased, the building industry has fragmented further and become more litigious, and the use of specialist languages (codification) has increased. A natural assumption would be that the Tavistock Institute's reports formed the catalyst for further research and led to improvements in the industry. Unfortunately, there is no evidence to suggest this was the case, indeed there is still little published advice on how to improve communications (Baden Hellard 1995). From a communications perspective the situation has become far more complex than was the case in 1965. A North American study commissioned by the Construction Industry Institute into the effectiveness of communications within project teams concluded that the major obstacle to project success was the 'lack of effective communications' (Thomas *et al.* 1998). Their research was based on analysis of 582 questionnaires completed by individuals representing 72 (mainly large) projects.

13.1.2 *Interpersonal communication*

Face-to-face explanation and demonstration (interpersonal communication) has long been recognised as the most effective means of conveying intent from one mind to another, especially when the participants of a building project are so different from one another. Carefully dimensioned drawings and expertly worded specifications allow the designer to be precise when conveying information impersonally to those charged with executing the work. But, as noted by Neutra (1954), it is difficult to adjust this information to the varying requirements of the 'chain of performers and artisans', seen as hindering teamwork and more suited to the courtroom than to the building site. When preparing the contract information the designer does not know the workers who will have to interpret his instructions or how well they will grasp his ideas. Indeed Neutra has argued that the designer is trained to ignore such 'subjective contingencies', and be more concerned with couching the contract documents in anticipation of a legal aftermath: the craftsman is scared off after reading it. There is a class difference between designer and worker, the former working in a warm office, the latter working in the cold wind and rain. Ill feeling is often present, which according to Neutra (1954) rises and becomes more hostile whenever there is a sharp differentiation between office work and site work. He also notes that the psychological division and antagonism is less in shop work which isolates the designer less. Antagonism and class differences accepted, the challenge is to communicate information from one organisation to another, to know whether or not the communication has been received by those who need it, and whether or not it has been interpreted correctly. Does the understanding of the receiver correspond with that of the sender?

Architects such as Wren, the master of the works, relied on interpersonal communication to get his ideas across to the craftsmen on site. With increased complexity of the building product and the building process the reliance on drawings and specifications grew. In 1900 Adolf Loos started to revolt against the practice of indicating dimensions on drawings, preferring to direct proceedings personally on site. He used a minimum of drawings and carried the detail of his designs in his head, the architect without a pencil (Neutra 1954). This was an admirable idiosyncrasy, but an approach which was out of step with the rest of his profession at the time. Nowadays, the designer is likely to be seen on site explaining a detail if a problem has arisen or if the detail was not anticipated at the design stage, which is not uncommon in work to existing structures. Working drawings need to anticipate such differences and be crafted with the same care as speech. Well crafted, they convey meaning and design intent with purpose; badly conceived, they can be confusing and the cause of antagonism between sender and receiver.

13.2 Codification

Organisations are important generators of new knowledge, either through research and testing or through the very act of carrying out their daily activities. This knowledge is 'tacit', understood and applied without being stated, and 'codified', i.e. arranged systematically into a code (Polanyi 1958, Boisot 1998).

From the perspective of the designer, the way in which they approach design problems will be tacit (indeed many designers find it difficult to explain 'how' they design) and the solutions will be codified in details, specifications and drawings, in effect a special language. Every subject area develops its own special way of doing things, special words and a special language, both as a means of cultural existence and as a means of identification. Building professionals, just like teachers and medical doctors, have developed a highly codified language that the uninitiated find difficult to access and hence understand. It is difficult to communicate within these cultures without having a clear definition of words and establishing and using a subject-specific language. This is one reason why clients considering a building project for the first time find it difficult both to read drawings and to understand the language being used by the design team. Designers do communicate in words, but primarily through drawings; thus typologies and standards become an important and integral part of their codified knowledge and hence language. In building design education a lot of time is dedicated to the pursuit of design excellence and the development of design skills, but less attention is paid to the receiver's perception of the codified message.

13.2.1 Architectural nomenclature

Different industries have different languages and some have traditionally used different scales, e.g. engineers prefer the 1 : 25 scale while architects prefer 1 : 20. This has caused difficulties in the past, but with the trend towards electronic interchange the scale one works at is not the problem, more the compatibility of the software used. A high profile and very expensive mistake was the loss of NASA's $125 million Mars Climate Orbiter in September 1998 simply because instructions were sent in metric (SI) measurements to a crafts operating in imperial units (one team had been working in imperial units, the other in SI units), a strong case for everyone using the same language on projects, whatever their size or complexity.

Expressions of desire for a common language in architecture have been voiced on many occasions. Building is awash with different spellings and different words for the same thing. Is it a 'lintel' or a 'lintol', a window 'sill' or 'cill', or even a window 'ledge'? Preference for one spelling over another usually depends on one's professional discipline. Regional variations in language usually produce some interesting names for familiar details. For example the sloping ceiling that follows the roof line from the vertical junction at the wall to the horizontal junction of the ceiling is known as a 'skeilling' in some parts of England. Control joints are frequently referred to as 'expansion joints' (which is incorrect since the joint should also be capable of accommodating contraction) or 'movement joints' (which is a little closer to describing its function). Some site based staff still talk about the sizes of structural members in feet and inches, not in metric units (as shown on the drawings): 'Just bung a bit of three by two in there with a couple of six inch nails' loses some of its charm when expressed in metric – roughly translated to a 75 × 50 mm piece of timber to be fixed with 150 mm long nails. It can become even more confusing when looking at the construction industry in other English speaking countries. For example, in the UK we refer to a 'leaf' of brickwork, but in the USA it is referred to as a 'wythe' of brickwork. Perhaps we should not get too precious about the precise use of words and technical terminology when conversing. Does it really matter if everyone in a meeting is talking about 'cold bridging' when what they really mean is 'thermal bridging', or 'movement joints' when they mean 'control joints'? Arguably, the answer has to be no, as long as everyone fully understands the issues being discussed and the action agreed. However, as noted in Chapter 10, when it comes to communicating design intent in graphical or written media then it is essential to use the correct technical language and be precise as to the intended meaning of the words used.

13.3 Language barriers – (in)compatibility

The vast majority of buildings are erected to house people, be it for work or pleasure; buildings are structures that are designed, assembled, maintained and eventually demolished and/or recycled by people. Mechanisation, standardisation and computer technology may have reduced the number of people involved in the process, but we still need people to produce the designs, work the machinery and communicate with one another in order to achieve a common goal, the realisation of a completed building project. The building industry is not a homogeneous industry, but made up of many diverse and competing companies and professional partnerships, the majority of whom are brought together for one, bespoke project, before transferring to the next. The industry is notorious for its adversarial behaviour and litigious orientation and it is questionable as to whether there is ever a real 'team effort' when it comes to designing and producing a building. Unlike buying a car, the procurement of a building is often a complex, time and resource consuming process. While some people prefer to buy structures that have been built speculatively, such as private house developments, the majority of building projects are designed and built to order, i.e. the product is bespoke regardless of the amount of pre-fabrication employed in its construction. From a communications perspective it is necessary to recognise that a number of diverse individuals and organisations come together for one project, forming communication networks in the process, but when the project is complete they will all go their separate ways to join new, often quite different, projects, forming new communication networks in the process. Thus, unlike manufacturing, the relationships are seldom stable and often very short lived. The project manager is faced with a difficult task since he or she will be dealing with different people; just as the project manager gets to know one set of consultants and deal with the issues specific to a particular project, the project ends, and with the new project come new relationships (often the same problems) and the 'learning curve' starts again (albeit from a slightly different starting point).

13.3.1 Temporary contract and contact

The traditional cast of characters, reinforced through academic subject specialisation, comprises a client (building sponsor), project manager, designer (architect), consultants, main contractor and sub-contractors. It is common to refer to *the* client or *the* architect, although in practice there will be an individual representing his or her organisation's interests; and just to confuse the issue further, the individual may change during the course of a project (move jobs). A good example would be of an architect's office where the individual who takes the client's brief (usually a senior member of the firm) will pass instructions to a design architect who will then pass the design drawings to a technologist who may then pass them to a project manager to oversee the contractual stages on site. The diversity and temporary nature of building brings about its own inherent problems; it is not easy to improve constantly the quality of the finished product or the consistency of the service delivered. Indeed, repetition and consistency have different meanings to manufacturing because contracts and, therefore, relationships are temporary. On small projects the interaction of project participants may be infrequent and short lived; at the other end of the scale on large building developments the relationships will last longer. It is where groups interact, the boundary condition, that needs to be effectively managed so that there is no loss in the quality of information transmitted from one group to another (Emmitt 1999a).

13.3.2 Boundary conditions

Anyone familiar with the field of geography and plate tectonics will know that when the plates under the earth's crust either collide or separate, friction results; it is at these boundary conditions where problems such as earthquakes occur. It is useful to draw a comparison between the science of plate tectonics and the building process because there are a number of distinct boundary conditions where friction and thus ineffective communication are most likely to occur, and they need careful consideration if communication is to be improved.

There are three major boundaries: first, the boundary between the sponsor of the building project (the client) and the designer; second, the boundary between designer and contractor; third, the boundary between contracts manager and tradesmen who actually assemble components, systems and products on site to form the finished building. These are the major boundaries where major faults in communication can and do occur, but there are many smaller boundaries, e.g. within the design office where it is common for a senior member of the firm to take the client's brief and communicate it to less senior members of the office who will work on the project (see Fig. 13.1). In many respects the issue of communication breakdown, gatekeeping behaviour and communication network has been a matter of conjecture, with little research in the field addressing such behaviour, which, admittedly, is difficult to observe.

13.4 Detail as a language – the morphology of joints

Every type of construction has its own mode of handling which must be understood if detailing is to be successful. For example, the detailing of a two-storey house in load bearing brickwork has different rules to that of timber frame construction. During their career designers tend to favour certain ways of doing things, and the manner in which they detail buildings often becomes part of their trademark or design signature – detail as a language. The importance of the detail was highlighted in Chapter 4 with a model for sustainable building developed by Schmid. His work has been developed further by Olie (1996) into a typology of joints to support sustainable construction. In effect, it is a language of details and principles that could be applied by designers to realise sustainable design.

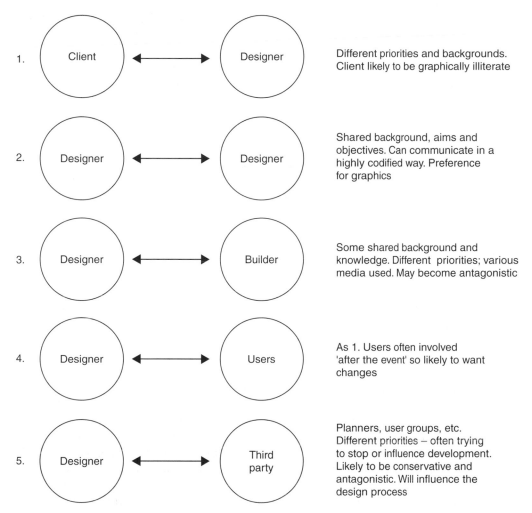

Figure 13.1   Communication between different parties to construction.

In essence Olie has addressed the layers of complexity that surround detail design, the typology, morphology and language of details. Through the deconstruction of the detail into its component parts (both its physical and procedural elements) identification of different layers of meaning – a language (or languages) – will emerge. It is this process of simplification that makes it possible to reconsider detailing from a new perspective, in this case a sustainable one, although the process holds true for different perspectives and for different priorities. From a greater understanding of the joint and its morphology we are better equipped to break new ground in our thinking and application of building details, i.e. we are better equipped to re-address our language of details and in doing so improve the manner in which we build, maintain and disassemble buildings. Once we start to think about the language of detail design we start to question some fundamental issues. For example, to what extent does the language of detail drive the conceptual thinking and conceptual design process? How does the designer's cookbook of standard solutions stand up to such analysis? In grappling with these and associated questions, combined with a greater understanding of the language of building details, we are better equipped to address detailing as an art.

13.5   Towards a common medium

With the move to a global economy and the increased ease of communicating via the world wide web the question as to whether or not construction needs a common medium naturally comes to mind. On an international level, language barriers do exist – as do cultural ones – which can affect the transfer of knowledge. Such differences also make comparisons between different countries particularly difficult, e.g. comparisons between the USA and the UK. Discussion in this book is confined to the more subtle, but equally challenging, differences between the different parties to a construction project. Is there a need for greater standardisation, conformity and equality through a common language? Or should diversity, idiosyncrasies, etc., be allowed and encouraged to flourish?

13.5.1   *The CI/SfB system*

A common language for the communication of information to all members of the building team is available in the CI/SfB system. This system was first used in

Figure 13.2 Communicating through sculpture, Barcelona.

Sweden – the SfB comes from the Co-ordinating Committee for Building (Samarbetskommitten for Byggnadsfragor) – and modified to suit the UK construction industry through changes initiated by the RIBA (the CI stands for Construction Index). Categorisation of technical literature was the main driver for the development of the system, with main headings suggested by the CIB, and development into the current system from the early 1960s. CI/SfB comprises five 'tables' which represent the design process as it proceeds from inception (Table 0) through increasing levels of detail (Tables 1–4). Each table has its own set of keywords and codes, summarised below:

- Table 0 – Physical environment
  Code 0–99
- Table 1 – Elements
  Code (–) – (99)
- Table 2 – Constructions
  Code A–Z
- Table 3 – Materials
  Code A–Z
- Table 4 – Activities, requirements
  Code (A)–(Z)

Whether or not the design team use this system in full, or only in part, will depend upon the approach taken by designers and the size of the project. Not all design offices use the CI/SfB system, although those that do usually incorporate it into their office management systems. Most manufacturers now use the system to identify and position their technical literature (used in product compendia). As with other languages the system has to be learned and used correctly, and this takes a degree of time, effort and dedication on behalf of all those connected with building. Making communication easy to understand and accessible for everyone is affected by historical and cultural factors, but it can be achieved given the will and the ability to manage the communication process from project inception to project completion and feedback.

13.5.2   A question of control

Before looking at some of the issues in project management, it is necessary to state the obvious. First, each project is unique, in that it differs from those preceding it. Second, the project is a temporary task for the project participants. Thus not only do the site, product, objectives and application vary between projects, but so, more importantly, do the project participants. Early work into project management tended to focus on project management techniques and tools to improve project delivery; indeed it is not uncommon to find that this is still a primary concern for project managers in construction. Whilst the effective application of project tools is still necessary, the focus of project management has started to move to the people involved in projects. The assembly of the project team is equally as important as the briefing process, since the culture of the project will be set by the people involved and their interaction during the project.

From a communications perspective, the project manager acts as a node through which all communication should flow, and as such it is without question the most important role in the project team. Empathy between project participants is desirable, yet rarely achieved in practice. If communication breaks down then it will lead to conflict, disputes and the need to resolve them. Control of information and communication routes is the key to control of the project, although whether or not it is effective will depend upon the talents of the individual(s) controlling the communication routes and their gatekeeping talents. From a managerial perspective a well-designed and well-implemented quality management system can assist in achieving effective communication. Quality management systems and communication are inherently linked. Without clear communication quality management systems will not operate effectively and the end product may well suffer, yet quality management systems may help to improve communication with a view to reducing the potential for misunderstanding and possible conflict.

Further reading

Kreps, G.L. (1990). *Organisational Communication: Theory and Practice* (Second Edition), Longman, Harlow.

14 Technological innovation

Technological innovation in building is an area of interest to clients, manufacturers, designers, builders and building users. Innovation can lead to quicker, safer and cheaper ways of doing things; it can also lead to expensive mistakes. The word 'innovation' is over-used and one that needs careful consideration in the context of building, simply because the word means different things to different sectors. This chapter looks at technological advancement and innovation in building. We then consider the development and diffusion of new products and the concept of gradual innovation before looking at the argument for returning to familiar techniques.

14.1 Technological advancement

When talking or writing about technologies in building it is very easy to overlook some significant technological developments that have influenced how most of us live and work. For example, the electric light bulb's development and widespread diffusion was closely linked to the availability of an electricity supply. The bulb was effectively useless until a reliable and safe electrical distribution network had been installed, a commodity most of us now take for granted. It is easy to forget that it is only 30 years since a person set foot on the moon, and the technologies employed to do so have had a major influence on our more mundane artefacts. The invention and rapid development of computers and more specifically the PC has transformed the way in which we live and work more than any other, yet we are still a long way from the paperless office and telecommuting in any major quantity.

Technology is a word used to describe the use of physical things to achieve tasks that unaided human bodies could not. Technology has played a major part in the evolution of human activity and the growth of society. Advances in technologies are widely associated with the competitive standing of individual organisations and collectively the industry in which they operate. Thus technological advancement is associated with economic growth and the standard of living. Benefits are related to the speed and extent of adoption, although not all new technologies turn out to be beneficial, only a small percentage of new technologies are widely adopted; the failure rate is high (see below). In a free market economy the decision to adopt major technological innovations, such as CAD, new manufacturing plant, etc., is taken at senior management level. Other decisions, such as the specification of a particular brick for a particular project, may well be taken on an individual level by a member of the design team with, or without, input from others who are party to the process. The numerous individual decisions will be taken in the light of the individual's existing knowledge and experience and choices of materials, products and details will have to 'fit in' with the overall building assembly. Thus the choice of possible solutions, and the chance to innovate, may well be limited by the overall vision for the building.

Figure 14.1 The 'Dancing House', Prague.

Innovations, and hence the range from which to choose, are constantly expanding as knowledge about innovations is transferred between organisations, from one industry to another and from one country to another. Where innovations are introduced from outside the building industry or from another country the industry can benefit from inventions made elsewhere, and directly or indirectly benefit from the practical knowledge required for their production (Bowley 1960). Detailing buildings to be energy efficient is considerably more advanced in some countries than it is in the UK at present. With the coming of the global market and easy access to information via the internet the transfer of these technologies should, in theory at least, be relatively easy if the climatic conditions are similar.

14.2 Innovation in building

The construction industry as a whole has a poor reputation for innovation, and is often accused of being slow to adopt new technologies. The implication is that productivity is less than it could be. In some regards this may be a fair observation, but in many instances such an observation is a long way off the mark. Ball (1988) has argued very convincingly that the building industry is not backward, merely different to other industries – an industry that has to 'innovate' on a daily basis in order to solve the problems building poses.

Marion Bowley, an economist, produced two significant and now famous books on innovation in building in the 1960s. Her first book, *Innovations in Building Materials: An Economic Study* (Bowley 1960), looked at innovations in major building materials, such as bricks, glass and asbestos sheet materials, and the industries producing them. Not only does this book provide a detailed historical account of the development of a number of materials and their industries, but also her conclusions have a certain amount of relevance today. By investigating the economic factors affecting the invention, introduction and subsequent development of innovations in the manufacture of building materials she demonstrated that the structure of the industry affected the way in which manufacturers innovated. Innovations in methods of production, market innovations, innovations in product, and changes in the structure of the industry formed the basis of her book. One of the many conclusions was that changes in the aesthetic, economic and sociological parameters affecting building demand were a major stimulus to launch innovations on the market, as were changes in the availability of resources. Bowley noted that innovations in building materials often pass through three stages: first, the actual invention of the material or introduction of the material to building from another industry; second, a stage of establishment of the material in the market, a stage that may include improvements to the product; and third, developments in variety of the material. Building organisations may also innovate through an interest in new materials that they themselves would find useful (Bowley 1960).

Her second book, *The British Building Industry: Four Studies in Response and Resistance to Change* (Bowley 1966), further emphasised pertinent issues facing the building industry at the time. Her work raised a number of questions about the relationship between design, the choice of materials, construction methods and the prevailing economic system. She also highlighted the fragmented nature of the industry and some of the barriers to change that existed at the time. Although things have changed since the 1960s many of the issues raised by Bowley are still topical, and although a number of papers and articles have appeared which have sought to tackle innovation in building the questions she posed still remain to be answered.

14.2.1 *A question of definition*

Before proceeding further it may be useful to look at what we mean by innovation. The *Concise Oxford Dictionary* (1990: 610) describes the verb innovate as 'bring in new methods, ideas etc; make changes' and innovation and innovator as 'make new, alter'. The synonyms listed against innovation in the *Oxford Thesaurus* (1991: 223) are 'novelty; invention; modernisation; alteration'. Innovation is a very useful word and one which tends to be over-used, especially in building. Design, invention and innovation are frequently confused, not least because those involved in building come from a wide background, each with their subtle interpretations of words and terminology. In architectural literature the word innovation tends to be used to describe either the design approach of the architect or the appearance of the finished building; hence the design of the building is 'innovative' or the designers have worked in a manner regarded as 'innovative' by their peers. The word is a substitute for 'creative'. In the context of this book innovation needs to be looked at from the perspective of the following five key groups, namely clients, manufacturers, designers, builders and users. Each group will have a different perception of innovation and the potential opportunity and/or threat it poses to them.

In her studies of innovation in the building industry Bowley divided innovations into two main groups, 'those that change the product and those that affect costs and availabilities'. She classified innovations in a range from those that result in new products to the consumer, to innovations that led to products that were, from the viewpoint of the consumer, no different from existing products, a perfect substitute. She went to great lengths to classify innovation (1960: 25–43) and concluded that 'there are innumerable ways of working out classifications of innovations, and the advantage of one rather than another depends on the particular purposes of the study.' Other authors have used different terminology. For example, Slaughter (2000) uses five types of innovation (incremental, architectural, modular, system and radical) when looking at the implementation of construction innovations. The use of different terminology is not particularly helpful, but it does emphasise the point made in the previous chapter about the need for clear definitions that are used by everyone in the industry. Indeed, Bowley made an important point: the word innovation needs to be defined for the purposes of a particular study if misinterpretation is to be avoided. In an attempt to avoid confusion the terminology used here follows the tradition of the large body of diffusion of innovations literature where an innovation is an idea or product that is perceived as new by the receiver of the information, regardless of how long it has been available (Rogers 1995).

14.2.2   *Innovation and diffusion*

A new idea or new process adopted by manufacturing industry has been described as a *technological innovation* (Utterback 1994) or a *process innovation* (Davies 1979). These innovations are concerned with the introduction of new machinery or production methods and their effect on productivity, and because of this they tend to be studied by economists. The development of new products has been referred to as the *innovation process*, by Parker (1978), for example, who divided the process into four functions: invention, entrepreneurship, investment and development. Other authors, such as Bradbury (1989), have made a distinction between the initial idea (invention) and the innovation process, which covers all stages of a product's development up to, and including, its launch onto the market, a phase also described as the 'generation of innovations' (Rogers 1995) which ends in a decision by the manufacturer to market the product to potential adopters (Fig. 14.2). It is the decision to market the product that is the start of the diffusion process.

To examine how a product is adopted a natural starting point would be to look at marketing literature, in particular that concerned with consumer behaviour (e.g. Chisnell 1995). The problem with this body of literature is that it is concerned with products that have recently been launched onto the market. While building designers may consider products that are new to the market, they may also consider products that have been on the market for many years, but which they have only just become aware of because they are faced with an unfamiliar building type or unusual detail. So products new to the market and the established

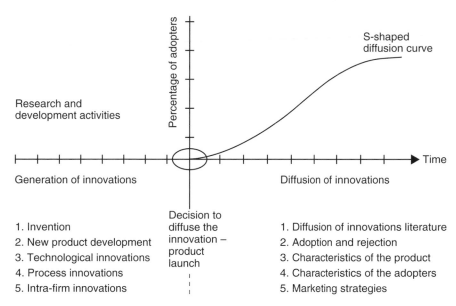

Figure 14.2 The generation and diffusion of innovations.

products may equally be perceived as new by the specifier. A more appropriate body of literature is to be found in work on the diffusion of innovations. This large body of research is concerned with an individual's reaction to something which is perceived as new, whether or not it is new to the market. It is the newness of the product, rather than the length of time it has been on the market, that sets diffusion literature apart from marketing literature (Rogers 1995). Based on a distillation of over 4000 independent studies, diffusion theory is concerned with the factors that influence the rate of adoption of ideas or products which are perceived as new by the receiver of the information, the potential adopter – in this case the adopter would be a specifier working in a design office. At the heart of diffusion research is the 'innovation–decision process' which describes the stages through which a potential adopter may pass, from first exposure to information about the innovation, through a period of gathering more information to consider its characteristics, and finally to its adoption or rejection.

14.2.3 *Movement for Innovation*

In July 1998 The Construction Task Force, chaired by Sir John Egan, published its report *Rethinking Construction* (the Egan Report). It urged the building industry to embark on radical change and a new approach to the delivery of buildings (it used the word product) if it was to improve its performance. Key drivers identified in the report were committed leadership, integration of the process and the team around the building, a quality driven agenda, commitment to people and a focus on the customer. The report also urged the industry to set clear, measurable objectives and to create a performance system to aid benchmarking and provide the tools for sustained improvement. The Movement for Innovation was set up in the autumn of 1998. According to its mission statement 'the Movement for Innovation aims to lead radical improvement in construction in value for money, profitability, reliability and respect for people, through demonstration and dissemination of best practice and innovation' (M4I 1998). Areas for innovation and change are categorised under four headings, also known as the four 'P's:

■ Product (building) development
■ Project implementation
■ Partnering the supply chain
■ Production of components.

The core feature of the Movement for Innovation project is the Demonstration Project Programme in which innovations can be developed, measured, tested and proven on live construction projects prior to dissemination. Applicants have to be willing to share their knowledge and experiences with others in the industry. Demonstration projects are featured on the Movement for Innovation's web site in an attempt to share and start the exchange of knowledge and apply it to future working practices. This, and other initiatives, are commendable and potentially very valuable. One of the drawbacks is that a false impression is often given. These demonstration projects by their very nature will be very small in number and, as proving to be the case, very specific in their remit. A balance would be to feature an equal number of average projects and equal number of poor projects. Not surprisingly, those involved in the average and poor projects are not so willing to share their experiences with a wider audience. For this sort of objective study it is necessary to consult research reports and doctoral work which by its very nature has to be more objective and balanced.

14.3　The development of new products

Technological advancement and innovation in building go hand in hand. If the economic process depends upon the capacity of industry to develop new products and new processes continuously (Druker 1985), it follows that it is equally dependent upon their adoption by the consumer. Products must first be developed and manufactured before they can be launched onto the market. As previously noted, this subject area has been covered extensively, from invention (e.g. Gilfillan 1935), through product development (e.g. Bradbury 1989) to marketing (e.g. Midgley 1977, Druker 1985). The question in the context of this book is who develops new products? Is it the manufacturers or the detailers and assemblers requiring something better than that currently available? A case study helps to illustrate some of the issues.

14.3.1　Case study – New product development

Product development managers from three building product manufacturers were interviewed to gain their views about new product development in construction. These three building product manufacturers were highly regarded by building specifiers and were active in the UK as well as mainland Europe. All three manufacturing companies had

(continued)

certified QC and QA systems in place, as did their suppliers and manufacturing sub-contractors. Furthermore, all three organisations adhered to a philosophy of TQM. The job of their trade representatives was to manage the existing product range through sales and technical assistance to specifiers and contractors. They also contributed to the development of their company's new products through feedback of their meetings with specifiers and builders to their research and development departments.

(1) *Product innovations.* All three organisations claimed to develop new products in-house through their research and development departments. One of the companies had recently launched a product that had been invented by an entrepreneur who took his ideas to the highest bidder. Views varied on the use of patents. Some patents were applied for, but the general view was that they were expensive to obtain and that the majority of their products would be copied. One manufacturer had sued a competitor (who marketed a very similar product at lower cost – and lower quality) and lost, despite having secured patents on the design. Interestingly, the same companies who were precious about protecting their own products were not shy about copying from others – dual standards. In an attempt to keep research and development costs under control, the manufacturers actively looked at other countries to see what they had and how they could be adapted (copied?) to the UK market. For example, the Scandinavian countries provided a good source of information with regard to thermal insulation (also humidity control from France and acoustic treatment from Sweden).

Certain products in their range were identified as having added value because they could be built on. For example, specifiers looking to select roofing tiles would also want products that helped the designer to achieve adequate ventilation as required by the Building Regulations, and, therefore, the manufacturer also sold ventilation products. The sales team had been trained to talk to specifiers about ventilation (and in doing so hopefully sell their products). All companies claimed to be actively developing and marketing further 'accessories' to their main range. The biggest problem facing these particular manufacturers was that of specification substitution. None of the companies would reveal the extent of the problem other than to say it was a major cause for concern. The companies believed architects and some of the main contractors to be unaware of the extent of the problem, rife in sub-contracting (supported by the Barbour Report 1993). In many cases the contractor had bypassed the formal communication routes and contacted the client directly in an attempt (often successful) to change products.

(2) *Specifiers as innovators.* The link between detail design and the development of new products is well known to manufacturers. Specifiers were seen as a major source of information about the suitability of building products. Enquiries from specifiers were taken very seriously, and requests for unusual configurations were investigated fully. The representatives felt that designers, technologists and builders had some good ideas that they had used in the past to improve their product range. However, they noted that this group was not particularly good at spotting an innovative idea themselves. So although designers and builders were frequently coming up with solutions to very difficult problems, it was the manufacturers who benefited from their ideas, simply because they could see the market potential.

(3) *Product development times.* The time period between the identification of an opportunity and bringing a new product to market varied depending upon the type of product. There was at least 2 years' lead-in time between identifying a market

(continued)

opportunity for a new product and the product launch. Manufacturers and supply chain sub-contractors and suppliers would have to make the tooling and they usually required some convincing before they would invest in the new tools, machines, etc., and commit themselves. All of those interviewed claimed to have innovative products in various stages of development, ready to launch when the market was ready, not before (too much risk of failure).

(4) *The influence of legislation.* Changing legislation was seen as both a threat to their existing market share and also an opportunity to develop new products. Building Regulations were the main driver for change, although changes to health and safety legislation and initiatives such as the European Product Directive provided further incentives to improve their products. Changing legislation was an important driver because the manufacturers were of the view that builders and designers would only do something if regulations applied, i.e. they must be forced to improve standards. An ability to keep an eye on changing legislation was identified as a major key to retaining competitive advantage and all three were contributing to the development of legislation which affected their particular market. They were represented on various working groups which fed into the Building Regulations and international standards, either through direct involvement or via the work of their respective trade association. In this way they were aware of the likely changes to current standards before consultation documents were circulated for comment and so they could identify the opportunity for new products early.

(5) *The consumers.* Builders and builder's merchants were seen to be interested in cheap products and/or products that the builder's merchants would give them most discount on (and hence most profit). Unfamiliar products were usually challenged and a more familiar alternative put to the designers for consideration and, they hoped, substitution. In contrast the designers were first and foremost concerned with aesthetics, then technical performance and, third, cost. High performance product specifications were preferred because they reduced the perceived risk of failure. Specifiers had become more cost conscious over the past 5 years. The sales force gathered information from specifiers, contractors and merchants about the awareness of their product range and the perception of it. 'We know how a specifier behaves. What we need to establish (know) is "why" a designer behaves in the way he/she does.'

14.4　Gradual innovation

Many practical inventions come into widespread use slowly. Manufacturers and producers are usually working in competition with one another and acceptance is by a diverse mass of consumers. Indeed Neutra (1954) concludes that the 'pioneering designer' would be wise to disclose the new features and consequences gradually rather than all at once, a series of steps rather than 'one' design. Manufacturers may well choose to follow similar strategies when introducing new products (as noted in the interviews reported above).

With the philosophy of total quality comes the desire to do the next project better than the previous one, a case of gradual improvement. For the designer such improvements may be procedural, to make more efficient use of the time available, and would not be reflected in the finished building, and/or constitute improvements in design which will be evident in the finished building. For designers working on similar building types, e.g. residential developments, it is a relatively natural task to look at the previous design and think about improvements. For designers working on a variety of different building types gradual innovation becomes more difficult for that particular designer because of the inconsistency between projects. Some designers would argue that innovative design solutions are more likely when they are working on unfamiliar building types (or with unfamiliar technologies) because they are not influenced by their previous knowledge of how to solve the problem. Thus they are unable to fall back on their own solutions, but must search and explore the possibilities as they see them.

The Eden Project in Cornwall could be viewed as an example of gradual innovation, albeit on a grand scale. The giant conservatories designed by Nicholas Grimshaw and Partners draw on the conservatory tradition of Paxton and the creative thinking behind Buckminster Fuller's geodesic domes. Here the architects have used new materials (e.g. triple glazed ethyltetrafluoroethylene foil instead of glass) in conjunction with lightweight galvanised steel tubular frames to form enormous self-supporting shells. The two giant conservatories reach 45 m at their highest point and span 100 m at their widest, being 200 m and 135 m long respectively.

14.5   A return to familiar techniques?

One of the questions which constantly confronts this author is one raised by Potter in the preface to *What is a Designer?* (1989). Should a designer be a conformist or an agent of change? The philosophy adopted in this book has been the latter. If, as designers, we merely conform then why bother? Surely the challenge for we designers is to push at the edges of accepted knowledge and be creative in the pursuit of our clients' goals and our concern for society at large, an argument pursued in this book with regard to designing, building and using buildings in an environmentally responsible manner. In practice the answer to the question posed above is rarely so polarised. Designers, like other workers, have to make a living and in a healthy market economy there is a place for the conformists and the agents of change to exist side by side and many positions in between. For example, diffusion of innovations literature categorises individuals under five headings, from the 'innovators' (the first to change and hence lead) and the 'early adopters', to the 'early majority', 'late majority' and eventually the 'laggards' (those least likely to change). In truth, even this answer is too general because the majority of designers work on projects at either end of the scale. Many well-known architects work on mundane projects in order to pay the bills and stay in business (they do not like to publicise or admit to the fact), choosing to publicise only their creative projects. Other designers known for their penchant for the mundane also produce some very competent, well-detailed, cost-effective buildings. However, such diversions do not help.

The question posed above has to be asked in the light of our growing awareness and concern for environmental issues. And in this regard designers have a responsibility to act as agents of change. Those clients who demand buildings with short design lives and who take a somewhat cavalier approach to environmental issues must be stood up to, advised and educated in the hope that they will consider building in the wider picture. As professionals concerned with aspects of building design, assembly and use we have a responsibility to our clients and to society at large. If we all do our bit then the achievement of sustainable design will become a reality sooner rather than later. We should not forget the dictum 'conventional thinking produces conventional results'. We must start to think and act differently to our predecessors for the sake of our host.

Further reading

Rogers, E.M. (1995). *Diffusion of Innovations* (Fourth Edition), Free Press, New York.

15 Towards a theory for practice

This final chapter discusses some of the challenges facing building designers as they attempt to build in an information driven, environmentally aware society. Research and its importance to academics and industrialists is discussed before looking at research methodologies for those working in this area. This naturally leads into an overview of new course provision specifically targeted at architectural technology and the need for continuing professional development. The chapter concludes with an attempt at developing a theory for practice.

15.1 Reports and buzzwords

Within the field of architecture and building, both students and practitioners are constantly bombarded with reports urging greater productivity, improved quality, improved service delivery, better value, better safety, greater adherence to programme and so on – for less money. Although well intended the reports display a surprising ignorance of the complex relationships and behaviour that make up the exciting culture of the building industry. The reports have failed to address the fact that *people* build and that these people must *communicate* with one another effectively in order to achieve their objectives. It is people who commission building projects, who do the designing, plan the programmes, design the project's culture and work together through a variety of communication media towards a common goal, a completed building project – be it a small domestic extension or a multi-million pound development, a point taken up in earlier chapters.

We are all urged to adopt x, y and z to 'improve' both the process and the product. Words such as 'partnering', 'quality management', 'supply chain management', etc., are bandied about with little thought for either their implementation or long-term effectiveness – as such, they tend to be ignored, with change driven by market forces rather than good intent. With every new idea or fad comes increased complexity, additional paperwork, more convoluted relationships, more consultants and even more sub-sub-contractors with the associated transfer of responsibility, i.e. lack of responsibility and questionable improvements in either service delivery or quality of the finished product. With increased complexity comes the spectre of ineffective communication, errors and disputes; the building industry is already littered with them. The reports alluded to above are the more recent ones produced by Sir Michael Latham (1994) and Sir John Egan (1998); neither is based on empirical research, but wrapped around personal opinion, rhetoric, prejudice and political dogma. The building industry has never had a strong research tradition, so perhaps we should not be surprised by the approach adopted by the reports' authors and, criticism aside, the reports do touch on some important issues such as project partnering, supply chain management and integration. If we are serious about trying to find out what is, or is not, being done in the architectural technology field then it is necessary to look at research work.

15.2   Innovation and research in building

In the previous chapter the word 'innovation' was explored in some detail because of the different meanings it has for different users. The word 'research' is equally problematic. Some have argued that research is an academic exercise, carried out by researchers working in universities and governmental research departments with questionable use to practitioners. At the other end of the scale the act of carrying out design has been described as a research exercise. Debates can (and do) fill books, but for research to be of any value to practitioners it must be accessible, a point taken up below. For the purposes of this book 'research' should be taken to refer to any exercise which results in a furthering of knowledge, whether it is published, codified in managerial systems or embodied in a building artefact. In the act of practising design we draw on many different sources, developing our understanding and knowledge base through the use of research reports, previous experience of building and design – a process of study which results in a state which did not previously exist.

Within the field of building there is an enormous amount of published research, a great deal of which falls within the technologists' domain. But for one individual, or even one organisation, to keep up with this information is a full-time challenge, as is its relevance to particular job functions and current projects in the office. Many research organisations exist throughout the world with the aim of improving knowledge through the activities of their members. In the UK the BRE is the prime producer of guidance for members of the industry, publishing a wide range of documents, holding an extensive library and employing experts. Other countries have their own equivalent organisations. On the international stage one organisation deserves mention for its dedication to research and its particular relevance to the field of architectural technology: that is the International Council for Research and Innovation in Building and Construction, known to many by the acronym CIB.

15.2.1   *International Council for Research and Innovation in Building and Construction*

This research organisation was established in 1953 as an association to stimulate and facilitate international co-operation and information exchange between research institutions associated with building. Under the name of the International Council for Building Research, Studies and Documentation, it held its first international conference in Rotterdam in 1959, since which time the organisation has evolved into the most significant research forum in the industry world-wide. From its base in the Netherlands the CIB has grown into a world-wide network of over 5000 experts drawn from industry and academia. CIB comprises a number of task groups (TGs) which have specific objectives and working groups (WGs) which have a wider remit. The TGs and WGs focus on a defined scientific area; combined they cover issues concerning construction materials and technologies, design of buildings and the physical environment, building science, legal and procurement practices, IT and management.

The CIB has a number of strengths. First, the organisation of conferences, symposia and congresses provides the opportunity for individuals to exchange ideas and share knowledge on a face-to-face basis, relationships which are often continued between meetings via use of the internet. Second, the publication of the WGs' and TGs' collective knowledge, in the form of proceedings, technical analyses and state-of-the-art reports, is important in expanding the knowledge base of building in an international arena. The task groups and working groups by their very nature do change over time, both in the composition of their members and in their specific aims and objectives, new ones being formed to tackle new challenges and established ones closed down, their task(s) completed. Current information can be obtained through the CIB's web site.

15.3 Research in architectural technology

There has been and continues to be a great deal of research carried out which falls under the general heading of architectural technology. More focused research into detail design (architectural technology) is more difficult to find. BIAT's Innovation and Research Committee was set up in an attempt to bring together disparate research under the common umbrella of architectural technology. Another initiative is the Detail Design in Architecture conferences. First held in 1996 these modest conferences aim to bring together researchers interested in detail design decisions (Emmitt 1996, 1999b, 2001). Despite the amount of time professionals spend on this activity, it soon becomes plain to researchers in this area that architectural technology, unlike design or structures, lacks a theory, a point taken up below.

15.3.1 *Link between research, practice and education*

Research, practice and education should form a synergistic relationship from which innovation can develop. These are issues revolving around the key areas of context, methods, professional relationships and reality (Fig. 15.1).

(1) *Context.* To be of any value research needs some form of contextual relationship. What are the underlying value systems of the architectural technology discipline? To answer this needs an understanding of the historical, political and cultural factors. History is important because it provides researchers with clearly identified benchmarks, e.g. the Oxford conference of 1958 was an important milestone in the development of the architectural technology profession and had a wide ranging effect on architectural education. Political issues (with a small 'p') concern the manner in which the professional institutions relate to one another as well as to the manufacturers, suppliers and trades associations. Culture will develop out of action, and inaction. As a culture, research is too important to be left to chance – culture needs to be fostered, moulded, sculptured, developed and nurtured, research needs to be directed by the professional bodies.

(2) *Methods.* In terms of methods the paradox between art and science that concerned researchers in the field of architecture is still present when focusing on architectural technology (discussed in more detail below).

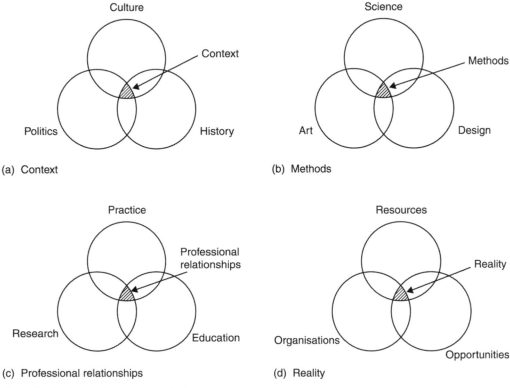

Figure 15.1 Research, practice and education.

(3) *Professional relationships.* These revolve around three key areas: synergy between practice, research and education. Practice provides researchers with a window on current techniques and procedures – some practices may be well ahead of published research, some lagging behind, but both ends of the spectrum are important areas to research. Practitioners also consume research, be it in the form of regulations, codes and standards, and/or reports and books.

(4) *Reality.* Issues of context, methods and professional relationships should be viewed from a realistic perspective. A balance is required between resources, professional opportunities and organisation. One of the most valuable resources is time – research takes a lot of it – and research projects need to be designed to be achievable in the time available. Finance is the other resource in short supply. Of course it is one thing to do the research, quite another to disseminate it to those who may require the information.

15.3.2 Research trends

Because the architectural technology discipline spans extensive disciplines of design, manufacture and assembly the opportunity for research is vast. The following list represents some of the areas relevant to the architectural technology field; it does not seek to be exhaustive, merely provide a few signposts for others interested in research. Some of these areas are attracting a lot of attention at the moment (such as sustainable building), others have been largely ignored to date (such as detail design decision-making).

- Sustainable construction, especially the challenge of detailing for disassembly
- Management of the detail design phase
- Detail design decision-making
- Linkage between conceptual design, detail design and operations on site
- Health and safety, fire engineering, secure by design
- Regulations and their contribution towards innovation
- Building products, their development and uptake by specifiers
- Impact of ITs
- Communication between parties to the construction process
- Knowledge management and application.

Combined, the areas identified above go some way to creating a solid knowledge base from which a theory for architectural technology can be developed. To consider this issue further it is necessary to look at some research methodologies available to students, researchers and practitioners.

15.4   Research methodologies

As mentioned above, the scope for research in architectural technology is vast and the range of methodologies that may be employed is equally wide. Therefore, a brief explanation of some of the methodologies which can be, and are, used may help those setting out on a research project, no matter how modest or ambitious its goals. Choice of research methodology will depend upon a number of factors, such as the scope of the project and the available resources, so the choice of methodology is often a compromise. It may also be based on strong research traditions associated with a particular field, i.e. the research follows a common methodology. Whether one approach is better than another is often open to debate and it is not uncommon for researchers to use a combination of both quantitative and qualitative techniques. For example, Dana Cuff's book on architectural practice was based on qualitative techniques (observational research) while the study by Symes *et al.* of architectural practice relied on an extensive postal questionnaire (largely quantitative) supported by three case studies (qualitative). Whatever method, or methods, used it is useful to remember that no matter how extensive and rigorous the research it only provides an indication of how things are at a particular point in time. It does not prove a point beyond reasonable doubt – there are guaranteed to be exceptions to every rule. Regardless of their scope, all research projects need to be designed and carefully planned to be achievable within the resources available. Thus time and money may well influence the methodology employed. The differences between quantitative and qualitative research are explored below.

15.4.1   Quantitative research

Quantitative research is based on the collection of data using scientific techniques, i.e. a numerical approach from which statistical analysis of the collected data allows conclusions to be drawn which may (or may not) be representative of the larger picture being studied. Engineering and materials science are examples of fields where quantitative methods are the principal investigative tool, essentially concerned with the world as it is (measurables). There are two main methods as follows:

(1) *Surveys.* Postal (and e-mail) questionnaires are a useful research tool for gathering information from a large, albeit remote, sample relatively cheaply and quickly. Although they are usually based on question design that requires answers that can be quantified, there is scope for asking and collecting a limited amount of qualitative data to support the quantitative responses. Typical questions require the respondent to tick or circle an answer to a question, ranging from a simple choice from Yes/Unsure/No to slightly more complex responses such as Strongly agree/Agree/Neither agree nor disagree/Disagree/Strongly disagree. Other questions may be designed that require the respondent to rank a list in order of preference, from 1 (first preference) to 10 (last preference). Telephone questionnaires serve a similar function, although they have the added benefit that respondents can ask for clarification if they do not understand a question and (depending on the design of the survey) there is more scope for asking questions that require qualitative answers. Response rates will vary, although the better designed and better targeted the questionnaire the more the likelihood of a good response rate. Surveys can be repeated relatively easily to gain comparative information at, say, a later date.

(2) *Experimental research.* Setting up a research project under controlled conditions, e.g. the laboratory, is relatively straightforward given a sound methodology, the correct equipment and accurate recording. Such experiments should be easy to replicate, by both the research team and others for verification of the findings. Again, the data generated are primarily numerical.

15.4.2   *Qualitative research*

Qualitative research is primarily concerned with individuals' perception of the world and is particularly well suited to research on management and design issues. Here the emphasis is on insights, using interviews (asking), observational techniques (looking) and case studies (looking and asking).

(1) *Interviews.* Interviewing people is an effective way of gaining opinion and perceptions and is widely used. A degree of caution is required because when professionals, such as architects, speak or write about their work they are portraying themselves as they wish to be seen, a professional image for public consumption (Ellis and Cuff 1989). Therefore, it would be sensible to use a second method of data collection to provide a cross-check to see that what people say they do is actually what they do, i.e. there is a need for observational research.

(2) *Observational research.* Looking at how people actually behave is potentially one of the most rewarding research techniques, but one difficult to conduct and difficult to repeat. The biggest problem with this type of research is that as soon as people know that they are being observed they tend to behave differently to how they normally would because they are conscious of the fact

that they are being observed. For example, people may behave differently if a researcher (a stranger) is present in their normal working environment or if they are being recorded on film, and this needs to be taken into account in the design of observational research. One way around this is to use discrete monitoring techniques, such as hidden cameras, although this approach raises a number of ethical concerns. A better and more honest approach is to use ethnographic techniques, essentially participant observation. The ethnographic approach is grounded in anthropology in that it allows the researcher to use naturalist modes of enquiry to account for the behaviour of humans.

(3) *Case studies.* Case studies are used in building to describe the process of building and to illustrate the outcome of that process. They may also be used to illustrate the behaviour of, e.g. design teams. For comparative purposes it is usually considered necessary to include four different case studies to ensure a degree of validity to the research. However, one case study may help to illustrate some of the main issues being discussed without seeking to be representative of the larger population.

15.4.3   *Ethical issues*

Research, by its very nature of enquiry, is invasive and care needs to be taken by the researcher at all stages in a research project to ensure that the interests of those associated with the subject being researched are not compromised, i.e. an ethical approach is required. The exact nature of the ethical issues will be related to the subject being investigated and the methodology employed. As a basic principle researchers must be open and honest with people and data. In the commercial world of building a number of areas may be sensitive and extra care is required. For example, research into the uptake of new technologies, especially where they are product specific rather than generic, can have implications for the manufacturer. Sometimes, e.g. in the case of research into the uptake of new building products, the research is not published in the public domain simply because of its commercial sensitivity. Likewise, research into the management of the detail design process in professional organisations could affect the organisation and individuals concerned, especially if the outcome is critical of those being studied. Thus researchers must concern themselves with ensuring that the people and processes involved are sufficiently well disguised to ensure anonymity. Not all research is anonymous, and some organisations and individuals may be keen to see their name in print. In such cases equal care must be taken to ensure that the completed research is not just an enhanced marketing exercise for those being researched – research should be a balanced enquiry and, therefore, criticism is expected. Gaining the adequate permissions to carry out a balanced research project is a constant challenge for researchers. It is ethical to

- inform affected parties about the scope and nature of the research and the likely outcome before starting it
- obtain consent to do the research and also consent to publish it (without too restrictive caveats)
- record all information accurately and in a manner that other researchers can follow should they wish to
- respect the organisation's and individual's wishes for privacy and anonymity

■ offer something in return, e.g. a copy of the completed report or publication, and not to forget to thank people for letting you into their private worlds.

15.4.4 *Research – an iterative process*

One of the biggest misconceptions about research is that it follows a predetermined, well-planned route, from identifying the scope, to reviewing the literature, deciding on a methodology, data collection, data analysis, and finally the presentation of findings, represented by the inverted pyramid in Fig. 15.2. Experienced researchers will be familiar with a much more iterative process. This is an important point to make because just as individuals have different learning styles they also have different approaches to data collection and presentation. Whether we start with a title, or with access to some data, is largely a matter of individual preference and circumstance; what is more important is not so much the order it is done in, but the outcome of the process, the deliverables. Figure 15.2 indicates the main phases in a research project and their logical progression over time, during which the scope for uncertainty should decrease. The iterative process is represented by the feedback arrows.

(1) *Title.* For reasons that should become clear from the discussion below, many research projects start with a working title which broadly describes the research being undertaken. The final title of the research is usually determined once the research is complete and may need adjusting simply because more is known at the end of a research project than was at the start.

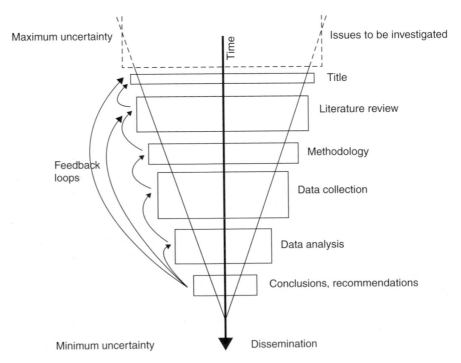

Figure 15.2 Research – an iterative process.

(2) *Literature review.* Searching for, finding, reading, analysing and criticising work already carried out on a particular field of study is necessary for a number of reasons. First, and most obvious, the literature review will provide an indication of the work already done in the field on which the new research project will build. Second, the literature review will reveal the methods used by other researchers and may well highlight shortcomings with the methodologies employed.

No literature review can ever be exhaustive, nor can it ever be complete, because during the duration of the research project other research may be published which cannot be ignored. Sometimes this new work can be helpful, (e.g. additional comparative data), sometimes it may necessitate an adjustment in the research being conducted. Either way, it is necessary to be aware of new developments in the field to ensure that the new research has validity.

(3) *Methodology.* It is not unusual for people new to research to confuse the literature search with the methodology and/or get confused as to what the methodology should be. It is very simple. The methodology describes how the data will be (and were) collected and how they are to be analysed. In essence, the researcher is telling the reader how the research was conducted. This allows the reader to make an informed opinion on the data and should also allow other researchers to repeat the research at a future date should they wish to do so. Once the methodology has been decided upon it is good practice to conduct a small trial (a pilot study) to test the design of the research. From this test an indication as to whether the data collection exercise is feasible can be established and any modifications made before data collection starts.

(4) *Data collection.* Whatever method is used for collecting the data it is essential that they are recorded legibly and consistently and time scales are adhered to. Different methodologies have different protocols for recording information.

(5) *Data analysis.* There are two different approaches to data analysis. The first is to complete the data collection phase and then analyse the findings. The second is a progressive approach to data collection where data are collected and analysed as a series of predetermined steps, with the results of the intermediate analysis informing future data collection. The approach used should be clearly stated in the methodology.

(6) *Conclusions and recommendations.* Once the data collection and analysis are complete the conclusion and any recommendations can be written and the new research findings discussed in relation to the work that has already been published (and identified in the literature review).

(7) *Dissemination.* The outcome of the research, the deliverables, should be disseminated widely. There is little point in doing research and then failing to communicate the findings to the parties that may need it.

15.4.5   *Research expectations*

A number of widely held expectations are expected from research projects. We should expect a piece of research to have the following characteristics:

■ The research should be meaningful and a catalyst for new work.

■ It should be well organised and challenge perceived notions and/or question assumptions.
■ The research should validate what has happened in the past.
■ An attempt should have been made to try and implement or test an idea (it does not necessarily have to break new ground).
■ It should have some value to its intended audience.

What constitutes a scholarly enquiry? Is it all text and diagrams or, e.g. a series of detail drawings that have been subjected to rigorous scrutiny? Architecture and the design process is special in that research may involve a high degree of analysis of graphical material, designs and details, and discussion of their implementation.

15.5 Education and training

Closely linked to research is the issue of education, training and lifelong learning. When we first start to question how buildings are created, assembled and used we begin a lifelong process of collecting, assimilating, adjusting and reinventing our practical knowledge base. This is a process given recognition with the concept of lifelong learning. In many respects creative individuals remain perpetual 'students' of their subject throughout their careers, constantly asking questions about what they are doing and why. Students just embarking on their chosen careers are confronted with what appears to be a daunting range of information, knowledge and skills which must be acquired quickly. Students further along their career paths are constantly confronted with new experiences and new problems that need rapid resolution and by their very nature require a certain amount of 'studying'. Students towards the end of their careers take on mentoring roles for the newer students, passing down knowledge and words of wisdom for new generations of professionals to take forward.

Criticism of architectural education has focused on the architecture schools' curriculum, especially its reluctance to teach management and more latterly the shift further towards design at the expense of technology, a trend to be found on both sides of the Atlantic (e.g. Symes *et al.* 1995, Fisher 1994). Crosbie (1995) complained that many architects did not know how technology integrated with design simply because the two were taught in isolation, and with reports (Latham 1994, Egan 1998) urging greater teamwork and greater efficiency the 'new' profession of architectural technology and its new undergraduate programmes appear very timely. The undergraduate degrees in Architectural Technology provide an ideal opportunity to develop these and other pertinent issues for the benefit of building as a whole.

15.5.1 The Architectural Technology degree

Although the introduction of the Architectural Technology degree has been a relatively quiet affair, it represents a significant development in architectural education. These degrees are being structured to cover a wide range of architectural issues, to include management, technology and design, the majority having an underlying philosophy of environmental responsibility. Until the 1990s students interested in architectural technology could only pursue the subject to BTEC

Higher National Diploma (HND) or Higher National Certificate (HNC). These were, and still are, highly regarded awards providing essential skills for the technologist in practice and which now form a bridge to the undergraduate degrees. At the start of 2001 there were over 140 institutions offering Architectural Technology at HND and or HNC throughout the UK and the Republic of Ireland (BIAT 2001) demonstrating the strength of the BTEC awards.

The first degree programmes were developed at Luton and Napier, and followed by Leeds Metropolitan and Sheffield Hallam Universities (Mason 1999). These pioneering institutions proved that there was an alternative to architecture (and building degrees) and the market has responded. Now there are 32 institutions offering degrees in Architectural Technology in the UK and the Republic of Ireland, 20 of which are accredited by BIAT (BIAT 2001). With others starting up around the world this represents a rapid growth in provision from modest beginnings. Curricula vary between different universities, although the three core areas of design, technology and management are the underpining characteristics of these degrees. In part, this is due to BIAT's deliberate policy of not being prescriptive, merely offering guidance (and an extensive checklist if accreditation is required), and in part due to institutions creating the degree out of existing modules from associated degrees, such as Architecture, Building Surveying and Construction Management. The effect of this is increased choice for students within the architectural technology discipline.

In May 2000 the Quality Assurance Agency for Higher Education (QAA) published separate benchmark statements for architecture and architectural technology (QAA 2000). The academic standards for architectural technology are based on subject knowledge and understanding of three core areas, namely:

- technology
- design, procedures and practice
- procurement and contracts (management).

Positioning is a challenge for the designers of the new undergraduate courses: where exactly does the technologist sit in the overall scheme of things? Anyone who has tried to answer this question (and hence justify the degree) will agree that it is not easy, since the technologist in practice can operate in the same role as an architect, or specialise in detailing or contract administration. In practice boundaries are constantly shifting. With evolution from architectural assistant, to technician to technologist, professional roles and responsibilities have also changed and it is sometimes difficult to find agreement on what an architectural technologist does in practice. To some observers, the technologist forms the link between design and production, detailer and project co-ordinator. At the other end of the scale some see the technologist in a similar vein to the traditional role of the architect, specialising in building design, construction *and* its management – the new 'master builders'.

When SAAT was formed in 1965 the technician's role was clear. Technicians were seen as performing a complementary role to that of the architect, seen as interpreting the architect's design vision and putting it into practice through detailing and efficient communication between design office and site. Technicians were primarily concerned with the technical elements of design, not the aesthetics, and were concerned with RIBA plan of work stages from 'E' onwards, a view consistent with that of the RIBA. Since the formation of SAAT there have been considerable changes in construction, not least the increasing fragmentation of the industry and increased competition between different professional groups. The transformation of SAAT into BIAT was consistent with competitive trends and the change of the word 'technician' to 'technologist' signalled a re-definition of the role. Technologists are now competing with architects and have extended their services into the design arena.

In industry some design firms operate very rigid boundaries, but the majority of these creative organisations are small and require a great deal of flexibility by their members if they are to respond to their clients and provide a quality service quickly and professionally. As such, individuals' qualifications and experience become blurred. Whatever position is adopted, the graduate architectural technologist will need to have a thorough understanding of design methodologies, be familiar with the latest developments in both building products and procurement, be fully conversant with IT, and be able to manage the detail design and construction programme effectively. Issues related to technological change and innovation, legal and economic issues as well as developments in environmentally responsible design complement the core themes. Furthermore, communication skills and the ability to work as an effective team player (or leader) are fundamental to the ethos of many of the architectural technology undergraduate programmes. On graduation the architectural technologist should possess the knowledge, self-esteem and transferable skills required to compete in an ever changing competitive marketplace, i.e. they should be capable of adding value to a firm's competitiveness. Purely on financial grounds the biggest advantage, as far as potential students are concerned, is that full membership of BIAT takes 5 years with 3 spent in education compared with 7 years for architects to become members of the RIBA, with 5 years spent in education. Since there is little difference in earning potential between the two professional disciplines it is likely that students may choose the BIAT route rather than the RIBA route once they (and their career advisers in the schools) are aware of the differences. The student financial debt will have 2 years less to build up and 2 years more to be paid off, a powerful incentive for prospective students.

When looking at these new degree programmes a couple of questions come to mind. Is this new development in architectural education merely a response to supply and demand, adding a further participant to the supply chain and fuelling the fragmentary agenda? Or does it represent the start of a real opportunity to integrate design and production through the catalyst of better education for architectural technologists? Providing answers to these questions is likely to upset other professionals; however, my own view is that this new discipline does provide the missing piece in the jigsaw (responding to market demands) and hopefully an integrating role. There will be fierce competition between architects, surveyors and technologists because there is limited work to go around, but ultimately this new role is about doing things differently and responding to the industry's challenges rather than perpetuating outdated stereotypes and ineffective modes of delivery. In forming the missing link between design, production and assembly, the architectural technologists' career prospects would appear to be very good.

For those unable or unwilling to attend university on a full-time basis a number of options exist. Part-time attendance allows the link between practice and education to be maintained during the course of a student's study (usually 5 years for an honours degree). Other options are distance or open learning, or to gain credit for workplace skills through the National Vocational Qualifications (NVQs) and Scottish Vocational Qualifications (SVQs).

15.5.2   NVQs and SVQs

The Construction Industry Standing Conference (CISC) was established in 1990 with the aim of setting standards of competence for professional, managerial and technical roles across all sectors of the construction industry. CISC is part of the government's initiative to introduce National Occupational Standards and NVQs/SVQs with the primary purpose of improving the performance of British industry through the development of individuals in the workplace through recognition of their workplace skills. The NVQs/SVQs are an assessment scheme, not a training scheme, aimed at honing the experience, understanding and competence of individuals. These awards can be used as part of a CPD programme, can help to identify future training and development needs during performance appraisals and are one way of demonstrating competence to clients. On the positive side these new qualifications provide individuals and employers with tools to assess and develop workplace competences through a national framework of recognised assessment. On the negative side there is still a great deal of confusion as to how they actually relate to the more established academic awards such as the HNDs and HNCs, degrees and postgraduate diplomas.

NVQs and SVQs are designed to reflect the skills, knowledge and understanding that an individual has in relation to a specific area of his or her work. Thus the focus is on demonstrating what individuals can do, not just on what they know. NVQs and SVQs may be pursued by individuals working in industry by demonstrating competence within a given occupation, e.g. architectural technology. These awards form a national framework and individual awards are accredited by relevant professional institutions. These awards have been developed to form a functional analysis of specific work roles and are available at five different levels. Level 1 covers varied, but routine, work activities, with increasing complexity through Levels 2–4 to Level 5 which involves the application of a significant range of fundamental principles in uncertain situations. Awards comprise a designated number of units that have to be passed at a designated level (see below). The Awarding Body for the Built Environment (ABBE) is a partnership of professional organisations and institutions which offers NVQ and SVQ awards across a wide range of built environment disciplines such as Architectural Practice (Level 5), Architectural Technology (Level 4) and Building Control (Level 4).

15.5.3   Architectural Technology NVQ/SVQ Level 4

This award is aimed at those who work in the architectural technology field and aims to promote best practice. The award is open to individuals with 'substantial experience, knowledge and understanding' of architectural technology and who 'have a substantial degree of personal responsibility and autonomy, whilst undertaking a broad range of complex, technical and professional work activities' (CISC 1997). Key roles and responsibilities are set out in the documentation. The award comprises eleven units:

AT1   Confirm a brief and design programme
AT2   Investigate factors affecting project design
AT3   Investigate and assess technical regulatory factors affecting project design
AT4   Develop and analyse technical design solutions
AT5   Recommend and advise on the selection of a project technical design
AT6   Recommend and advise on the selection of a detailed project plan
AT7   Prepare specifications
AT8   Monitor construction requirements
AT9   Facilitate meetings (MCI)
AT10 Provide solutions to and advice on problems within an ethical framework
AT11 Contribute to advances in occupational knowledge.

Although there is a certain element of management skills inherent in the Architectural Technology award these issues are covered in parallel NVQs/SVQs such as Architectural Practice (Level 5) and Construction Project Management (Level 5). The NVQ/SVQ Level 5 in Architectural Practice is based on the RIBA plan of work and has been designed to appeal to a wide range of individuals who may wish to increase their management skills within the context of the workplace. Candidates for this award will have already demonstrated comprehensive technical knowledge.

15.5.4   *Continuing professional development*

Technological advances in manufacturing and new product development raise the prospect of new opportunities to be creative. Regulations evolve and put a different emphasis on the way in which things are done, often necessitating a change in established and familiar procedures. Until quite recently professional development was often left to individuals and as a consequence was self-directed and not always particularly relevant to the organisation in which they worked. The move to more formally instigated continuing professional development (CPD) programmes has, to a certain extent, shifted the responsibility in the direction of the employer and made the requirement to continue to learn after qualification (the constant student) an explicit component of being a professional. As trained, qualified and experienced professionals it is no longer possible to rest on one's professional laurels, nor is it a sensible policy in the increasingly litigious environment of construction. Clients expect their professional advisers to be competent and knowledgeable about recent developments. Lifelong learning, or continual learning, is, therefore, an essential component of a professional's commitment to his or her vocation.

With the world-wide drive to demonstrate professional competence has come the need for individuals, regardless of individual skills, experience and ability, to conform to professional institutions' schemes and thus demonstrate continual learning. The concept of CPD, or lifelong learning, is not new to building professionals. The RIBA's interest started in 1962, although it was not until January 1993 that the institution made participation a duty of membership and made

Figure 15.3 New and old, Montreal.

compliance obligatory in 1999 (with spot-checks). If one were to be cynical, such initiatives could be seen to be more about professional institutions generating additional fee income through such schemes than about professional confidence. A more realistic view would probably be that the professions have been having a crisis of confidence and the possession of certificates and filling in of CPD diaries restores some of that lost faith amongst clients, the public and fellow profession-als. A more positive view is that to become and remain competitive professional service firms must invest in the development of their members' skills and educa-tion. As people businesses, staff are their biggest asset, and one that should be invested in for the benefit of the organisation.

15.6   A theory for practice

We build to create shelter, containers for living in, and in doing so we make our mark on the earth. We are dependent on our planet for food, water and building materials yet we continue to ignore well-understood ecological principles and live our lives with little regard for future generations or respect for our host. Our temporary presence on the earth leaves a much longer impression than some would be prepared to recognise and address. Sustainable building is still consid-ered by the majority to be something different from normal, well-established, practice. It is frequently taught as a separate module to other architectural subjects rather than being integrated throughout the syllabus. Many barriers to change do exist and need to be challenged and re-defined by students and practitioners alike. Throughout this book sustainable design principles have, quite deliberately, been used as an underlying philosophy, sometimes expressed explicitly, often implicitly, with the intention of breaking down these barriers.

For designers working in a pluralistic society, with no dominant design thread or coherent framework, it is, arguably, difficult to challenge established protocols when clear typologies for sustainable building fail to empathise with current thinking. If we are to move towards sustainable architecture then the way in which we teach building construction needs urgent reassessment. Are we really comfortable with teaching standard details for standard solutions? Do we really encourage students to think about what they are doing and question conventional wisdom? Carpenter's *Learning by Building* (1997) explores the link between design and construction through the integration of construction studios into the design studio. His book emphasises the link between thinking and making, collaboration and communication skills. Drawing on examples from American schools of architecture he makes a strong argument for linking technology to the design studio, bringing the excitement of building into the education process instead of students merely 'observing' construction. It is an interesting approach, and one that has a lot of potential for bringing sustainable building techniques into mainstream thinking, with environmentally responsible ideals and practices forming an underlying philosophy across the whole syllabus.

15.6.1   *A (borrowed) theory for practice*

Analysis of the work of other designers (either through personal visits or through reports in journals) can help individuals to develop an insight into the profession and their own learning process, as can the process of doing research and practising. In attempting to put forward a theory for practice there has been a natural gravitas to a series of observations in Michael Brawne's book *From Idea to Building* (1992). He makes the clear distinction between three aspects of all design problems, namely the parts which can be taken as given, making decisions and the building (the most important). These are explored briefly in relation to the themes developed in this book and expressed in Fig. 15.4.

(1) *The parts which can be taken as given.* At any given time and in any particular place, a range of building materials and techniques exists which is equally available to all. Financial restrictions may reduce the choice, while legislation may influence the shape, orientation and use of the building, but again these restrictions apply to all. Ten years earlier than the point in question the range of materials and methods would have been different, just as it will be 10 years on from our chosen point. Thus the technologies and methods available to designers are not the most critical factor – the ability to select the most appropriate for the given time and particular place is critical.

(2) *Making decisions.* Design problems involve making decisions: the vast range of decisions made from briefing through to completion of the building by designers, consultants, managers, contractors and sub-contractors. The technologies available may limit choice, and the models available may limit the approach, but the success of the building will be determined by the decisions

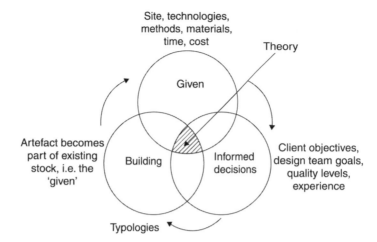

Figure 15.4 A theory for practice.

made by individuals, by teams and collectively by all the parties to the building process. Selecting and deciding is the pleasurable and agonising process of design. Thus the ability to make informed decisions is the most critical aspect. Designers will work within a framework based on their own particular interests and ways of searching for information and thus individual designer's knowledge of the parts that can be taken as given will vary, i.e. designers will not be aware of all the options available to them.

(3) *The building.* The result of this complex set of considerations is the building, the ultimate goal, and the result of the entire process. It will be experienced through sensory perception, primarily visual, tactile and auditory, while moving in and through the physical spaces, and is thus different from its earlier representation in drawings, specifications and models. This new addition to the building stock will influence the actions of those who use it on a daily basis. It also becomes part of the existing stock, part of the 'given', and hence adds to existing typologies. As an influence on design decisions the 'given' has considerable influence, largely as a conservative critical mass from which designers may choose well-established solutions to design problems. As the number of sustainable buildings increases as a percentage of the given, so does the likelihood of other designers selecting these typologies.

Humans, and hence building activity, interact with and depend upon the natural world; thus designers must accept responsibility for the consequences of their actions upon natural systems and human health (well-being). We need to understand the limitations of design. No building lasts for ever and design cannot solve every problem. We need to create safe and healthy buildings with a long-term view, which are easy to maintain, recyclable and functional for a long time. The success of buildings, and ultimately the success of those involved in building, depends on attention to detail – attention to joints and details, and attention to the interaction of the various parties to the building project and the ensuing product. Continual improvement can be sought by sharing knowledge. Communication between clients, designers, manufacturers, assemblers, users, etc., is encouraged so that information and knowledge about sustainable building can be shared.

15.6.2   *Final thoughts*

Architectural technology as a discipline evolved rapidly during the last decade of the 20th century and in doing so started to re-establish synergy between design, technology and management. Now, at the start of the 21st century, the opportunity to deal with complex challenges such as sustainable construction through the detail design process is greater than ever. The role of the architectural technologist, both the official role promoted by BIAT and that of other building designers (such as architects and surveyors) operating in this professional field, will continue to evolve, shaped and reshaped by the industry and the society in which they live and work. Regardless of technological advancement, changing regulations and fashions there will always be a need for individuals and organisations who are able to interpret conceptual design into a series of details that work, communicate information efficiently and effectively to the fixers and fitters, and manage the process.

Demands on buildings have changed over the years and will continue to change in the future. Technological and social developments, e.g. industrialisation, globalisation, increased mobility, IT, extended (and divided) families, etc., continue to influence the design, use and re-use of our building stock. Professional designers need to be aware of changing user demands, able to respond and shape technological developments for a specific point in time. Functionality, time, cost, quality and value will continue to be important. Designers need no reminding that the process of producing good quality buildings on time and to budget is a complex affair, influenced by a multitude of different people and shaped by legislation and tradition. Buildings are designed by people (qualified or otherwise), assembled by people (skilled or otherwise) and financed by people (well intended or otherwise). We must not forget that building is a commercial activity and those involved in the industry are attempting to make a healthy return on their investment. Thus economic and commercial pressures will shape our built environment, simply through the size of the budget available and the time in which to complete the task. There is a price to pay for all building activity and altruistic aims to deliver sustainable building need to be accommodated within this framework. Building design is a service provision that everyone has an opinion about, yet few are qualified and experienced to do it professionally. Designers need to master the technologies available to them and apply technology in such a way as to improve our built environment for present and future generations. The ability to make life better (or worse) for building users is, quite literally, at our fingertips.

Further reading

Gill, J. and Johnson, P. (1997). *Research Methods for Managers* (Second Edition), Paul Chapman, London.

APPENDICES

A1 Recommended reading – a note

At the end of each chapter are a couple of recommended books that my students and I have found to be informative and which provide additional information to that provided in this book. Throughout the text references to the work of others have been provided where appropriate with full details in the References. In addition to these references, and especially for those students embarking on a career in building, the following books are recommended as essential study aids.

Design

Metric Handbook: Planning and Design Data (1999) edited by David Adler, Architectural Press, Oxford.

Understanding Architecture: An Introduction to Architecture and Architectural History (1994) by Hazel Conway and Rowan Roenisch, Routledge, London.

Architecture: The Story of Practice (1991) by Dana Cuff, MIT Press, Boston, MA.

The Idea of Building: Thought and Action in the Design and Production of Buildings (1992) by Steven Groák, E & FN Spon, London.

Design Thinking (1991) by Peter Rowe, MIT Press, Boston, MA.

Technology

The Mitchell's Series published by Longman, namely:

Structure and Fabric, Part 1, Sixth Edition (2000) by Jack Stroud Foster.

Structure and Fabric, Part 2, Sixth Edition (2000) by Jack Stroud Foster and Raymond Harrington.

External Components (1994) by Alan Blanc.

Internal Components (1994) by M. McEvoy.

Finishes (1996) by Yvonne Dean.

Materials Technology (1994) by Yvonne Dean.

Management

The Architect in Practice, Eighth Edition (2000) by David Chappell and Christopher Willis, Blackwell Scientific, Oxford.

Architectural Management in Practice: A Competitive Approach (1999) by Stephen Emmitt, Longman, Harlow.

Managing the Professional Service Firm (1993) by David Maister, Free Press, New York.

Architect's Legal Handbook: The Law for Architects, Sixth Edition (1996), edited by A. Speaight and G. Stone, Butterworth Architecture, Oxford.

Project Management in Construction, Third Edition (1996) by Anthony Walker, Blackwell Science, Oxford.

Periodicals

Architects' Journal, Architectural Review, Architectural Technology, Building, Building Design, Detail.

A2 Milestones in architectural technology

A few (very selective) dates and events are noted below.

1400–1830 The Renaissance

1671   French Academy of Architecture founded

1714–1837 Georgian period

1768   Royal Academy founded
1769   Coade factory starts producing terracotta in London
1779   The Iron Bridge at Coalbrookdale, Shropshire, built
1818   Institute of Civil Engineers formed
1824   Portland cement patented by Joseph Aspdin

1830   Liverpool to Manchester railway opened

1832   Charles Babbage built the first 'computer'
1834   Institute of British Architects formed
1834   Launch of the *Architectural Magazine* (folded 1839), the first periodical for the building industry

1837–1901 The Victorian era

1843   Launch of *The Builder*
1851   Great Exhibition, Crystal Palace, London
1854   Elisha Graves Otis demonstrates his safety device at the New York World's Fair
1858   Introduction of the Hoffman continuous brick kiln
1868   Surveyors' Institute formed
1875   Public Health Act

1903   First powered flight

1903   First British Standard applied to building (BS 4)
1946   Electronic analogue computer invented
1952   Pilkington Brothers Ltd. starts experiments leading to the float process
1958   'Oxford Conference' on architectural education
1965   SAAT founded, forerunner of BIAT

1969 Neil Armstrong walked on the moon (20 July)

1984   SAAT publish *Architectural Technology: The Constructive Link*
1987   *Agenda 21* published
1992   Rio Earth Summit
1992   RIBA strategic study of the profession
2000   Architectural Technology subject benchmarking document published

A3 Conversion tables

For readers involved in work to historic buildings and buildings built before SI units (also known as the metric system) were adopted in the UK some conversion tables may be useful. American readers may also find the tables of assistance.

Imperial

8 × 1/8 inch = 1 inch (1″)
12 inches   = 1 foot (1′)
3 feet   = 1 yard

Typical scales used were
12″ = 1′ (1:1), 6″ = 1′ (1:2), 4″ = 1′ (1:3), 3″ = 1′ (1:4), 2″ = 1′ (1:6), 1″ = 1′ (1:12), 1/2″ = 1′ (1:24), 1/4″ = 1′ (1:48), 1/8″ = 1′ (1:96).

Metric

10 millimetres (mm) = 1 centimetre (cm)
1000 millimetres   = 1 metre (m)
1000 metres   = 1 kilometre (km)

Typical scales used by building designers are
1:1, 1:2, 1:5, 1:10, 1:20, 1:50, 1:100, 1:200, 1:500, 1:1000, 1:1250, 1:2500.
Some engineering disciplines also use 1:25, 1:33 and 1:75.

Conversion

1 inch   = 25.4 mm
1 foot   = 304.8 mm
1 yard   = 914.4 mm
1 mile   = 1.609 km
1 square foot = 0.0929 sqm
1 square yard = 0.8361 sqm
1 acre   = 4046.9 sqm (0.40469 ha)
1 square mile = 259 ha

A4 Useful addresses

Below is a short list of addresses that readers may find useful:

British Institute of Architectural Technologists (BIAT)
397 City Road, London EC1V 1NE

Chartered Institute of Builders (CIOB)
Englemere, Kings Ride, Ascot, Berkshire SL5 7TB

CIB
PO Box 1837, 3000 BV, Rotterdam, The Netherlands

Construction Industry Board
The Building Centre, 26 Store Street, London WC1E 7BT

Royal Incorporation of Architects in Scotland (RIAS)
15 Rutland Square, Edinburgh EH1 2BE

Royal Institute of British Architects (RIBA)
66 Portland Place, London W1N 4AD

Royal Institution of Chartered Surveyors (RICS)
12 Great George Street, London SW1P 3AE

References

Adler, D. (ed.) (1999). *Metric Handbook: Planning and Design Data*, Architectural Press, Oxford.

Akin, O. (1986). *Psychology of Architectural Design*, Pion, London.

Alberti, L.B. (1472). *Ten Books on Architecture*, translated into English by Leoni, J. and edited by Rykwert, J. (1755), London.

Antoniades, A.C. (1992). *Poetics of Architecture: Theory of Design*, Von Nostrand Reinhold, New York.

Baden Hellard, R. (1995). *Project Partnering: Principle and Practice*, Thomas Telford, London.

Ball, M. (1988). *Rebuilding Construction: Economic Change in the British Construction Industry*, Routledge, London.

Barbour Index (1993). *The Changing Face of Specification in the UK Construction Industry*, Barbour Index, Windsor, Berks.

Barbour Index (1994). *Contractors' Influence on Product Decisions*, Barbour Index, Windsor, Berks.

Barbour Index (1995). *The Influence of Clients on Product Decisions*, Barbour Index, Windsor, Berks.

Barbour Index (1996). *Communicating with Construction Customers: A Guide for Building Product Manufacturers*, Barbour Index, Windsor, Berks.

Bartlett, E. and Moss, G. (1999). 'Durability data for building design: the whole life perspective', Emmitt, S. (ed.), *The Product Champions*, LMU, Leeds.

BIAT (2001). *Your Career as an Architectural Technologist* (2000–2001 Edition), British Institute of Architectural Technologists, London.

Blanc, A. (1994). *Mitchell's Internal Components*, Longman, Harlow.

Boisot, M.H. (1998). *Knowledge Assets: Securing Competitive Advantage in the Information Economy*, Oxford University Press, Oxford.

Bowley, M. (1960). *Innovations in Building Materials: An Economic Study*, Gerald Duckworth, London.

Bowley, M. (1966). *The British Building Industry: Four Studies in Response and Resistance to Change*, Cambridge University Press, Cambridge.

Bradbury, J.A.A. (1989). *Product Innovation: Idea to Exploitation*, John Wiley & Sons, Chichester.

Brawne, M. (1992). *From Idea to Building: Issues in Architecture*, Butterworth-Heinemann, Oxford.

British Standards Institution (1999). *BSI Catalogue: Products and Services*, BSI, London.

Brown, R. (1988). *Group Processes: Dynamics Within and Between Groups*, Blackwell, Oxford.

Brunskill, R.W. (1990). *Brick Building in Britain*, Victor Gollancz, London.

Building Industry Communications (1966). *Interdependence and Uncertainty: A Study of the Building Industry*, Tavistock, London.

Building Research Establishment (1975). *BRE Digest 176, Failure Patterns and Implications*, BRE, Watford.

Cadogan, G. (2000). 'Making sure our heritage has proper protection', *Financial Times*, Weekend 29/30 January, p. 4.

Carpenter, W.J. (1997). *Learning by Building: Design and Construction in Architectural Education*, Van Nostrand Reinhold, New York.

Carson, R. (1962). *Silent Spring*, Hamish Hamilton, London.

Chermayeff, S. (1933). 'New materials and new methods', *Journal of the Royal Institute of British Architects*, 23 December, pp. 165–173.

Chisnell, P.M. (1995). *Consumer Behaviour* (Third Edition), McGraw-Hill, London.

Chown, G.A. (1999). 'Requirements for durability and on-going performance in Canada's objective-based construction codes', Lacasse, M.A. and Vanier, D. (eds), *Durability of Building Materials and Components 8*, Vol. 2, pp. 1527–1536.

CISC (1997). *Architectural Technology NVQ/SVQ Level 4*, Accreditation Edition, January, CISC, London.

Cmnd (1981). *The Future of Building Control in England and Wales*, HMSO, London.

Coade, E.A. (1748). *A Descriptive Catalogue of Coade's Artificial Stone Manufactory … with Process Affixed*, London.

Cole, R. (1998). 'Emerging trends in building assessment methods', *Building Research and Information*, Vol. 26(1), pp. 3–16.

Cole, R. and Cooper, I. (1988). 'British architects – accommodating science and technical information', *Journal of Architectural and Planning Research*, Vol. 5(2), Summer, pp. 110–128.

Coleman, A., Brown, F., Cottle, L., Marshall, P., Redknap, C. and Sex, R. (1985). *Utopia on Trial*, Hilary Shipman, London.

Construction Industry Research and Information Association (1983). *Buildability: An Assessment*, Special Publication 26, CIRIA Publications, London.

Cooper, D. (1992). *Drawing and Perceiving* (Second Edition), Van Nostrand Reinhold, New York.

Cox, P.J. (1994). *Writing Specifications for Construction*, McGraw-Hill, London.

Cox, S. and Hamilton, A. (1995). *Architect's Job Book* (Sixth Edition), RIBA Publications, London.

Crinson, M. and Lubbock, J. (1994). *Architecture – Art or Profession?: Three Hundred Years of Architectural Education in Britain*, Manchester University Press, Manchester.

Crocker, A. (1990). *Building Failures: Recovering the Cost*, BSP Professional Books, Oxford.

Crook, J.M. (1972). Introduction to John T. Emmett, *Six Essays*, Johnson Reprint Corporation, New York, p. xvi (first published as a collection 1891).

Crosbie, M.J. (1995). 'Why can't Jonny size a beam?', *Progressive Architecture*, June, pp. 92–95.

Cruickshank, D. and Wyld, P. (1975). *The Art of Georgian Building*, Architectural Press, London.

Cuff, D. (1991). *Architecture: The Story of Practice*, MIT Press, Cambridge, MA.

Curwell, S.R. and March, C.G. (1986). *Hazardous Building Materials: A Guide to the Selection of Alternatives*, E & FN Spon, London.

Curwell, S., March, C. and Venables, R. (1990). *Buildings and Health: The Rosehaugh Guide, to the Design, Construction, Use and Management of Buildings*, RIBA Publications, London.

Daniels, C.N. (1994). *Information Technology: The Management Challenge*, Addison-Wesley, Reading, MA.

Davies, S. (1979). *The Diffusion of Process Innovations*, Cambridge University Press, Cambridge.

Day, L.F. (1903). *Pattern Design*, Batsford, London.

Dean, Y. (1994). *Materials Technology*, Mitchell's Building Series, Longman, Harlow.

DoE (1994). *Evaluation of Environmental Information for Planning Projects: A Good Practice Guide*, HMSO, London.

Druker, P.F. (1985). *Innovation and Entrepreneurship: Practice and Principles*, Heinemann, London.

Edmonds, G. (1996). 'Trade literature and technical information', Nurcombe, V.J. (ed.), *Information Sources in Architecture and Construction* (Second Edition), Bowker Saur, London.

Edwards, B. (1996). *Towards Sustainable Architecture*, Butterworth Architecture, Oxford.

Edwards, S. and Anderson, J. (1999). 'Environmental profiles of construction materials and components', Emmitt, S. (ed.), *The Product Champions*, LMU, Leeds.

Egan, J. (1998). *Rethinking Construction*, DETR, London.

Ellis, R. and Cuff, D. (eds) (1989). *Architects' People*, Oxford University Press, Oxford.

Emmerson Report (1962). *Survey of the Problems before the Construction Industries*, HMSO, London.

Emmett, J.T. (1880). 'The profession of an "Architect"', *British Quarterly Review*, April, pp. 335–368.

Emmitt, S. (ed.) (1996). *Detail Design in Architecture*, BRC, Northampton.

Emmitt, S. (1997a). 'The diffusion of innovations in the building industry', PhD thesis, University of Manchester, Manchester.

Emmitt, S. (1997b). 'The diffusion of environmentally responsible ideas and practices', Gray, M. (ed.), *Evolving Environmental Ideals: Changing Ways of Life, Values and Design Practices*, Royal Institute of Technology, Stockholm, pp. 41–49.

Emmitt, S. (1999a). *Architectural Management in Practice: A Competitive Approach*, Longman, Harlow.

Emmitt, S. (ed.) (1999b). *The Product Champions*, LMU, Leeds.

Emmitt, S. (ed.) (2001). *Detailing Design*, LMU, Leeds.

Emmitt, S. and Wyatt, D.P. (1998). 'The product's milieu: towards an effective information domain to deliver sustainable building', *Construction and the Environment*, CIB, Rotterdam.

Emmitt, S. and Yeomans, D.T. (2001). *Specifying Buildings: A Design Management Perspective*, Butterworth-Heinemann, Oxford.

European Community (1985). *Council Directive 85/337/EEC on the Assessment of the Effects of Certain Public and Private Projects on the Environment*, OJ No. L 175, 5 July 1985.

Fisher, T. (1994). 'Can this profession be saved?', *Progressive Architecture*, Vol. 75(2), February, p. 84.

Fitchen, J. (1986). *Building Construction before Mechanization*, MIT Press, Cambridge, MA.

Frampton, K. (1995). *Studies in Tectonic Culture: The Poetics of Construction in Nineteenth and Twentieth Century Architecture*, Cava, J. (ed.), MIT Press, Cambridge, MA.

Friedman, A. and Cammalleri, V. (1995). 'The environmental impact of building materials in the North American building industry', *Building Research and Information*, Vol. 23(3), pp. 162–166.

Gann, D.M., Wang, Y. and Hawkins, R. (1998). 'Do regulations encourage innovation? – the case of energy efficiency in housing.' *Building Research and Information*, Vol. 26(4), pp. 280–296.

Gibbs, J. (1728). *A Book of Architecture, Containing Designs of Buildings and Ornaments*, London.

Gilfillan, S.C. (1935) (1970 imprint). *The Sociology of Invention*, MIT Press, Cambridge, MA.

Gill, J. and Johnson, P. (1997). *Research Methods for Managers* (Second Edition), Paul Chapman, London.

Glasson, J., Therivel, R., Weston, J., Wilson, E. and Frost, R. (1997). 'EIA – learning from experience: Changes in the quality of environmental impact statements for UK planning projects', *Journal of Environmental Planning and Management*, Vol. 40(4), pp. 451–464.

Goldsmith, S. (1963). *Designing for the Disabled*, RIBA, London.

Goldsmith, S. (1997). *Designing for the Disabled: The New Paradigm*, Architectural Press, Oxford.

Goodey, J. and Matthew, K. (1971). 'Architects and information', Research Paper 1, Institute of Advanced Architectural Studies, University of York.

Government White Paper (1999). *Saving Lives: Our Healthier Nation*, The Stationery Office, London.

Grant, J. and Fox, F. (1992). 'Understanding the role of the designer in society', *Journal of Art and Design Education*, Vol. 11(1), pp. 77–78.

Greed, C.H. (1996). *Introducing Town Planning* (Second Edition), Longman, Harlow.

Groák, S. (1992). *The Idea of Building: Thought and Action in the Design and Production of Buildings*, E & FN Spon, London.

Gumpertz, W.H. and Rutila, D.A. (1999). 'Building durability: know what you know or let's use the knowledge we already have, before we improve upon it', Lacasse, M.A. and Vanier, D.J. (eds), *Durability of Building Materials and Components 8*, Vol. 3, NRC Research Press, Ottawa, pp. 2068–2077.

HAPM (1991). *HAPM Component Life Manual*, E & FN Spon, London.

Handisyde, C.C. (1976). *Everyday Details*, Architectural Press, London.

Harris, C.M. and Dajda, R. (1996). 'The scale of repeat prescribing', *British Journal of General Practice*, November, Vol. 46, pp. 649–653.

Harvey, R.C. and Ashworth, A. (1993). *The Construction Industry of Great Britain*, Newness, Oxford.

Heath, T. (1984). *Method in Architecture*, John Wiley & Sons, Chichester.

Herbert, G. (1978). *Pioneers of Prefabrication: The British Contribution in the Nineteenth Century*, Johns Hopkins University Press, Baltimore, MD.

Hesselgren, S. (1972). *The Language of Architecture* (Vols 1 and 2), Applied Science Publishers, London.

Higgin, G. and Jessop, N. (1965). *Communications in the Building Industry: The Report of a Pilot Study*, Tavistock, London.

Highfield, D. (1991). *The Construction of New Buildings Behind Historic Facades*, E & FN Spon, London.

Hillier, B. and Jones, L. (1977). 'Architecture at the crossroads', *New Scientist*, Vol. 74 (1052), pp. 390–392.

Holness, A.N. (1996). 'A methodological account of detail design in architecture: some preliminary findings', Emmitt, S. (ed.), *Detail Design in Architecture*, pp. 115–123.

Huovila, P. (1999). 'Managing the life cycle requirements of facilities', Lacasse, M.A. and Vanier, D.J. (eds), *Durability of Building Materials and Components 8*, NRC Research Press, Ottawa, pp. 1874–1880.

Hutchinson, M. (1993). 'The need to stick to the specification', *Architects' Journal*, 20 October.

Jacobs, J. (1961). *The Death and Life of Great American Cities*, Vintage Books, New York.

Janis, I.L. (1972). *Victims of Groupthink*, Houghton Mifflin, Boston, MA.

Kreps, G.L. (1990). *Organisational Communication: Theory and Practice* (Second Edition), Longman, Reading, MA.

Kwakye, A.A. (1997). *Construction Project Administration in Practice*, Longman, Harlow.

Latham, M. (1994). *Constructing the Team*, HMSO, London.

Leatherbarrow, D. (1993). *The Roots of Architectural Invention*, Cambridge University Press, Cambridge.

Lovelock, J. (1990). *The Ages of Gaia*, Oxford University Press, Oxford.

Lyons, A.R. (1997). *Materials for Architects and Builders: An Introduction*, Arnold, London.

Mackenzie, D. (1997). *Green Design: Design for the Environment*, Laurence King, London.

Mackinder, M. (1980). 'The selection and specification of building materials and components', Research Paper 17, Institute of Advanced Architectural Studies, University of York.

Mackinder, M. and Marvin, H. (1982). 'Design decision making in architectural practice', Research Paper 19, Institute of Advanced Architectural Studies, University of York.

MacLeod, M.J. (1999). 'Teaching prescribing to medical students', *Medicine*, Vol. 27(3), pp. 29–30.

Mainstone, R. (1998). *Developments in Structural Form* (Second Edition), Architectural Press, Oxford.

Maister, D.H. (1993). *Managing the Professional Service Firm*, Free Press, New York.

March, J.G. (1994). *A Primer on Decision Making; How Decisions Happen*, Free Press, New York.

Martin, B. (1977). *Joints in Buildings*, George Godwin, London.

Mason, R. (1999). 'Innovating to excel: the role of innovation and research in architectural technology', Emmitt, S. (ed.), *The Product Champions*, LMU, Leeds, pp. 5–15.

Matthews, R.A.J. (1997). 'The science of Murphy's Law', *Scientific American*, April (cited in *Visions of Technology*, p. 187).

McEvoy, M. (1994). *Mitchell's External Components*, Longman, Harlow.

Midgley, D.F. (1977). *Innovation and New Product Marketing*, Croom Helm, London.

Munn, R.E. (1979). *Environmental Impact Assessment: Principles and Procedures*, John Wiley & Sons, New York.

M4I (1998). *Movement for Innovation*, London.

Neutra, R. (1954). *Survival Through Design*, Oxford University Press, New York.

Newell, A. and Simon, H.A. (1972). *Human Problem Solving*, Prentice Hall, Englewood Cliffs, NJ.

Newman, O. (1972). *Defensible Space: People and Design in the Violent City*, Architectural Press, London.

Nicholson, P. (1792). *The Carpenter's New Guide*, London.

Olie, J. (1996). 'A typology of joints: supporting sustainable development in building', PhD Thesis, Technical University of Eindhoven.

Palladio (1570). *Four Books on Architecture*.

Parker, J.E.S. (1978). *The Economics of Innovation: The National and Multinational Enterprise in Technological Change*, Longman, London.

Patterson, T.L. (1994). *Frank Lloyd Wright and the Meaning of Materials*, Van Nostrand Reinhold, New York.

Pawley, M. (1990). *Theory and Design in the Second Machine Age*, Basil Blackwell, Oxford.

Pevsner, N. (1976). *A History of Building Types*, Thames & Hudson, London.

Polanyi, M. (1958). *Personal Knowledge: Towards a Post-critical Philosophy*, Routledge & Kegan Paul, London.

Porter, R. (1993). 'Diseases of civilization', Bynum W.F. and Porter, R. (eds), *Companion Encyclopedia of the History of Medicine*, Routledge, London.

Potter, N. (1989). *What is a Designer?: Things, Places, Messages* (Third Edition), Hyphen Press, London.

Poyner, B. (1983). *Design Against Crime: Beyond Defensible Space*, Butterworths, London.

Poyner, B. and Fawcett, W.H. (1995). *Design for Inherent Security: Guidance for Non-residential Buildings*, Construction Industry Research and Information Association, Special Publication 115, London.

Pugh, S. (1991). *Total Design: Integrated Methods for Successful Product Engineering*, Addison-Wesley, Reading, MA.

Pye, D. (1968). *The Nature and Art of Workmanship*, Cambridge University Press, Cambridge.

QAA (2000). *Academic Standards: Architectural Technology*, Quality Assurance Agency for Higher Education, Gloucester, May.

Quiney, A. (1989). *Period Houses: A Guide to Authentic Architectural Features*, George Philip, London.

Rainger, P. (1983). *Movement Control in the Fabric of Buildings*, Mitchell's Series, Batsford, London.

Ramaswamy, R. (1996). *Design and Management of Service Processes: Keeping Customers for Life*, Addison-Wesley, Reading, MA.

RIBA Journal (1997). August, Vol. 104(8), p. 52.

Rich, P. and Dean, Y. (1999). *Principles of Element Design* (Third Edition), Butterworth-Heinemann, Oxford.

Rogers, E.M. (1995). *Diffusion of Innovations* (Fourth Edition), Free Press, New York.

Rowe, P.G. (1987). *Design Thinking*, MIT Press, Cambridge, MA.

Royal Institute of British Architects (1962). *The Architect and His Office*, RIBA, London.

SAAT (1984). *Architectural Technology: The Constructive Link*, Society of Architectural and Associated Technicians, London.

Salisbury, F. (1990). *Architect's Handbook for Client Briefing*, Butterworth Architecture, London.

Schaffer, T. (1983). 'Site architect's guide', *Architect's Journal*, 20 April, 27 April and 4 May.

Schmid, P. (1986). *Biologische Baukonstruction*, Rudolf Muller, Cologne.

Schmid, P. and Pa'l-Schmid, G. (1999). 'A detail model', Emmitt, S. (ed.), *The Product Champions*, LMU, Leeds.

Schmitz-Gunther, T. (ed.) (1998). *Living Spaces: Sustainable Building and Design*, Konemann, Cologne.

Shillito, D. (1990). 'The assessment of risk', Curwell, S., et al. (eds), *Buildings and Health: The Rosehaugh Guide*, RIBA Publications, London.

Simon, H.A. (1969). *Sciences of the Artificial*, MIT Press, Cambridge, MA.

Slaughter, E.S. (2000). 'Implementation of construction innovations', *Building Research and Information*, Vol. 28(1), 2–17.

Sliwa, J. and Fairweather, L. (eds) (1968). *AJ Metric Handbook*, London.

Symes, M. and Pauwels, S. (1999). 'The diffusion of innovations in urban design: the case of sustainability in the Hulme Development Guide', *Journal of Urban Design*, Vol. 4(1).

Symes, M., Eley, J. and Seidel, A.D. (1995). *Architects and their Practices: A Changing Profession*, Butterworth Architecture, Oxford.

Thomas, S.R., Tucker, R.L. and Kelly, W.R. (1998). 'Critical communications variables', *Journal of Construction Engineering and Management*, Jan./Feb., Vol. 124(1), pp. 58–66.

Thompson, S., Treweek, J.R. and Thurling, D.J. (1997). 'The ecological component of environmental impact assessment: a critical review of British environmental statements', *Journal of Environmental Planning and Management*, Vol. 40(2) pp. 157–171.

Tomlinson, P. (1990). 'Environmental assessment and management', Curwell, S. *et al.* (eds), *Buildings and Health: The Rosehaugh Guide*, RIBA Publications, London.

Utterback, J.M. (1994). *Mastering the Dynamics of Innovation*, Harvard Business School Press, Boston, MA.

Wackernagel, M. and Rees, W. (1996). *Our Ecological Footprint*, New Society Publishers, Gabriola Island.

Wade, J.W. (1977). *Architecture, Problems and Purposes: Architectural Design as a Basic Problem Solving Process*, John Wiley & Sons, New York.

Wakita, O.A. and Linde, R.M. (1999). *The Professional Practice of Architectural Detailing* (Third Edition), John Wiley & Sons, New York.

Walthern, P. (ed.) (1992). *Environmental Impact Assessment: Theory and Practice*, Routledge, London.

WHO (1995). *Guide to Good Prescribing*, World Health Organisation, Geneva.

Woolley, T., Kimmins, S., Harrison, P. and Harrison, R. (1997). *Green Building Handbook: A Guide to Building Products and Their Impact on the Environment*, E & FN Spon, London.

World Commission on Environment and Development (1987). *Our Common Future* (The Brundlandt Report), Oxford University Press, Oxford.

Worthington, J. (1994). 'Design in practice – planning and managing space', Spedding, A. (ed.), *CIOB Handbook of Facilities Management*, Longman, Harlow.

Yeomans, D.T. (1992). *The Trussed Roof: Its History and Development*, Scolar Press, Aldershot.

Yeomans, D.T. (1997). *Construction Since 1900: Materials*, BT Batsford, London.

Index